Time for Telling Truth Is Running Out

Vera Schwarcz

TIME FOR

TELLING TRUTH IS

RUNNING OUT

Conversations with

Zhang Shenfu

Yale University Press

New Haven & London

The author gratefully acknowledges permission
to use excerpts from the following poems:
"Crazy Jane Talks with the Bishop" by William
Butler Yeats, reprinted with permission of
Macmillan Publishing Company from *The Poems
of W. B. Yeats: A New Edition*, edited by Richard
J. Finneran, Copyright 1933 by Macmillan
Publishing Company, renewed 1961 by Bertha
Georgie Yeats; and "Through Nightmare" by
Robert Graves, reprinted with permission of
Oxford University Press Inc. from *Robert
Graves: Collected Poems 1975*, Copyright 1975
by Robert Graves.

Designed by Sonia L. Scanlon
Set in Times Roman type by Marathon
Typography Service, Inc.
Printed in the United States of America by
Vail-Ballou Press, Binghamton, New York

Schwarcz, Vera, 1947–
    Time for telling truth is running out :
    conversations with Zhang Shenfu / Vera
    Schwarcz.
        p.   cm.
    Includes bibliographical references and index.
    ISBN 0-300-05009-7 (alk. paper)
    1. Chang, Shen-fu, 1893–   2. Communists
    — China — Biography.
I. Title.
DS778.C4966S38   1992
951.05'092—dc20
[B]   91-817
                                              CIP

The paper in this book meets the guidelines for
permanence and durability of the Committee on
Production Guidelines for Book Longevity of the
Council on Library Resources.

10 9 8 7 6 5 4 3 2 1

In memory of my father Elmer Savin 1911–1984

CONTENTS

NO WAY IN BY

HISTORY'S ROAD

The untameable, the live, the gentle. Have you not known them? Whom? They carry Time looped so river-wise about their house There's no way in by history's road To name or number them. —Robert Graves, "Through Nightmare"

In 1979 Zhang Shenfu, one of the last surviving founders of the Communist Party in China, took the risk of talking to a Westerner. Over the next five years, it was my privilege to become Zhang Shenfu's partner in conversation. We met for more than seventy hours in his home on Wang Fu Cang Lane in Beijing. We talked alone, in Chinese, with tea cups and a tape recorder between us. Our friendship developed as I learned the story of his life.

Zhang's life, like his story, challenged my training as a historian of China. Here was a founder of the Communist Party. Here was the man who introduced Zhou Enlai, China's renowned premier, into the Communist movement. He should have been a familiar public figure. And yet his life story required me to look beyond the well-known events of the twentieth-century revolution into forgotten or repressed corners of the living past.

Our dialogues opened for me a world I had not known before. Away from the main road of modern Chinese history, I wound my way through side alleys where love affairs, mathematical logic, and Bertrand Russell took up as much space as Confucianism, dialectical materialism, and Mao Zedong. It was in these alleys that Zhang Shenfu managed to find and to maintain the integrity of his personal worldview.

Neither standard history nor conventional biography, this book mirrors Zhang Shenfu's life through the circuitous pattern of conversation. It is not a thread that follows one theme or idea but, rather, a web that enfolds its subject in layers and fragments. I leave it to the reader to savor, to judge, and to recompose these fragments. Each person may discover a different Zhang Shenfu in peeling back the layers of the tale. But I have identified my own point of view along the way and have provided the reader with concrete signposts along the route that took me into the house and life of Zhang Shenfu. That path, like the book that emerged, is marked by a tension between public history and personal memory.

I first met Zhang Shenfu on November 12, 1979, at an appointment arranged by officials from the National Beijing Library. Zhang's name had caught my interest during my research on the May Fourth movement of 1919. He was listed among survivors of a student association (*New Tide*) founded at Beijing University in 1919. Public events loomed large in our encounter. The year 1979 marked the sixtieth anniversary of the May Fourth movement of 1919, a patriotic student movement canonized in Chinese Communist historiography. In 1979 I was a member of the first scholarly exchange between China and the United States, and I had official approval to do research on the May Fourth movement. Zhang Shenfu was a recently rehabilitated survivor of that event.

We met in the guest parlor of the National Library to talk about the public past. Within moments it became clear to me that other doors were opening in this ceremonial space. In spite of the presence of Communist Party officials in the room, in spite of the historic subject that was the focus of conversation, Zhang Shenfu began talking about something else. He was bent on telling me his own story.

The eighty-six-year-old man in the cushioned armchair facing me had seemed frail as he walked up the library steps with the aid of a cane and his young daughter. Now, inside the parlor, he was full of vigor and humor. Zhang Shenfu had a surprisingly sharp memory. During our first meeting he insisted on bringing up all sorts of odd details about himself, his philosophical interests, and his love life.

These fragments had no relevance to the public history of the May Fourth movement commemorated in the People's Republic of China. But for me they were an unexpected gift, and I wanted more. At the end of our public interview, I therefore took a risk and said to Zhang Shenfu, "I hope we can meet again. May I come and visit you at your home to continue our conversation?"

Foreigners were not yet allowed to visit Chinese homes at will in 1979. So Zhang Shenfu looked at the Party secretary in the opposite armchair and answered, "I hope so. Very much. We must talk frankly. Time for telling truth is running out."

During the next five years, Zhang Shenfu welcomed me into his home on Wang Fu Cang Lane over and over again. There, away from the watchful guardians of the public past, I learned the facts of his long life. Some of what I heard was so intriguing that, for a while, I considered writing a novel about Zhang Shenfu. But other details, including long-lost texts from his life, turned out to be too real, too important for the historian in me. Like rough stones in a river, they scraped me each time I crossed into the realm of pure imagination.

I had to come up with something else, something that conveyed the flow of dialogue as well as the arresting power of rough stone. While on this quest for narrative form, I was fortunate to find Saul Friedlander's *When Memory Comes*. This personal work by a survivor and historian of the Holocaust enabled me to find a middle ground between history and memory. It helped me place my story of Zhang Shenfu in a space between public amnesia and personal recollection. In Friedlander's book, present-day life in Israel is used to interrogate the painful dilemmas of a European childhood. The graceful atonality of Friedlander's voice allowed me to hear what lay beneath my own conversations with Zhang Shenfu.

I became convinced that these dialogues provided the most meaningful entry into the life of Zhang Shenfu. They became a springboard into the corpus of his essays. His writings were scattered in a variety of periodicals. On reading them, I found that they sometimes corroborated, sometimes challenged, sometimes distorted the "history" presented in our conversations. These texts, in time, became part of the living past. They were a ballast that kept recollection from drifting too far from the complexity of actual experience.

The rhythm of Zhang Shenfu's remembrance and of our deepening friendship shaped the content of each chapter. Because that rhythm was circular and episodic, the chapters do not follow a chronological line. Rather, they unfold around certain knots, certain conflicts that marked our dialogues. Questions that could not be answered, more often than coherent historical events, led me to dwell on the dilemmas of Zhang Shenfu. Some of the dilemmas that I explore in this book concern Zhang as a feminist womanizer, as a Communist interested in mathematical logic, as a follower of Bertrand Russell who also admired Confucius, as a philosophically inclined political activist.

This book does not untie the knots; it only locates them and seeks to convey the struggles they engendered. These struggles, however, did not overshadow Zhang Shenfu's pleasure in recollection. Delight in dialogue, in the end, overcame his rancor about the tragic fate of intellectuals in modern China.

From 1979 to 1989, while this book was in gestation, many colleagues and friends—both in China and in the West—were generous with their time and thoughtful counsel. I owe my greatest debt of gratitude to Zhang Shenfu. From our first encounter in 1979, during the tentative reopening of United States–China relations, he made his willingness to converse with me amply apparent. I taped sixty hours of conversation with Zhang at his home in Beijing's Wang Fu Cang Lane, sometimes with uneven results owing both to his tendency to mumble (especially after his ninetieth birthday) and to the poor quality of recording equipment available in the initial months of these interviews. These tapes are preserved in my personal collection of materials concerning Zhang Shenfu.

In Beijing, members of Zhang Shenfu's family graciously aided my research—especially his daughters, Zhang Yanni and Liu Fangqing, and his younger brother, professor of philosophy Zhang Dainian. In addition, several xii

PREFACE

of Zhang Shenfu's friends and acquaintances granted me interviews. Among the many to whom I talked over the years I would especially like to thank Xu Deheng, Liang Shuming, Wang Yao, Wu Xiaoling, Xu Yin, and Li Jiansheng. Without their frank, extensive, and thought-provoking commentary on the life and times of Zhang Shenfu this book might have been limited to the views and recollections of its subject. In China, too, I benefited greatly from critical comments by Tang Yijie, Li Zehou, and Yue Daiyun, who helped me better understand the philosophical and historiographical dilemmas in the thought of Zhang Shenfu. In France, where Zhang Shenfu spent critical years as founder of the Paris cell of the Chinese Communist Party, I received generous help from Yves Chevrier, Nicole Duloist, and Geneviève Barman, who introduced me to the archives relating to the activities of Chinese students in France.

Closer to home, Marilyn Levine shared with me her ideas about Chinese radicals in Europe and her contacts with scholars in the People's Republic of China; Guy Alitto helped by providing an introduction to Liang Shuming (Zhang Shenfu's schoolmate and fellow philosopher); and Jonathan Spence and Frederic Wakeman helped shape the manuscript with their welcome comments. Christina Gillmartin, a friend and fellow China traveler during the years of this oral history project, helped by being an emissary to and from Zhang Shenfu's family in Beijing, as well as by providing me with sources and insights about Liu Qingyang, Zhang Shenfu's lover, who is part of Gillmartin's research on women in the Chinese Communist Party. Paul Cohen deserves special mention for his lengthy review of the entire manuscript at a turning point in its evolution. His generous-spirited friendship over the years and, in particular, his thoughtful, detailed comments on this book have been critical to my work on modern Chinese intellectual history. My Chinese research assistants—Mao Tong, Ma Shaozhong, and Xu Hang—worked for many months indexing and summarizing the corpus of Zhang Shenfu's essays.

Among the non-China specialists who have enabled me to take a less conventional approach to the life of Zhang Shenfu are Dr. Dori Laub, Sarah Glaz, and Jan Willis. My editors at Yale University Press, Charles Grench and Karen Gangel, made this book more artful and coherent than it might have been otherwise. Debbie Sierpinski typed numerous versions of the manuscript with care. Finally, I wish to thank my husband, Jason Wolfe, for his interest in Zhang Shenfu, for accompanying me during my last visit with Zhang in October 1984, as well as for his patience during the past few years, when Zhang's memory became such a concrete presence in our home.

I also wish to acknowledge supporting grants provided by the Committee for Scholarly Communications with the People's Republic of China, the Social Science Research Council, the American Philosophical Society, and Wesleyan University.

Time for Telling Truth Is Running Out

THE LAUGHING VOICE

OF ZHANG SHENFU

Memory is our wound. But greater than the wound of memory is what seems the contemporary failure of memory. As memory fades, so does its healing and recuperative powers; and as these ebb away, we also lose our sense of history and culture.

—Bruce Duffy, "The Do-It-Yourself Life of Ludwig Wittgenstein"

My encounter with Zhang Shenfu began in November 1979. The book about that encounter began in the middle of the night of December 17, 1988. At home, in my study, I finally understood what I had learned from Zhang Shenfu. In the opaque language of the night I wrote: In public, we begin to forget. Alone, or with friends, we begin to remember. Memory, however, cannot be consummated privately. It will not count unless it spills forth into communal life. Memory's weight cannot be measured; its worth in gold remains unknown, unless it makes its mark upon the present. The personally recovered past must, in the end, make a dent in public history. It must dislodge (even if just a bit) official memories—those public myths rooted in historical amnesia.

Zhang Shenfu's life is, for me, a parable about forgetting and remembrance. Both in the way he lived his life and in the way he talked about it, Zhang proved that memory can outwit amnesia. Did I go to China in 1979 to look for this parable? Not consciously. Retrospectively, however, I realize that it was almost inevitable that the parable would find me. It lay there, waiting, below my conscious intentions. In Beijing, just out of reach of an ever-changing public past, I sought and found the story of a man who broke through the domain of official forgetfulness.

Zhang, the subject and narrator of this story, is a survivor experienced in the ways of forgetfulness and remembrance. I am the child of survivors. The Holocaust, I used to think, was another event, another place—far from Wang Fu Cang Lane, where Zhang Shenfu narrated the story of his life. But as I listened to this story, the world of my parents in Eastern Europe became less and less removed from Zhang's in Beijing. Messages about forgetting and remembrance began to cross the cultural and historical divide.

At first, certain details captured my imagination. In the spring of 1980, for example, I found myself bringing the conversation back to the little boy that Zhang Shenfu had fathered in Paris in 1921. Though this child was but one of Zhang's six offspring, he puzzled me more than the rest. For the next three years, I probed Zhang's memory about the child's name, about how the boy had been given up to a French family while his parents engaged in philosophical studies and Communist Party building. I wanted to know more about how the little boy died shortly after Zhang Shenfu brought him back to China in 1923.

Much later, after Zhang Shenfu's death in 1986, I realized that two story lines had crossed here: a Chinese line and a European one. Through Zhang's life, I had allowed myself to wonder about the fate of my own missing sister, born in 1944 just before the Nazis marched into Budapest. This was the child my mother was forced to give away in order to save my older sister. This was the child never mentioned while I grew up in Romania after the war. Nothing that Zhang Shenfu remembered or forgot about his Paris-born son could answer my questions about the child left in Budapest. Nonetheless, Zhang's story opened doors I had not ventured through before. Once one door opened, others beckoned not far beyond.

My father, like Zhang Shenfu, was a survivor. He, too, wanted to tell me a story. He was full of reminiscences about his youth, about his experience during the Holocaust, about his adventures in Romania after the establishment of Communism in 1944.

For several years, I used my work with Zhang Shenfu as a screen against my father's tales. Then, after both men had died—my father in 1984, Zhang Shenfu in 1986—I returned to their stories on my own terms. First, I edited the hundred odd pages of scattered memoirs my father had assembled over the last years of his life. This project became *Encounters Dictated by Fate*, a book I finished in 1987. After 1987 I was able to disentangle Zhang Shenfu's voice from that of my father. But still their words kept crossing in my mind, forcing me, finally, to acknowledge the echoes, the convergence.

Both Zhang Shenfu and my father had lived through war and revolution: my father through the Holocaust in Europe and the establishment of Communism in Romania, Zhang through the anti-Japanese War and the consolidation of the People's Republic under Mao Zedong. Each was a sensualist with a taste for women and the finer things in life. Both treasured memory, even when the world conspired to make them forget.

This became clear for me much later, when I was given a copy of Zhang Shenfu's self-criticism, written during the Cultural Revolution of 1966–69, which sought to destroy old traditions as well as the memories of old people. Yet the text of Zhang's self-criticism preserved some bit of memorial truth in spite of the pressure to defile the personal and the public past. Through the 1967 text I entered a life that challenged and overcame the political pressure toward historical amnesia.

SEPTEMBER 21, 1967. The seventy-four-year-old Zhang Shenfu has completed a thirty-three page manuscript entitled "My Education, Professions, and Activities."[1] Here in the middle of the Cultural Revolution, in the heat of Red Guard attacks on intellectuals, Zhang reaffirms his covenant with memory.

The self-criticism produced by Zhang contains a year-by-year account of his political life from 1904 to 1967. It includes the required self-castigations against the "shortcomings of petty bourgeois intellectuals" and praises Chairman Mao's works as "the truth, and not only the truth, but the sunshine and air without which we cannot live." All this is familiar terrain for hundreds of thousands of Zhang Shenfu's colleagues forced to distort their own pasts during the Cultural Revolution.

Zhang's manuscript, though, concludes on a note of pride. In the midst of chaos, he dwells on the past few months, "during which I have been repeatedly interviewed by various people about certain historical events. I try my best to help them. I am told that I can help more than others because I have a good memory. Although these interviews are not good for my blood pressure, I feel happy doing them. This is because I can make a contribution to the people. And because I like to use facts to clarify an individual's history."

AUGUST 1987. The thirty-three pages of cramped, handwritten characters are in front of me, a belated gift from Zhang Shenfu's youngest daughter, Zhang Yanni. "Use facts to clarify an individual's history"—what a strikingly simple combination of words in the 1967 essay, given all the dogmatic talk about class struggle that lay so thickly on the tongue of the Chinese people during the Cultural Revolution! More astonishing still is the image of Zhang Shenfu writing these words in the presence of the Red Guards. These inexperienced young men and women sat in judgment over his memory, trying to channel it toward a few political incidents in his life that were considered "revolutionary" at the moment.

And yet, Zhang Shenfu wrote and lived by his own credo: "Use facts to clarify an individual's history." The skeleton of his political career is there in the manuscript now before me, one year after his death. I am left alone with the challenge of piecing together the bits: this text, our conversations. The 1967 text, full of details, might have saved me months of work in 1979, at which point I knew little about Zhang's long, confusing political career. But it can never replace the years of conversation. In talking with me Zhang revealed all the living, loving, doubting, and thinking that had no place in his 1967 self-criticism.

The Cultural Revolution manuscript is not animated by laughter. Though Zhang wrote that he was happy to be interviewed by the guardians of public memory, this was a happiness eked out on the edges of a world ruled by the truths of Chairman Mao and imprisoned by Red Guard notions about the "short-comings of petty bourgeois intellectuals." There was not much room in 1967 for the rambling tone in which Zhang Shenfu told his nonpolitical tales at the oilcloth-covered table on Wang Fu Cang Lane.

And yet the chronology from 1904 to 1967 tells its own story—that of a man who managed to be faithful to his own experience against all odds. In 1967 Zhang Shenfu wrote what was expected of him, without changing a single fact about his life. To be sure, he left out many details that he knew would be incomprehensible and intolerable to his Red Guard interrogators. Yet he maintained his fidelity to the facts as he remembered them. Even in the 1967 text, Zhang Shenfu retained his right to distinguish truth from falsehood.

Was this integrity, the spirit of traditional *qinggao* (high-minded purity) for which Zhang Shenfu castigates himself in 1967? Or was integrity the by-product of an eccentric life lived on the periphery of public events? The puzzle of Zhang Shenfu's balancing act—of how he managed to live in keeping with his beliefs—is not solved either in the 1967 document or in our conversations. The puzzle of the man endures beneath the diverse, often dissonant faces that he wore as a public and private rememberer.

"Time for telling truth is running out" was his credo at our initial meeting. It arches back to his self-criticism in 1967 and provides the connecting thread to the tales freely shared in his home from 1979 to 1984.

On Wang Fu Cang Lane

NOVEMBER 26, 1979. This is my first visit to Zhang Shenfu's house on Wang Fu Cang Lane. What do I expect to find here? Truth? From such a practiced survivor? A survivor is, by necessity, a two-faced—or is it many-faced?—person. Without yet knowing much about Zhang's intellectual or political journey, I sense he is more than what he calls himself: "an incorrigibly simple-minded man."

This was the phrase he used in our public interview two weeks ago to describe his lifelong addiction to truth. Even in the reception hall of the library, I sensed that Zhang's insistence on "truth telling" does not place him in opposition to official truth. He cannot afford to displease the authorities who have just "rehabilitated" him. His "crime" as a "rightist" in 1957 was forgiven just a few months before our meeting at the library.

Today I make my way slowly to the narrow alley near the large, graying White Tower Pagoda—an enduring sign of the Lamaist faith of China's Manchu rulers. I know Zhang Shenfu has no reason to risk his fate in China by telling secrets to a foreigner. If not secrets, then, what am I going to hear? Bits. I am hoping for details about the life of an old man, which I will use to enliven my narrative of the May Fourth movement of 1919. I am tired of canonized "heroes" like Lu Xun, the modern writer whose museum I also pass on the way to Zhang Shenfu's house.

Beyond the White Tower Pagoda and the Lu Xun Museum, I arrive at 29 Wang Fu Cang Lane. After passing workers who had settled in the compound during the Cultural Revolution, I find, in the innermost courtyard, Zhang Shenfu's house—a series of six rooms. I visit only one today.

Zhang is waiting by a curtained window. His face is half hidden by late autumn shadows. The coal stove casts a small circle of warmth over a square table and two chairs. Across the table, graced with candies in my honor, we begin the conversation. An unspoken contract begins to take shape between us: Zhang will lead me off the well-traveled road of China's public memory. I am to be a mirror for his playful self-assessment in old age.

None of this is said. Instead, we share a lighthearted moment early on. Zhang leans his head back and laughs from deep within his throat—so unlike the choked, nervous laughter I have heard in the company of other intellectual-survivors whom I have been interviewing for the May Fourth project. What provoked this outpouring of mirth? A turn of phrase about the May Fourth intellectuals who were Zhang's friends? Something about Mao Zedong's proverbial wrath? About Bertrand Russell's romantic adventures? About Zhang Shenfu's?

The catalyst for Zhang's laughter is lost. This was our first and only unrecorded session. The sound is gone. But not the impact of this moment when we lost sight of the public past, thick as the fog just outside the window. For one moment, Zhang Shenfu's version of his life prevails. For one moment, a veil falls from the face of official China's vengeful forgetfulness.

JANUARY 21, 1980. I arrive a little late after taking photographs of the White Tower Pagoda—a detour intended to calm my nerves about the meeting. Zhang continues to agree to see me, week after week. This is my fourth visit to Wang Fu Cang Lane. Yet each time is like the first. Nothing is taken for granted: not our growing intimacy, not our ways of testing each other, not the invitation to come back again.

Today he is again waiting for me at the table. I catch his eyes searching the courtyard through the lace curtain. It is a sunny winter day. Our eyes meet as I approach—the old philosopher is waiting to tell me his story.

He has prepared gifts for me: a set of New Year's bookmarks with little goddesses on them, as well as two photographs taken of him by a doctor friend in 1967 and in 1979. Later, his wife, Guan Suowen—a short, stocky, rather uneducated woman with one arm paralyzed by a stroke—brings out a larger photograph of Zhang Shenfu. It is an official faculty portrait taken at Qinghua University (circa 1934–35). "Doesn't he look great as a professor?" Guan asks, passing the image to me, along with snapshots of herself "in my prettier days, before grey hair, before the political misfortunes."

The tape recorder repeatedly malfunctions, producing lots of blank, muffled spaces. I'm furious with myself. Then I remember that I can still write. I force myself to be less scared of this project. So many details keep pouring out, a confusing mass of scattered bits. For now, they are a counterpoint to the broad generalities of publicly recorded history.

Zhang Shenfu has a strong personality. Underneath the whimsical laughter lies a tough will. He is still testing me. He wants to tell his story, but in his way. He will not be bound by my chronological questions or by any theme I try to follow. When we talk about politics, he always brings in his philosophy. When we talk about philosophy, I find myself drawn off on some tangent about Liu Qingyang, who in 1920 was the first woman invited to join the Communist Party and then became the main love of Zhang Shenfu's life after 1921.

Today Zhang jumps from the National Salvation Movement, and his resulting imprisonment from February to May 1936, to another love affair, this time with Sun Junquan, the principal of Beijing's Normal School for Women. Then he leaps to a 1940 argument with Jiang Kaishek and back again to 1925 and the disputes that led to his withdrawal from the Chinese Communist Party.

It is hard for me to follow his verbal meandering. I need a place to stand outside of Zhang's story. A concrete place other than my own ignorance.

FEBRUARY 11, 1980. Zhang is waiting behind the lace curtain again. He makes me feel welcome, as if I'm a bit late for a task that only I can complete. Today the room around us is especially intimate. Zhang's wife leaves us alone until about 4:00 P.M. Again and again his laughter punctuates our conversation. Today Zhang dwells on his addiction to all things new and strange. He confesses an aesthetic, all-devouring curiosity.

As often before, Zhang Shenfu is prepared for our meeting. Today he brings out three letters that Bertrand Russell wrote to him in 1920. "These are my greatest treasures."

We also go over some photographs taken in Germany in 1923. One shows a Göttingen drawing room full of Chinese Communists dressed in Western clothes. Liu Qingyang is wearing a fox-collared coat. Zhu De, the man who later became Mao's guerilla chief in the 1930s, sits stiffly in a formal Western suit.

A new world opens for me in these photographs, offering a more nuanced sense of what Chinese "Communists" looked like in Europe in the 1920s. This is an aspect of the Party's past that has been swept under the rug in official chronicles of revolutionary peasants led by Mao Zedong.

Zhang repeatedly goes over the tale of how he and Liu Qingyang began their love affair on the boat to Marseilles: "Maybe we were a bit extreme," he laughs.

"She was a fine person, but bad-tempered, you know. I had another girlfriend before that boat ride. I don't know how my feelings changed so quickly. I'm so much like Russell with women."

Zhang's openness and his laughing, rambling voice are pulling me deeper into his story. Our story? The one not yet written? I am touched by his invitation to keep coming back, to continue asking whatever I want, even if he answers only partially or roundabout or not at all. I have to stop and realize just how much I am growing to like this old man!

MARCH 24, 1980. A fine afternoon with Zhang Shenfu. "He is not well," the wife announces as I enter the room. Indeed, his eyes are cloudy, evasive under the dusty old hat. But by the time I leave, his eyes are shining, excited again. Memory can heal. I see that literally today. Zhang is coming alive not just in the stories he tells, but here, in front of my eyes. And something awakens in me, too. I become more alert, more involved as we go on.

At times during our conversation today, my Chinese falters. Certain words evade me; others get lost in Zhang's tired, mumbling voice. But I keep trying to listen. He jumps from stories about Mikhail Borodin, Sun Yatsen's Soviet adviser, to comments about his own glasses: "I never needed them. I just liked how they look on me."

I now see the dandy in this man who insisted on stylishly cut clothes in Europe in the 1920s. While working for the Communist Party in Canton, Zhang left in the summer of 1924 because it "was too hot." The comforts and the sensuality of this intellectual's life are amply apparent here. What bothered him most about his being fired from Qinghua University in 1936 (for political activism in the National Salvation Movement) was "having to give up the fine house I had on the Qinghua campus."

Today I ask about changes, developments in his thought: "Not many," Zhang answers. I shoot back with a smile, "Yes, there were several; I'll prove it to you." I point to a lessening emphasis on analytical reason after the 1930s. On today's tape I talk almost as much as Zhang Shenfu. I'm inside the picture whose outline I have yet to define.

At dinner with friends tonight, I hear myself saying that I will do a book on Zhang Shenfu, maybe even before finishing the one on May Fourth. There is something urgent, concrete, delightful in this project that is missing in the other one.

JUNE 16, 1980. I come to say goodbye. This is my eighteenth visit to Wang Fu Cang Lane. I feel like a member of the family, especially after taking part in yesterday's birthday celebration. Zhang's friends and family gathered for his eighty-eight *sui*—a year having been added on to his eighty-seven years, according to Chinese tradition. I promise to come back to China to celebrate his next birthday with him. I feel ever closer to Zhang Shenfu's inner circle.

Yesterday I met the woman who has been at the center of that circle for many years: Li Jiansheng, the loyal, fierce, animated widow of Zhang Bojun, China's foremost "rightist" in 1957. Li Jiansheng is here today. She kept a promise given at the birthday party to come and talk with me about struggles she shared with Zhang Shenfu from the 1920s onward.

For most of our two hours together, I simply listen and take pictures of Zhang Shenfu and Li Jiansheng. The two of them are deeply involved in a heated conversation about the failure of revolution in 1927, about their "clumsy efforts" to build the Third Party (something between the Guomindang [GMD] and the CCP) in 1928–29, about the "brutal, unfair" charges leveled against Zhang Bojun in 1957.

I hear and feel the pain that Li still carries inside her. She has great loyalty and affection for Zhang Shenfu, who knew her husband in Berlin in 1923 and who defended him repeatedly, always at great cost to himself. Today I am an outsider to the vibrant connection across the small square table. This configuration reminds me of what happens in my parents' living room when the old Hungarian group gathers to trade labor camp stories. They know the dates, the jokes. They continue to ask each other how it might have been otherwise. They are intimate, anguished rememberers most at ease in their own company. Here, in Beijing I have come upon a similar scene.

Although I am an outsider, perhaps I have a role to play among these history-ladden rememberers. As in my parents' living room, perhaps it matters that I am present to witness and to record the outpouring of memory. My gift to Li Jiansheng today is an article by Zhang Bojun that I found buried in the Beijing University Library. It is a piece about democracy dated June 16, 1948. Thirty years after its publication, a snippet of the past—so precious and so forbidden to Zhang Bojun's widow—finds its way into her hands. As an outsider, I have access to what is still off-limits for Chinese survivors themselves.

Am I really outside the Chinese picture? Not in the Western sense of the word *objective*. I certainly do not see my subjects from without. Chinese words come to mind now, classical terms for the unity of subject and object.

In traditional China, to be *subjective* was to be *pianmian*: one-sided, limited by partiality and prejudice. Its opposite was never some point beyond the subject, but *quanmian*: all-around, having an inner ability to see things from many sides.

JUNE 7, 1981. I am back on Wang Fu Cang Lane, as I promised. Last year I told Zhang Shenfu I would be here for his birthday celebration. Today the family planned a festive gathering to correspond with my arrival. At 9:00 A.M., as I make my way across the courtyard, Zhang is waiting for me outside the door of his newly refurbished house.

"It took three months of work," Zhang tells me, "to repair the damage done during the 1976 earthquake and the Cultural Revolution of the 1960s." Now the job is completed. I wonder who authorized these extensive repairs. How does this new sense of material well-being relate to Zhang Shenfu's ongoing political rehabilitation? Is it a "payment" for his willingness to become an increasingly prominent voice in China's revisionist historiography? Zhang's memoirs of Zhou Enlai are now helping party historians to reorient the Communist Party away from the legacy of Mao Zedong.

Zhang Shenfu looks plump, withdrawn. He appears sleepy before our eyes meet. Then the familiar, animated warmth returns to his face. Our mutual delight at this reunion is great. He brings me up to date on the details of his daily routine: "I can still eat and sleep well, but my memory is slipping. Still, I have better and better thoughts about dialectics. It all goes back to *xiangfan*, *xiangcheng*, the basic Chinese idea of mutually attracting opposites."

The arrogance of the aging philosopher is more apparent to me now than it was last year. The desire to distill his life's thought into a few words has also grown more acute.

By 11:00 A.M. the other guests arrive. In their company, I present my gift to Zhang Shenfu: a hundred index cards listing each of the articles by him that I have collected over the past three years. The guests express appreciation and admiration for my efforts.

Only Li Jiansheng's face shows more sorrow than pleasure. She is thinner than last year, smaller somehow. Gone is the spirited voice in which she had debated with Zhang Shenfu the details of their shared past. Before her arrival, Zhang's daughter pulls me into a side room: "It would be best not to seek out Li Jiansheng this time, though she would probably welcome you out of her warm heart. The question of Zhang Bojun's 'crimes against the people' has not been settled yet. She's been fighting for his posthumous rehabilitation. But no success at all."

Behind this well-intentioned warning, I sense a deeper anxiety. My other intellectual friends, too, are nervous about the current campaign against Bai Hua, a writer accused of being too critical in his revelations about Cultural Revolution horrors. Bai Hua stands accused of a lack of "patriotism," or a "lack of faith in socialism."

Such charges could easily be turned against any of the guests gathered here in Zhang Shenfu's house. At the same time, there are rumors of new regulations to curb relations between foreigners and Chinese. The government seems to be losing confidence in its own population. Old charges against Westerners as a "contaminating" presence are being revived in newspaper editorials. Here, on Wang Fu Cang Lane, I am an "old friend" of the family. But is this enough to reassure the guests at this lunch?

During the meal Li Jiansheng sits next to Zhang and me. She gives him the best morsels from the table. She remains his loyal, loving friend. But the shadows of disillusionment are deeply etched in her face. She moves her fingers slowly through the cards listing Zhang Shenfu's works. Wordless grief engulfs her eyes. Although all traces of her husband have been wiped from public life, she guards his memory with fierce fidelity.

During lunch I also talk to Zhang Shenfu's younger brother, Zhang Dainian, a philosophy professor from Beijing University, who shares with me stories about Qinghua University in the 1930s. He was a student and then a faculty member there, and his time overlapped with Zhang Shenfu's. Zhang Dainian gives me the names of the professors who wanted his older brother fired for political activism in 1936. He reveals to me the pen name that he himself used to write essays on Chinese and Western philosophy in the early 1930s. Zhang Dainian, too, turns out to have been a fervent follower of Bertrand Russell for a while.

Zhang Congnian, the youngest brother, a physicist from Shandong, answers my questions about their early family life. He confirms that none of the children knew their mother's personal name. In keeping with old Confucian traditions, she was called simply Zhao Zhang—a combination of her father's and her husband's last names. From Zhang Congnian, I also learn the exact date of Zhang Shenfu's birth: June 16, 1893, or May 2 in the lunar calendar.

JUNE 13, 1981. I come to Wang Fu Cang Lane daily, as we agreed at the birthday celebration. For this month that I am in China, Zhang is making himself fully available to me. The voluminous file cards, my return to Beijing —everything cements my commitment to our conversations in his eyes. From his side, Zhang is making his commitment increasingly explicit. Today, yet another breakthrough. More openness from him, and more confusion for me.

We are talking about Dong Guisheng, the young secretary who lived with Zhang Shenfu during the anti-Japanese war. He still claims that theirs was a platonic relationship. But hints of a love affair with his former student abound. At one point today, Zhang looks up from the tape recorder between us: "I think I still have some of her letters. Let me show them to you." We get up slowly because he has trouble walking, even with his cane. He leads me into an inner room, past the study that was revealed to me during my last visit in 1980. Today we walk into a corner of the house that I never knew existed.

Zhang looks for a key in a dresser drawer and proceeds to open the door to "my old study." Here, dust filled but orderly, lies an extraordinary collection of works on Chinese and Western philosophy. My eyes roam over American, Ger-

man, French, English, and Japanese journals from the 1930s. They are arranged in rows next to numerous stacks of cloth-bound Chinese texts, many of
them from the Qing dynasty. From the drawer of his old desk Zhang takes
several packages of letters: about ten from Dong Guisheng, two from Liu
Qingyang, and three from another lover, Sun Junquan.

I ask to borrow the letters to make copies. Zhang agrees and also gives me
more old photographs to reproduce. Among them is one of his first wife, Zhu
Denong, the child bride who died in childbirth. I carry away more primary
sources than I had ever hoped for. The number and variety overwhelm me.

I don't know what to do with this plethora of detail. I feel as if I am drowning in puddles. The question of the significance of it all—of what I am to
select and why—is growing more urgent. For now, I fumble along on pure
intuition. I am like a blind person in need of a Seeing Eye dog.

Struggling with the details of Zhang's life brings back memories of my
panic last summer in Romania. After China and Nepal, I stopped off to see my
aunt in an old-age home in Timisoara. For a week my father's sister overwhelmed me with stories and photographs from a world buried by the Holocaust. Out of shoeboxes, she excavated details that had no place in the history I
knew. I was especially taken aback by pictures of my father's first wife, who
had died in Auschwitz. That is all I had heard before. Then I jotted down my
aunt's words: "She gave birth to a daughter named Vera, dead just a few days
after being born. The mother was pregnant again when she was deported."

Too many pictures, too much information in Romania, as in China. No
context in which to fit it all. No context with which to tame it all. My back
hurts. I can hardly stand as I leave Wang Fu Cang Lane. I go on blindly.

MAY 5, 1983. Two years have passed since my last visit on Zhang's birthday.
This is the year he reaches ninety! On the walls I see lots of fine new paintings
filled with the traditional symbols of longevity: peaches and Tang dynasty poems.
These are tributes from Zhang's friends and colleagues. All around him I see
even more abundant signs of material well-being than in 1981. A newly refurbished sofa and formal sitting chairs now grace the freshly painted "reception
room." The inner rooms have also been cleaned up and are used as the daughter's bedroom and study.

Zhang Shenfu is as peppery as ever, but his memory has seriously weak-
ened. His thoughts are more and more disconnected. His voice drops into an
almost inaudible mumble. Daily interviews with him are not so useful now. He
seems to come back to one theme and one theme only: "I am the greatest
philosopher in twentieth-century China."

His arrogance, there all along, now comes out unadorned by his once fe-
cund memory. There is something unattractive, unreliable about him these days.

In 1984 Zhang Shenfu describes his latest rehabilitation in China's official memory: he has
been asked to contribute to a volume on the Whampoa Military Academy. (Courtesy of
Jason Wolfe)

If this were my first meeting with him, nothing could persuade me to begin this
project.

As it is, though, the story of his life has opened many doors for me. I am
now able to follow the Zhang Shenfu thread in conversations with other
survivor-participants of China's revolution. Tomorrow, for example, I will see
Liang Shuming, the eminent philosopher and social reformer who has been
Zhang Shenfu's friend from middle school on. Were I not following the thread
of Zhang Shenfu's life, I might not have found my way to Liang Shuming's
door. It might have never opened to me.

OCTOBER 23, 1984. A rushed visit to Wang Fu Cang Lane. This is a morning taken out of an official visit to China with the president of Wesleyan University. I am bringing my husband to meet the old man who has occupied my
thoughts for the past five years. Zhang Shenfu is frail now. But the warmth
between us is still strong, perhaps even more tender, today. His youngest daughter, Zhang Yanni, gives me a book of essays about the Whampoa Academy, the
military and political training ground for Communist and Nationalist cadres in

the early 1920s. Zhang has been included in its history—another sign of his rehabilitation in Communist Party historiography.

Zhang himself, though he gives frequent interviews about China's political history, wants to talk to me about philosophy. He delights in the prospect of an article I wrote entitled "Zhang Shenfu: China's Foremost Russell Expert." He goes on about how much more he knows about both Chinese and Western philosophy than any of his contemporaries. He is as arrogant as ever about this.

His wife, Guan Suowen—more debilitated by the stroke than before —complains that I spent too much money on the new radio that is my gift to Zhang Shenfu. I do not tell her that I would have bought nothing less for my father if he were still alive, if he had no pleasures left but to listen to music and news on the radio. Zhang Shenfu is an explicit father figure to me now. My father's death in March this year has brought me closer to Zhang.

At the door Zhang holds my hand a long time in his dry, thin palms: "I know that your presentation of me will be different from my image of myself. This is all right. That is how I want it to be. That is what it means to be objective." I leave encouraged, blessed somehow. I'm free to write *my* story of Zhang's life.

AUGUST 26, 1986. I'm back in Beijing. Zhang Shenfu died on June 20. I have come for ten days, hoping to learn a few more details, a few more stories, as his friends and family now openly mourn him.

A dream fragment from last night: a prominent Communist diplomat, Gong Pusheng, grants me a guarded interview. The burden of silence lies heavy between us, a silence that borders on lies. Waking up, I realize what Zhang Shenfu's gift to me was, why I kept going back to Wang Fu Cang Lane. He told me what he could, and he often got mixed up about the various versions of a story. So did I. But there was never a sense of some huge "forbidden" zone between us. All aspects of his intellectual, personal, and political life were fit for conversation, and laughter. This is a gift I had never received before—either at home, from my parents, or from anyone else in China.

Rather Break Than Bend

I found what I was looking for on Wang Fu Cang Lane: an old hunger for true stories was assuaged there. But what of Zhang Shenfu? What made his eyes search the courtyard with expectation before each of my visits? What made them sparkle, even on days when he was tired, sick, and lost in the fog that began to invade his once-lucid logician's mind? Pride at the prospect of being written about in the West? An impish delight when he managed to embarrass his foreign interviewer with tales of his amorous adventures?

Arrogance and eros certainly played a part in Zhang Shenfu's decision to continue talking with me. But there was also the desire to vindicate himself in a forum that was not bound by the whims of Communist Party historiography. Although he was being rehabilitated in China's public memory, newly fashioned chronicles of revolution had little room for Zhang's philosophical ideas and even less for the odd details of his personal life. Finally, there was something else: a determination to size up his life in his own terms.

By the time Zhang and I met, the guardians of China's official history had already begun writing about him. The modestly dressed, often well-informed cadres that came to Zhang's home before and after my visits asked new questions about the founding of the Chinese Communist Party, about Zhou Enlai's youth, and about other luminaries in modern history, such as Beijing University president Cai Yuanpei and Communist Party founder Li Dazhao.

The questions these historians posed to Zhang Shenfu were firmly rooted in twentieth-century events. At the same time, these men stood in a long lineage with Confucian officials who had compiled China's voluminous dynastic annals. Year by year, reign by reign, dynasty by dynasty, orthodox historians had sought to fashion a narrative that would instruct future generations. Their intentions were moralistic and political—much like revisionist scholars who are seeking to "correct" Communist Party history after the death of Mao Zedong.[2]

Even in traditional China, however, literati had devised ways to preserve unofficial history. Didactic intent, though linked with the sacred names of Confucius and the Grand Historian Si-Ma Qian, was never so encompassing that someone somewhere did not get the urge, or the opportunity, to laugh at himself. And through irony, Chinese intellectuals managed to acknowledge ambiguity, ambivalence, and self-deceit.

One traditional form for such candid explorations of the self was *zizan*, an ironical autobiography. Started by Buddhist monks who inscribed self-mocking eulogies on the margins of their formal portraits, the zizan tradition spread to Confucian intellectuals who sought to break with the conventions of moralistic historiography.[3]

For Zhang Shenfu, I now realize, our conversations provided just such marginal space. With words addressed as much to himself as to me, he continued inscribing and revising the one-dimensional portrait of himself being painted in Chinese public life. After 1949 the possibilities for fashioning zizan were almost obliterated. Irony had little room in China's public life and was eventually squeezed out of individual recollections as well.

A vast literature of made-to-order memoirs proliferated instead. But its aims and form remained every bit as didactic as the Party's official histories or the dynastic annals of former times. Even after Mao's death in 1976, forays into oral history (that awkwardly named domain of *koutou shi*, literally, mouth-spoken history) sought to impart "lessons from the past." It was as if a lessonless past was a meaningless one.[4]

Zhang Shenfu knew nothing about koutou shi when we began our conversations in 1979. But he did sense that there were aspects of his experience and corners of his mind that could not be explored in the essay that he published or in the interviews he granted to Chinese scholars during the last decade of his life. Our conversations gave him an opportunity to explore those corners, to linger there at his leisure. And in the process something occasionally crystallized that was very much like a zizan.

APRIL 28, 1980. One such ironical epiphany occurs today. We are talking about two decisive moments in Zhang Shenfu's political career: 1925, when he withdrew from the Communist Party, and 1948, when he was expelled from the Communist-supported Democratic League. Both events have come up before in our conversations. Both actions, Zhang concedes, were the result of "mistakes" on his part. But on this day, we circle parts of the story that are beyond the reach of political commentary. On this day, Zhang is not interested in passing judgments on his political career, not interested in *pingjia* (literally, weighing and deciding)—that act of moralistic appraisal so familiar to Communist and Confucian historians.

Instead, Zhang tells the story of a day in early January 1925, when he walked out of a stormy debate at the Fourth Chinese Communist Party Congress. Zhou Enlai, his friend from the European sojourn, followed him out and expressed support for Zhang's point of view. Zhou also counseled Zhang against leaving the Party in a fit of anger. He argued that they must go back and create common ground in keeping with Party discipline.

"But I left, you see, and Zhou Enlai stayed. I guess I'm the kind of man who would rather break than bend (*ning zhe bu bian*)." Zhang Shenfu leans back his head and laughs aloud. His delight mounts, now that he has hit upon four ideograms that explain to him something about his own character. He writes them down on the paper for me. Then, another self-satisfied chuckle: "Yes, I was always like that—in 1925, in 1948, in 1957. Now Zhou Enlai, you see, was different. He was the kind to always bend without ever breaking. His character was that of the compromiser who makes endless concessions (*wei qu qiu quan*)."

More laughter. Zhang's eyes narrow, becoming more inward-looking, as he stops to savor this contrast. Zhou Enlai has been such a prominent figure in his life: friend, then supporter, and finally protector. But never before had Zhang Shenfu used this man as a negative mirror for his own character. Zhou had been an almost sacred topic of conversation, with me as with the Chinese historians who come to interview Zhang Shenfu. Today, however, Zhang lets himself stray toward the margins of the formal portrait of China's premier. There he glimpses and inscribes something about himself.

A few moments after this delighted discovery, Zhang Shenfu's eyes cloud over: "Zhou Enlai bent so much, it finally killed him. During his last years he just gave in too much." With this, Zhang Shenfu pulls himself out of the pleasures of zizan and takes another look at his friend's life. He will not dwell on the details of Zhou's endless compromising. That would betray Zhou's memory, perhaps even lead Zhang into the dangerous realm of political criticism. (Only a foreigner like Simon Leys could and did call Zhou Enlai the whore of the Chinese Communist Party, when analyzing the same character trait that Zhang called "rather bend than break.")[5]

Instead, Zhang Shenfu goes on to talk about their fathers: "Mine was a scholar; Zhou Enlai's was a merchant. Different temperaments, you know: one was firm, moralistic, the other mild, forgiving. Yet, here is how it ended: though Zhou was five years younger than I am, his health was ruined before mine." Zhang stops again. Silently, he reflects upon something he cannot, will not, speak to me about.

I write in my notes, "Who is the brittle one, the breakable one: Zhang or Zhou?" At this point, Zhang Shenfu's garrulous wife enters the room, interrupting our conversation with her summary: "Zhou Enlai was a really good man, really good." The voice of public, official judgment is reasserted once again, right here on Wang Fu Cang Lane.

But Zhang Shenfu's determination to break through the confines of public memory endured. In each of our conversations he tried to glimpse some part of his own character, especially when talking about his "political mistakes." He had confessed these in public many times. On Wang Fu Cang Lane, however, he was after something else. At home, he explored his temperamental disability to tow any political line.

JUNE 9, 1980. We are talking once again about how Zhang Shenfu left the Communist Party. Suddenly, Zhang starts on an entirely different story—that of his friendship with Zhou Zuoren, the younger brother of China's famous writer Lu Xun. I had sensed during earlier conversations that Zhang Shenfu did not like Lu Xun, in spite of the public veneration of this writer, because Chairman Mao praised him as the foremost revolutionary fighter on the cultural front. But I had not heard the details of Zhang Shenfu's friendship with the lesser-known brother.

Zhang describes how they continued to write to each other throughout the 1940s. "After the war with Japan, Zhou Zuoren was accused of being a traitor for his supposed collaboration with the Japanese in North China. Everyone held him in contempt. But I always had respected him. Why stop now? So I visited him often, brought him the books he needed. I am not swayed by what most people think, you see. [He laughs.] Most people paid no attention to Zhou

Zuoren. But I did. Even if a hundred people oppose someone, it makes no difference to me. Even if someone is in trouble, I welcome him. To me, a good person remains good, no matter the twists of political fate. I guess I just don't know how to be an opportunist, like Guo Moruo [a prominent Communist writer and archaeologist and another of Mao Zedong's favorites]."

This image of a man constantly at odds with his contemporaries is embroidered with more stories: with details of Zhang's ill-fated support for Zhang Bojun in 1957, with details about his conflict with the Chinese education minister in France in 1921. Then there is another thrust of his head backward, another peal of laughter: "I guess I am just too unworldly [tai bu shigu]. . . . Whenever I disagree with the majority, I just go my own way. I pull out [Wo butong, suoyi wo bugan]."

The significance of these simple words for Zhang Shenfu is not apparent to me until two years later, when I read his published recollections of the founding of the Chinese Communist Party. He describes his withdrawal in 1925, with a summary judgment of his own character: "I am just a bad tempered man. When the majority approves of me, then I do anything. When they disapprove, I just roll on out."[6]

This is a lie masquerading as half-truth. It is printed in an official historical collection sponsored by the Party. Zhang certainly did "roll on out" repeatedly during his long political career. He certainly brushed up against the majority more than once. But something is missing, something is distorted here. Without the echo of Zhang's self-mocking laughter, without the stories of his risk-laden fidelity to friends in trouble, this pingjia is a fake confession intended to satisfy official historians accustomed to squeezing required political conclusions out of the memory of survivors like Zhang Shenfu.

Just how laughter can change the meaning of words also became clear to me in yet another contrast, this time between Zhang's 1967 self-criticism and one of our conversations in 1980, both of which contain the same phrase, I note. In the text written during the Cultural Revolution, Zhang confesses, "I have always liked to be totally free. I have lived all my life for three loves [san hao]: fame, books, and women. Still, under Chairman Mao's guidance, I began criticism of my tendency toward individual heroics. The more I studied, the more I realized how wrong I had been. I grew aware that I had always liked to seek the limelight, to show off, to consider myself a wise hero, as if nothing could be done without me. This is the result of my rotten, petty bourgeois temperament."[7]

Precisely the same three loves come up in our conversation on March 10, 1980: fame, books, and women. But everything else is different—how Zhang Shenfu speaks about these weaknesses, in what order, with what emphasis. In the end it all comes down to laughter, to another moment in the zizan that Zhang Shenfu goes on embroidering on the margins of our conversation about politics.

On that March afternoon, Zhang Shenfu dwells on his lifelong attachment to books: "I loved my books too much, I suppose. I just could not be too far from my library, ever. You see, I have had three weaknesses, three loves all my life: books, women, and fame. I even had a seal carved with these three loves, my san hao, in the 1920s. And I never gave them up. My love of books cost me dearly in 1948. My love of women got me into trouble even more often, with Liu Qingyang and others. I'm really embarrassed by this, but I can't help it. Not even now." Zhang Shenfu looks at me directly, then throws his head back and laughs at himself. He looks out the window, momentarily silent, as he ponders the price paid for his three weaknesses.

There is nothing in this conversation about Zhang Shenfu's love of fame —the main crime for which he castigated himself in 1967. There is no mention here of the "shortcomings of petty bourgeois intellectuals." The word Zhang uses in 1980 is *weakness* (*ruodian*), not the public currency of *shortcomings* (*quedian*). In public the much-confessed shortcomings of Chinese intellectuals are like a hem that is too high, shows too much, and must be let down with proper, Maoist alterations. In China during the 1950s and 1960s such alterations were called "thought reform" and "ideological remolding."

But Zhang Shenfu was, and knew himself to be, unalterable. He had enjoyed his weaknesses through the end of his life. My presence across the small square table gave him a chance to think about and talk about his san hao in a new way. It must have pleased him to watch me blush when I realized that I was included in his incurable weakness for women.

An Unheroic Survivor

Interest in individual character and individual foibles constituted our common ground. Zhang Shenfu himself guided me in the exploration of his limitations. Early in our conversations he began to talk to me about his favorite classical Chinese text, the *Ren wu zhi*, which he described as a "forerunner of modern psychology, a valuable aid to me in understanding myself and others."

I read the Han dynasty section of the text in spring 1987, after Zhang Shenfu's death. Its title, "The Record of Individuals" (or "The Study of Human Abilities"), points away from the moralistic categories of character judgment in both Communist and Confucian historiography. The preface by Liu Shao, a logician who composed the text around A.D. 250, claims that the *Ren wu zhi* is nothing more than an elaboration of Confucius's own dictum: "Examine what gives a man pleasure, and observe where he comes from."[8]

But the bulk of Liu Shao's text goes beyond Confucius. It develops a meticulous typology of character and ability intended to give rulers a road map to the proper use of bureaucratic personnel. Each chapter contains explicit advice on what kind of man is best suited for what kind of job. Liu Shao also warns against the consequences of applying a certain type of talent to a task for which it is not suited.

In a chapter entitled "Types of Personality" I come upon a passage that decodes some of the enigma of Zhang Shenfu. The passage concerns the generalist, the man who is never narrow-minded but suffers from being too *za*, too scattered: "When a man is broad and all encompassing, his greatness lies in loving all, but his defect lies in being muddy. The all embracing man pervades all things with his benevolent feelings. He does not refrain from muddiness and the mixed nature of his friendships, but regards rectitude as one-sided. . . . So one can use him to pacify the mass of people, but it is hard to uplift vulgarity with him."[9]

Though I read this after Zhang Shenfu's death, I can still hear his voice describing his friendship with the "traitor" Zhou Zuoren and his contempt for Zhou's overly righteous brother Lu Xun. I hear Zhang's amused, regretful laughter at how he never finished any schooling, at how he jumped from grade to grade and, later, from one philosophical subject to another, from one woman to another, from one political commitment to another. He knew himself to be za: broad-minded and muddy.

The *Ren wu zhi* does not solve the puzzle that was Zhang Shenfu. It only helps me thread my way past all the judgmental talk about weaknesses and shortcomings. It helps me sift through the record of our conversations as we went back and forth over the same events, the same people, the same story. During each conversation Zhang Shenfu added one or another detail here, a nuance there, that complicated earlier versions of his life.

The plethora of ill-fitting details, in the end, makes it impossible to follow one narrative line. These conversations are as decentered as Zhang Shenfu's history-torn life. All that remains are pieces of a puzzle. All I can do is gather fragments around the polarities that marked Zhang Shenfu's life—a life lived on the margins of China's revolutionary history, a life snatched back from the forgetful annals of public history. A life laughingly shared at the end, when little mattered but the pleasure of story telling itself.

1

THE MAKING OF

A BOOKISH REBEL

He had fancied himself an educated youth. He even believed that reading books might save the nation. Little did the schoolmaster know that he would not reach his goal with such a soft-mannered occupation.
—Ye Shengtao, *Schoolmaster Ni Huanzhi*

JUNE 10, 1981. The morning sun cuts through the thick dust on Wang Fu Cang Lane. Much new construction is under way in this new age of prosperity and rehabilitation brought on by the death of Mao in 1976. Not only is Zhang Shenfu's house being rebuilt, so is the whole neighborhood. A tall, new, for-foreigners-only hotel is to be erected across the street from the White Tower Pagoda. Zhang has lived to see China reborn.

Around the table another, an older world is being called up from the shadows, the world of his boyhood years eighty years before cars, before mechanized cranes and fifty-stories-high hotels. Searching the distant past with mischievous eyes, Zhang concludes our conversation: "All my life, I have loved new ideas. I loved the idea of the new. As soon as I encountered something new, I would drop the old subject that had interested me earlier. Thus I became hopelessly scattered [*fensan*]. I have been diffuse [*za*] in my scholarly concerns, as in all my political activism. No wonder I was less well known in intellectual circles than some of my friends."

A tired, regretful old man dissects his fragmented, novelty-ridden life. With the steam shovel still grinding beyond the window, Zhang falls into silence. He looks at me across the table. He's finished for today. For me, the puzzle deepens: how to link the self-styled "revolutionary" philosopher in front of me with the thoroughly conventional youth he has described to me. Little in Zhang Shenfu's early years foreshadowed a thirst for new ideas. In fact, he told me earlier today: "Until the revolution of 1911, I lived out the Confucian role of the elder son in a traditional literati household without any inner rancor at all."

A Confucian Boyhood in Gratitude County

JUNE 15, 1981. "Were it not for war and revolution, I would have never strayed from my home in the North China plain. I am a native son of Gratitude County [Xian Xian], in Hebei province, you know. Our hometown of Xiaoduokou was located about a hundred miles from China's imperial capital. Even with all the upheavals of the revolution, I have managed to spend most of my life in the two cities closest to my childhood home: Beijing and Tianjin. Only nine years out of my ninety did I spend away from these cities, and then only because of the war against Japan. Those years were the most difficult ones for me."

The burdened voice of the old man testifies to the truth of his words. Yet he is one of the most cosmopolitan intellectuals of his generation. Why this melancholia about his native place now?

"Yes, yes, I have lived in other cities, too. Paris, Berlin, then Shanghai and Guangzhou. But whenever I had a choice, I stayed close to Beijing. Not out of nationalism, mind you, but out of old cultural habit. This is hardest to shake. Even when I quarreled most intensely with China's traditional values, I liked to stay close to its historical terrain."

He catches traces of disbelief in my eyes and goes on: "You probably think it odd, this attachment of mine to native place. It certainly cost me a great deal, especially during the political turmoil of 1948–49 when I refused to leave Beijing to go to Hong Kong. . . . But the pull of my origins has been great. . . . I have always been interested in the history of Gratitude County and its most famous native son, Ji Yun, a Qing dynasty scholar. I have collected as many of his poems and essays as I could, you know. In my library, even now, I have a nearly complete collection of works by this fellow provincial of mine."

The name of Ji Yun keeps coming up in our conversation. Here sits Zhang Shenfu—a cultural rebel, a modern scholar interested in mathematical logic and dialectical materialism. Yet he has spent months, "indeed years," he says, correcting me, finding and collecting the works of Ji Yun. What lies behind Zhang's attachment to this eighteenth-century Confucian? Compensation for his own injured pride?

Zhang Shenfu himself did not become a famous native son of Gratitude County. His family's intellectual genealogy stretched no further than his grandfather, a wealthy peasant who had saved enough to hire Confucian tutors for his sons. Zhang Shenfu's uncle, his father's older brother, had been the first family member to take the imperial examination. Zhang Shenfu's father, Zhang Lian, was the second.

But the more we talk about Ji Yun, the more he grows in stature in Zhang's eyes. And in my own. In Ji Yun, it appears, Zhang has found a kindred spirit. In the years when Zhang Shenfu had difficulty balancing internal convictions and outer obligations Ji Yun provided him with some precedent, some way out of the thickets of a cultural tradition obsessed by politics.

Before I leave today, I ask to borrow one of Zhang's books by Ji Yun. From the introduction I learn that Ji Yun first attracted national attention in 1747, when he came in first at the provincial-level examination. Within a few years Ji rose to the top of the central bureaucracy, so high in fact that he became exposed to charges of bribery and favoritism. Whatever the basis of these charges, Ji Yun never contested them. Instead, he accepted exile to the farthest northwestern corner of the imperial realm. On his way to and from Urumchi, Ji wrote the collection of poems that Zhang Shenfu quotes to me today. Then he adds, "Whenever I was cast out from the center of political revolution, Ji Yun's poems gained new meaning for me."

Zhang Shenfu's parting words as he hands me the volume of poetry at the door make his attachment to this eighteenth-century Confucian clearer. "Ji Yun, too, had to learn how to walk the public tightrope. But he was more successful than I. He came back from exile to become an important official.[1] He managed to thread his path between politics and scholarship more gracefully than I did. He was a close friend of the philosopher, Dai Zhen. Together they took on many battles against the moralists who pretended to be the true heirs of Confucian tradition. . . . For us twentieth-century Chinese intellectuals, the battle was not so clear, nor so easily won. We could no longer claim to be the true heirs of Confucianism. Though at times I was tempted to try."

JUNE 16, 1981. I try to bring our conversation back to Zhang Shenfu's childhood. I want to learn more about his father and his uncle, not just Ji Yun. But Zhang Shenfu's parental world stays opaque. Though his account is clothed in formalities, I sense pain buried beneath the genealogical recitation: "My eldest uncle had taken and passed the *zhuren* examinations at the provincial level. This opened the path for my father, Zhang Lian. He passed the highest examination for the *jinshi* [the metropolitan degree] in 1906. The next year, my father was sent on an official visit to Japan to oversee the educational progress of government students there. He returned convinced of the practical value of a modern education. So my father promptly enrolled me in a modern style primary school in Beijing."

I am not ready to jump over the first thirteen years of Zhang's life, and I ask more about what happened at home in Gratitude County, before the new schooling in Beijing.

"Before that? Well, before that I had a thoroughly Confucian upbringing, I suppose. My father was the overseer of my education, but he left the details to the family tutor. My father, I remember, was very strict with me. Here, take a

Zhang Shenfu's father, Zhang Lian, in 1906, the year in which he obtained the jinshi degree. (Courtesy of Zhang Shenfu)

look at these old photographs. They were taken right after my father passed the jinshi examination."

Two small portraits are laid out on the table—the father and the son, a stiff, thoroughly Confucian pair. Zhang Lian, wearing his official robes and cap, looks out with a severe gaze and sports the long mustache of a military official. In fact, as Zhang Shenfu tells me, most of his father's assignments for the Qing dynasty revolved around the military. In 1906 Zhang Lian began to serve as tutor at the Manchu military academy. During the next five years, the men who became Zhang Lian's closest associates were military officials: "Foremost among these was Feng Guozhang, the Chinese general who took over the Manchu Nobles' College in 1906. My father and Feng Guozhang remained close throughout the upheaval of the 1911 revolution. Zhang Lian went on to share a brief moment of glory when Feng came close to suppressing anti-dynastic rebels in the late fall of 1911."

The other little portrait shows Zhang Shenfu at thirteen. The boy's face is as severe as that of the father. The child's gaze projects the kind of seriousness expected of the eldest son of an official who just passed the jinshi examination.

Zhang Shenfu at age thirteen, on the eve of his enrollment in a modern primary school in Beijing. (Courtesy of Zhang Shenfu)

Dressed in a silk gown with fur collar, the boy wears his little scholar's cap with awkward dignity over protruding ears. His eyes are unflinching, as if he has just won a battle against an inner foe.

"Were you afraid of your father?" I ask softly. I may be transgressing on protected domain, but the portrait of the fierce father coupled with the overserious boy edges me on. Zhang Shenfu stops in mid-sentence. He had been rambling on about the open-air market that took place in his native village every four days or so. He interrupts the story of how his great-grandfather started this village after running into trouble with his own clan just a few miles away. He looks at me with pained eyes:

"I was six or so when my father beat my head into the *kang*—you know, the kind of North China stove that also serves as bed and oven for village families. . . . He came into the room in which I was supposed to be memorizing my daily lessons and caught me playing idly with the pages of a classical dictionary. This was a big book, a huge compendium of classical learning that served as a reference work for officials. For my father, this was a sacred text. For me, a boy, it was a toy. Without warning, my father smashed my head into the kang. Blood pumped from the wound a long time. To this day you can see the scar on my forehead."

I lean closer to look for some visible sign of the wound. There is none. But the withdrawn look of the old man in front of me lets me know that the little boy inside is still smarting from the father's violence. The silence between us stretches on longer than usual. Then Zhang Shenfu goes on to assimilate this momentary recollection into the broader picture that he is painting for me.

"You see how early I exhibited my pleasure in playing with books. I always liked books, but I didn't like to study."

Zhang leans back and tries to let a smile wash away the gloom hanging over the memory of his father's beating. "By the time I was fourteen, playtime was over. I was sent to Beijing to study under my uncle's supervision. I went there alone, in a small, horse-drawn cart." Zhang's voice trails off, leaving me no way now to return to the subject of his childhood pain. Clearly he has locked most of it in a place words cannot reach. He wants to go on to talk about himself as an easygoing (*buzaihu*) man.

Toward the end of this afternoon's conversation, however, one more trauma slips through the net of selective remembrance. We are talking about other members of his family. Zhang starts listing his various siblings, adding a few more to the two younger brothers, Zhang Dainian and Zhang Congnian, whom he had mentioned before (and whom I have met). A couple of sisters now enter Zhang's world, "uneducated, as all women were at the time." Then, another cloudy look: "My youngest brother drowned when he was five years old. He was much younger than I was. Still, his death shook me deeply."

Again, the conversation moves on. Another subject, another time. A brief gaze of pain and loss lingers in spite of Zhang's chatty voice. I realize that I have seen the same look come over Zhang's face whenever he speaks about the death of his Paris-born son in 1924. At such times, part of Zhang slows down to countenance old aches. But the conscious, rational, storytelling voice moves on. His losses, unlike the "mistakes" that thread through his marriages and political life, do not hold Zhang Shenfu's interest for long.

Although he allowed the pain of the kang beating and the loss of his brother's drowning to enter our conversations, Zhang Shenfu really wants to tell me about something else today. He finally comes around to his mother, that vague character whose first name he can never quite recall. He always refers to her by the family name, Zhao Zhang. Though illiterate herself, this daughter of a renowned scholar-official brought considerable prestige to the recently educated Zhang household.

The story of Zhao Zhang takes up a bit more time than usual, mostly because her son Zhang Shenfu is counting his blessings. "My mother," he recalls, "was only twenty-two when I was born. Because she was so young and healthy, I benefited both within and outside of the womb. She continued to bear children every three years or so. None of them was as strong or as healthy as I."

This boast does not quite fit the picture of Zhang Shenfu's younger brothers, with whom I shared a table at the birthday celebration last week. Zhang Congnian, the physicist from Shandong, is a tall, vigorous man of seventy-five. Zhang Dainian, the eminent professor of philosophy from Beijing University, also has the robust bearing of a healthy, cared-for man who grew up on the

Zhang Shenfu on his eighty-eighth birthday with his two younger brothers: *left,* philosophy professor Zhang Dainian; *right,* physicist Zhang Congnian. (V. Schwarcz)

North China plain. Only time will tell whether these brothers will live to the ripe age of their oldest sibling. But even in their seventies, the young Zhang brothers cast a questioning light on Zhang Shenfu's vision of himself as the healthiest, strongest offspring of Zhao Zhang.

JUNE 17, 1981. One last detail about Zhang's early childhood comes out today. He embroiders it fully in the telling: "My father took great care in naming me Zhang Songnian. I was, after all, the first son of an aspiring scholar-official. So he used the occasion of my birth to commemorate one of the five sacred mountains of Confucianism, Mount Song. In a departure from traditional practice, however, it was not my grandfather—who was barely literate—or my elder uncle who picked the name. It was my father himself.

"I kept my given name of Songnian for about twenty years. But I never liked the fact that there were countless sons of scholar-officials with the same name. I always wanted something different. Therefore, as soon as I could, I chose another name. I named myself Shenfu—recalling a famous minister of ancient times who saw himself as a protector of all under heaven. I wanted a name that would suggest determination in the governing of the nation.

"Thus I became known as Songnian to my tutors, and Shenfu to my friends. I was a slow-budding rebel, you see. Even in my name, I modeled myself on an ancient, virtuous minister. My father had chosen an obvious symbol of Confucian respect. I wanted something a little more unusual. It was not my intention, though, to break with my father's worldview. At home I continued reading the Confucian classics with a hired tutor. In keeping with my father's orders, the tutor emphasized the memorization of the *Book of Rites*. This classic had more prescriptions for virtuous behavior than any of the other books in the Confucian canon.

"I did not get a taste of livelier education until my father became a Hanlin scholar and I began to attend a modern primary school in Beijing. In 1909 I was enrolled in one of the best new style middle schools in Beijing, the Shuntian Academy, one of the first schools to combine Western knowledge with Confucian principles. The Shuntian Academy offered courses in Japanese and English, as well as in basic science and mathematics. This last was my favorite. . . . Of course, we still studied Chinese history and literature. I think I still have an essay from my Shuntian days if you want to see it." And with the familiar shuffle, the old man goes to recover his boyhood notebook.

AUTUMN 1910. In this schoolboy's essay, Zhang Songnian speaks in the voice of a Qing general sent to pacify peasant rebels who have taken over the city of Wuhan.[2]

The topic is an assigned one and is meant to test the students' knowledge of nineteenth-century history, especially of the great upheaval caused by the Taiping Rebellion of 1850–64. Inspired by the foreign idea of Christianity, this uprising had come close to overthrowing the Qing dynasty. Its suppression was assumed to contain important lessons for pupils in the Shuntian Academy. In this exercise, they are asked to write an ultimatum to the peasant rebels trapped in the besieged city of Wuhan. Zhang Songnian's essay offers pardon in exchange for submission:

"In the name of our glorious dynasty and His majesty's army, I ask you to lay down your arms. . . . You have committed crimes against the people and the Will of Heaven. Your cruel reign is now at its end. If peace is not recognized as the ultimate principle of the people, then the day when all of our realm will fall is not far. It does not pay to fight the forces of the government. Before you could win any victories, you will surely meet your end. Therefore, I advise you to submit to imperial orders and I will grant you pardon. Do not attack government troops. Do not think that your actions have been effective or that they correspond to the needs of the people."

Nothing in this student essay is revolutionary. Rather, a Confucian-minded schoolboy condemns, as expected, all armed resistance to imperial rule. In 1910 Zhang Shenfu—who went on to help found the Chinese Communist Party a decade later—mocks the notion that rebels could be heroes. He rules out the possibility that revolutionaries might represent the interests of the people better than those currently in power.

JUNE 19, 1981. Seven decades after his schoolboy essay, Zhang looks at the yellowed pages with a mixture of pride and embarrassment. "Look," he tells me, "look at the style of the essay. Not bad, huh? My teacher always singled out my examinations for bold calligraphy. The content? Well, the content is something else altogether."

He then moves closer to me with an impish smile. He anticipates my question: "What are we to make of this thoroughly conformist voice?" The pages lie between us, proof of Zhang Shenfu's determination to document his past objectively. Looking more closely at the essay, I notice that the last page carries a new inscription. At the end of the meticulous, forceful brush strokes of the young boy come the following words—dated June 1977—in the trembling fountain pen of the aged philosopher: "Peace will not come but in a land where all men are as kings."

Zhang follows my eyes down the page and adds: "I feel a certain satisfaction in having written this phrase. After all these years, it sticks in my mind. I remember quite clearly that I included it in the school exercise itself. But in rereading the text later I could not find it. So I added it in 1977. It speaks to my early yearning for democracy in a land where all are sovereign. . . . In my school days I paid no attention to such essays. I just left them anywhere. One of my schoolmates must have picked this one up and torn out the pages with 'peace' on it."

The corrective urge of memory breaks through here. Not content merely to preserve a fragment of the past, Zhang seeks to embroider it, to bring it into harmony with the persona of the boy who longed for a "land where all men are kings." Without the 1977 addition, the pages reveal nothing more than an unquestioning perspective of the Taiping Rebellion. With a few extra words, the essay accords more smoothly with the aged iconoclast's image of himself. It allows him to imagine a schoolboy who was Confucian and democratic at once.

Reprehensible in imperial China, the phrase "all men are kings" is no more acceptable in present-day China. I try to follow out the implications of this belief upon Zhang's career in the Chinese Communist Party. But Zhang Shenfu does not want to pursue the political twists of his school essay. Instead, he dwells on women again—this time on Zhu Denong, his child bride.

Marriage and Revolution

JUNE 19, 1981. "The year 1911 changed my life. Of course, it also changed the lives of most Chinese who were aware that the Qing dynasty had fallen. I was on the side of the republican revolution that started with mutiny by young army officers in Wuhan. At the same time, though, I went home to get married."

Zhang Shenfu's face becomes somber as he retells the story of his first marriage. Today is not the first time that I hear about how his wife died in childbirth. But it is a more detailed, more tender story of their brief years together: "Zhu Denong was only sixteen when we married. Her given name was Zhu Huinong and she was the daughter of a well-known district magistrate. Her family came from Baoding County, not far from us. . . . How did we meet? It was all arranged by our parents, of course. The matchmakers were well paid. She turned out to be very kind and proper. She treated my parents and me with the greatest respect. Never a harsh word or an impetuous desire. If she hadn't died, I would have never looked at other women. I would have never become involved in women's liberation."

The wistful note in Zhang's voice echoes that of his younger brother Zhang Dainian, who also spoke with reverance about Zhu Denong's presence in the Zhang household: "She was like a mother to me," Zhang Dainian told me at his eldest brother's birthday party. "So pretty and so caring at the same time. I felt quite orphaned when she died."

I try to listen to what lies beneath the loss-tinged ruminations of these old men. Does the face of Zhu Denong float over them with such sweetness because she died shortly after entering their lives? Is she their apotheosized link to a Confucian youth later overwhelmed, even in memory, by Communist politics? What did Zhang Shenfu feel when he was called back home from the Shuntian Academy in the fall of 1911 to marry the woman his family had chosen for him? He was only eighteen years old at the time. Other schoolmates had married even earlier. Very few managed to escape parental pressure to propagate. Fewer still could dedicate themselves to revolutionary activities fulltime. The dynasty was collapsing when Zhang Shenfu was ordered home to Gratitude County to meet his bride with bound feet and a neighborly accent.

Zhang's voice breaks through my musings with the rest of the story: "By the winter of 1911–12, I was back in Beijing, a married man trying to finish middle school. I saw my wife rarely—mostly on vacations, because she stayed back in my mother's house as expected by Confucian rules. . . . Was I in love? In a way, I suppose. But that was not our expectation then. Later, you know, I wrote a lot about the trap that romantic love is for men and women alike. No, Zhu Denong and I were bound by something else. I was the eldest son. I had married her as was expected of me. Then I began to refashion our relationship on my own terms. I started to educate my wife.

"Zhu was bright but had been held back by the Confucian view that absence of learning is a positive virtue in women. But I managed to persuade my mother to allow this daughter-in-law out of the house several days a week to attend classes at one of the newly opened schools for girls. My mother resisted quite a while. After all, she was uneducated herself and could see no way that schooling could make a woman more virtuous. . . . In the end, my mother gave in.

Zhang Shenfu and schoolmate Zhu Xizhou on an outing in Beijing in 1914, a few months after the twenty-one-year-old Zhang Shenfu became a father and widower. (Courtesy of Zhang Shenfu)

"To shut the mouth of gossip, I chose a particularly Confucian name for my wife when she enrolled in school—Denong, meaning 'ample virtue.' The schooling of Denong did not last long, however. She was already pregnant when her education began. In the spring of 1914, she had to stop her trips outside the family compound. Everyone waited for news about a son. I was away at school in Beijing when the telegram came. It announced the birth of a girl. My parents were surprised that I was not disappointed in the child. They were also displeased when I choose a foreign-sounding name for her. I called her Yali, because I liked the sound of the English name Alice. In Chinese Yali means 'beautiful Asia.' Just a few days after giving birth to Zhang Yali, Zhu Denong died."

I tried to imagine Zhang Shenfu at twenty-one, simultaneously a father and a widower. Whenever we talk about his first wife, he likes to dwell on Zhu Denong's life, her virtues and purity. The year after her death remains enveloped in silence. . . . Back in my room I look through my files. Here, I find two photographs from 1914. They capture the change in the boy who so suddenly became a man.

Memorial portrait of Zhang Shenfu's first wife Zhu Denong, who died in 1914 after giving birth to Zhang Yali (Alice). The inscription, written by Zhang Shenfu's school-mate Zhu Xizhou, praises her virtue and intelligence. (Courtesy of Zhang Shenfu)

In the first, Zhang Shenfu is posing in a Beijing park with a Shuntian Academy schoolmate, Zhu Xizhou. Zhu was three years older than Zhang and had been active in the anti-Manchu revolution of 1911. By 1914, however, Zhu appears to be younger, stockier than Zhang Shenfu. Both young men are wearing heavy silk jackets over long silk gowns. It must have been a bitter, windy spring in Beijing. Zhu Xizhou stands straight in front of the camera. Zhang Shenfu is leaning against some rocks, his round face drawn. There is no sign here of the stylized severity of his Confucian boyhood, nor of the casual dandy in Zhang Shenfu's European photographs. In 1914 Zhang's face is tired, stamped by the recent death of his bride.

From the same year, I find a portrait of Zhu Denong printed after her death. It shows a full-faced young woman with hair coiled on top of her head and over the ears. A shy propriety veils the eyes that, nonetheless, face the camera straight on. Zhu Xizhou, Zhang's closest friend that year, inscribed the border of the portrait. Giving words to Zhang's loss, Zhu wrote: "What a pleasant face had she! What worthy grace and beauty! What an intelligent and virtuous woman, who left this life so soon! Alas, but why?" Neither Zhu Xizhou nor Zhang Shenfu had the answer to this question. They were young and inexperienced, even though they had styled themselves as revolutionaries and fathered children —all before they turned twenty-one.

I also read in their faces a certain impatience. These young men were not to be consoled by Buddhist notions of the impermanence of all existence. After all, both Zhu Xizhou and Zhang Shenfu had just begun to take charge of their own lives. Each had begun to define his own intellectual interest. Each was working to refine a style of writing and thought. Only three years earlier, during the revolution of 1911, they had imagined themselves in charge of the nation's destiny. Now they were powerless in the face of death and the erosion of republican ideals.

In autumn 1911, Zhu Xizhou had been out on the streets distributing anti-Manchu pamphlets. Zhang Shenfu had kept in touch with revolutionary comrades even as he readied for marriage back home. Social conformity had not prevented Zhang from taking a political position against the dynasty. Three years before the death of Zhu Denong, Zhang had already experienced the magnetic force of the most ardent revolutionary at the Shuntian Academy, a schoolmate named Guo Renlin.

JUNE 20, 1981. When he talks about Guo Renlin seventy years after the 1911 revolution, Zhang Shenfu's voice still echoes the excitement of youth: "Guo Renlin, oh yes. Guo Xiaofeng, as we used to call him then. He was from Hunan, the same province as the Communist Party founder Li Dazhao. It was Guo, you know, who introduced me to Li. I suppose I owe him a debt of gratitude for launching me on the path that led to the founding of the Communist Party.

"Guo was a French major at Shuntian. So good looking! His marriage was arranged when he was only eleven—to a girl four years his senior! At school he was our most fiery speaker. Though he was an expert in Buddhist and Daoist texts, what influenced me the most was his support for Sun Yatsen and the Revolutionary Alliance. It did not take me long to realize that Guo Renlin was right. Revolution was the only alternative. And I have stuck to that view ever since."

As often before, I bemoan aloud the absence of any of Zhang Shenfu's writings from the time of the republican revolution of 1911. As always, Zhang adds his pensive regrets to mine: "I wish I had saved some of my writings from *The Republic*. This was one of the boldest new magazines edited in Tianjin, you know. But I still remember the title of one of my essays: 'Glimmers of Gold and Jade.' . . . These were my first revolutionary essays. I signed these with a new pen name, Chizi [the kid]. The pen name protected my identity from my father. Imagine if he knew then that I supported the antidynastic rebels while he was close friends with the Qing generals who were suppressing the revolution! . . . The pen name was not just a cover though. It also suggested the unfinished quality of my point of view then. I had just began to form my political opinions in exchanges with comrades at Shuntian Academy."

Revolution and marriage—these events connect the lives of Zhang Shenfu, Zhu Xizhou, and Guo Renlin in the year 1911. All were Confucian schoolboys on the threshold of a new world. They all stand to one side of the picture that now has a new figure in it, Liang Shuming:

"With Guo Renlin, I always felt open, safe somehow. Forced into a marriage himself, Guo knew all about the need for pen names. He had many identities himself: a scholar of Daoism, a revolutionary, a married man. Liang Shuming, the man who has endured as my best and oldest friend from the Shuntian days, was different. Marriage and compromise were the furthest thing from this idealist's mind. . . . Liang also felt the heat of Guo Renlin's presence. But he was not content with friendship. He looked up to Guo as a spiritual mentor. He wrote down our schoolmate's every word in a notebook called 'Quotations from Teacher Guo.' "

Zhang's recollections of the ardent, worshipful friendship between Liang Shuming and Guo Renlin are supported by Liang's own published memoirs.[3] Born in 1893, the same year as Zhang Shenfu, Liang's life crossed and mirrored that of his friend. Both Shuntian graduates became philosophers, but Liang Shuming achieved far greater renown with his magnum opus, *Dongxi wenhua ji qi zhexue* (culture and philosophy, East and West), published in 1921. Furthermore, while Zhang Shenfu joined and then withdrew from the Chinese Communist Party, Liang Shuming gained fame and respect as the leader of a rural education movement. Finally, while both men emerged as champions of democracy on the eve of Communist victory in 1949, it was Liang's voice that carried the greater weight—to the point that he was noticed and later loudly denounced by Mao Zedong.

But all this trouble lay far ahead when Zhang Shenfu met Liang Shuming at the Shuntian Academy on the eve of the republican revolution of 1911. In that year, Liang Shuming was still single. He was free to throw himself full-time into revolutionary activism. The recently married Zhang Shenfu, by contrast, had to content himself with the more distant role of sympathetic supporter. In the winter months of 1911–12, Liang Shuming was running secret ammunition missions for the revolutionaries, while Zhang Shenfu was confined to writing secret essays for *The Republic*.

Crisis and Commitment: Two Friends, Two Paths

MAY 1, 1983. May Day, Workers' International Day. This day also marks my fifth year of conversation with Zhang Shenfu. On this day politics seem remote from Wang Fu Cang Lane. Instead, we return once again to an old subject, Zhang Shenfu's friendship with Liang Shuming. Today Zhang lingers over the differences between them. Each appears to have followed his own drummer. Zhang seeks the source of their divergence. He retells, in the ironic voice usually reserved for his own foibles, the story of Liang Shuming's overly serious manner at the Shuntian Academy: "Liang was a young man grown old before his time. He seldom laughed or even smiled. A joke was beyond him."

Zhang calls up for me the picture of a simply dressed, gloomy-faced Liang; whereas he, Zhang Shenfu, wore colorful silk gowns and, later, Western-style suits. Yet the two became close friends: "For three years, between 1913 and 1916, we saw a great deal of each other. These were the years in which Liang Shuming moved toward suicide. These were also the years I married, then mourned for Zhu Denong. We commiserated endlessly in those hard years. I recommended lots of books to Liang Shuming. I was trying to cheer him up, to cheer myself up. Liang Shuming discovered Russell through me."

I have already heard the story of how Liang Shuming, an avowed Buddhist, discovered Western philosophy through Zhang's books on Bertrand Russell. But I sense something new in the retelling today. Zhang is trying to describe what led Liang Shuming and himself to look at life so differently after the 1911 revolution. I probe on. I ask more about their shared years at Shuntian, about their disparate approach to friendship with Guo Renlin. Zhang talks about his own, easygoing admiration for Guo. Liang Shuming, by contrast, was engaged in an intense discipleship. Neither Zhang nor Liang was a follower by nature: "Liang Shuming's schoolmates had nicknamed him Ao—the proud one —because he was so determined to achieve moral perfection. . . . I already called myself Chizi—the kid. Worldliness, not perfection, was my goal.

"Liang Shuming, by contrast, was a purist, perhaps because he was so deeply marked by his father's suicide in 1918. Even before the suicide, his father, Liang Ji, was very different from mine. Liang Ji, you see, came from a distinguished line of scholar-officials. Liang Shuming's grandfather was already a famous scholar, and Liang Ji had many high official positions. Having passed the imperial exams at a young age, Liang Ji became a secretary in the Grand Secretariat, then chief of the Metropolitan Bureau of Poor Relief. . . . But he gave up all his official posts before the revolution of 1911 because he was sickened by the corruption of the late Qing.

"My father, on the other hand, remained in the Qing bureaucracy. Zhang Lian was only the second son of his family to receive an education in the classics. He felt a responsibility to succeed in his official position."

Zhang Shenfu leans back. He is not willing, for the moment, to follow this line of thought any further. It might lead toward a criticism of his father.

I linger for tea and try to piece together in my mind the chronology of the two fathers: Zhang Lian was a late comer to bureaucratic success. He passed the jinshi examination in 1906, only two years before Liang Ji left official service altogether in 1908. Zhang Lian's political fortunes were consolidated during the last years of the collapsing dynasty. Liang Ji, by contrast, emerged as an articulate proponent of imperial reform. In spite of their differences, both fathers—unlike their sons—were opposed to republicanism during the revolution of 1911.

After 1911 the temperamental and political differences between Zhang Lian and Liang Ji became even more striking: Zhang Lian remained involved in gentry politics and became a member of the parliamentary assembly in 1918. This was the same year in which Liang Ji committed suicide to protest corruption among his intellectual and political contemporaries.

Liang Ji's suicide note had a great impact on the radical intellectuals of his son's generation. In it, Liang Ji had castigated officials of the warlord government for forsaking the ancient virtues of loyalty, fidelity, chastity, and righteousness. Although radical youth were no longer bound by these "virtues," they found in Liang's gesture a compelling call to moral conscience. Rereading Liang Ji's suicide note, I wonder whether he was thinking of Zhang Lian and the military men who were his friends when he castigates the "evils of contemporary officials." I have no way of knowing.

From conversations with his son Liang Shuming, I know that Liang Ji encouraged his children to disagree openly with him—a far cry from the stern, authoritarian Zhang Lian, who smashed the head of his six-year-old son into the kang. The fathers provide different images of the cultural conservative. Liang Ji was reform-minded in the actual practice of parenting. In spite of his staunch Confucian values, he had educated his sons *and* his daughters. Zhang Lian, by contrast, remained a stern authoritarian all his life.

The two sons, Liang Shuming and Zhang Shenfu, supported the republican revolution of 1911, but each had his own emotional and political outlook. After one year, both Liang and Zhang became disillusioned with the "republic" created—and undermined—by warlords. For Zhang Shenfu, the new husband who had limited himself to writing essays in support of revolution, the disillusionment was easier to bear. For Liang Shuming, the ardent idealist who had plunged himself into the world of secret societies and arms trading, the failure of revolution was a more traumatic event. In 1912 Zhang Shenfu began sending his young bride to school. He had found something else to do, something other than political revolution. Liang Shuming, on the other hand, began to contemplate suicide.

MAY 5, 1983. We are back to the subject of Zhang's friendship with Liang Shuming. The worried tone that colored our conversation about the two fathers has faded. Zhang Shenfu now leans his head back, looking away from me as if searching the face of some impersonal judge: "Liang and I represent two different views of the world. Shuming, you see, took a different path toward China's salvation. His was a more Eastern path than mine. I only cared about the new, whereas he knew how to combine the old *and* the new. He was broad-minded and so was I. But his broad-mindedness was hidden beneath simple words and an honest face. This won him a much broader hearing than I ever got. He

Liang Shuming in
1983, during our
interview at his
home in Beijing.
(V. Schwarcz)

always had lots of students, lots of disciples. I only had one or two. So he
ended up having more influence than I. But it is widely known, as Liang acknowledged, that everything he knew about the West came from me."

He lets his voice drift off, seemingly with the hope that this time history
might find them equal. The quest for parity through recollection goes on in the
late afternoon sun.

MAY 14, 1983. Today is my third visit to Liang Shuming's home. The ninety-
year-old philosopher lives on the ninth floor of a modern apartment building. A
young housekeeper answers the bell. Behind her I glimpse the short, thin old
man in a woolen cap. His bony face does not break out into a smile easily. He is
a seeker who is serious, even severe, with the world. And with himself. His
deep-set eyes remain fixed on mine as we sit down to talk.

First about himself: "I am a Buddhist first and foremost, no matter if some
—like your American colleague Guy Alitto—would call me 'the last Confucian.'
I still eat no meat. I still seek to understand the cause of suffering and try to
root it out in my life and in the lives of those around me." Liang's voice fades
away, as if sucked up by the thirsty red cactus between us.

Slowly, this fierce vegetarian, this contemplative social activist who with-stood Mao Zedong's rage in the 1950s, returns to tea and to details of his friendship with Zhang Shenfu. We go over the long course of their association, from before 1911 through the Cultural Revolution. Liang Shuming is quite precise about when and where they have met: the Shuntian Academy in 1909, at Beijing University in 1919, in jail, where he visited Zhang Shenfu briefly in 1936, in Chunqing during the anti-Japanese War.

Until today my host has shied away from talking about Zhang Shenfu's work as a philosopher. I sense a reluctance to pass judgment on an old friend. But now, Liang Shuming appears willing to talk about his own philosophy, and so we drift toward Zhang's. We begin with Liang's journey through Buddhism and Confucianism toward what concerns him now: "the foundations of our native psychology." While tracing his own intellectual evolution, he comes back to Zhang Shenfu, always mindful of their differences, always respectful of his friend, whom he insists on calling "Mr. Zhang":

"Mr. Zhang Shenfu, you see, knows far more about the West than I. He has seen and read more about it firsthand. I can't read foreign languages, though I have studied English for years. I haven't used it for so long that I have quite forgotten how to read it. Mr. Zhang helped me a great deal in this. He knew many foreign languages and he knew them well. So I could rely on him to lend me books and talk to me about authors who were being translated, but trans-lated unreliably, into Chinese. We were interested in different things, even back then, at Beida. I was working on Buddhist epistemology, Mr. Zhang on mathe-matical logic. As for Mr. Zhang's own philosophy, well . . ." Liang Shuming's voice trails off. We must stop for today. After two hours this afternoon, I sense that he is growing tired, weak, vague with words. He invites me to come back again. We have another chance to talk about Zhang Shenfu.

I leave, mindful of their differences. Unlike his old schoolmate, Liang Shuming is in no rush to sum up his own life. Maybe that is because Liang has already written and talked about it in so many different ways at various stages of his political career. He gives me a manuscript copy of a 1942 essay, "A Brief History of My Self-Education." Four decades later, Liang Shuming is still at work on his memoirs. He does not need conversation to take the place of written recollection in the same way as Zhang Shenfu does.

But I need and treasure these hours with Liang Shuming. His soft-spoken, lucid, detailed recollections have a rhythm and integrity all their own. They are so different from the boastful, increasingly rambling quality of Zhang Shenfu's memory these days. Liang's shaven head brings home his monkish reserve. His slow, focused movements bespeak a long-standing effort to curb worldly de-sires. In this, too, Liang Shuming is different from Zhang Shenfu—with his finely combed grey hair, his idle yet still pleasure-seeking ways.

Even if Liang Shuming does not want to comment on Zhang Shenfu's life and their disparate perspectives, I cannot help but be drawn to the contrast. Their relationship to women, their views about Russell, their commitment to the Democratic League in the 1940s, all suggest significant divergences. Beneath their time-tested loyalty to and respect for each other, I sense a parting of the ways, not just in the number of disciples or books written but in the inner force that propelled each one along the troublesome course of a long life. And so I go back to old texts, to the words each wrote as a young man.

Crisis and Recovery

MAY 1916. Liang Shuming is publishing his first major essay after the revolution of 1911. Entitled "On Tracing Origins and Solving Doubt," it appears in one of the most forward-looking magazines of the day, *The Eastern Miscellany* (*Dongfang zazhi*). This work celebrates a young man's self-healing after two suicide attempts and a long period of seclusion. It also carries a public acknowledgment of his indebtedness to Zhang Shenfu: "Ever since I was 20 sui [in 1912] I had made up my mind to enter into the path of Buddhism. During the next four or five years, I concentrated all of my energies in Buddhist studies, along with reading small volumes about Western philosophy brought to me by my friend Mr. Zhang Songnian."[4]

After these introductory words, Liang Shuming goes on to dissect the origins of his desires and disillusionments. He describes, quite frankly, his retreat into Buddhist theory for therapy. (After his mother's death in 1912 and the last of his suicide attempts, Liang shut himself up in his father's house for three years. He emerged from this period of incense burning and prayer a changed man.) Now, in 1916, he offers the world a new plan for spiritual salvation. Using Western philosophy and concepts such as "willed determination" and "instinct" (carefully spelled out in English), Liang sets out to prove the ultimate validity of the Buddhist approach to consciousness and to human suffering.

Zhang Shenfu also faced a personal crisis after the revolution of 1911: his wife's death in childbirth. By 1915 Zhang emerged from widowerhood with the discovery of "mind." A voracious reader of everything new, Zhang found a balm—not in Buddhism but in mathematics and Bertrand Russell.

FEBRUARY 1915. Zhang Shenfu is publishing his first essay since the death of his wife a year earlier. It is a biography of a nineteenth-century Russian mathematician, Sofia Kovalevsky, and appears in the recently established *Ladies Journal* (*Funu zazhi*). Addressed to a literate, well-to-do urban population, this journal has some of the same readers as *The Eastern Miscellany*, though a far smaller circulation. Unlike the more established *Miscellany* (full of news, literature, and thought), the *Ladies Journal* has a narrower aim: to provide information that would make its readers better wives and mothers.

Both the subject and the approach that Zhang Shenfu takes in this essay, however, contradict these sedate aims. Here he has chosen to write about a professional scholar who managed to overcome the many obstacles put in her way. Zhang tells Kovalevsky's story with the impassioned sympathy of a young man who is beginning to look for broader horizons himself.

After the death of Zhu Denong, Zhang Shenfu had begun to develop a more intense interest in mathematics. Through his uncle he eventually met Feng Zexun, the chairman of the Beijing University mathematics department. Zhang Shenfu was beginning to think about studying at Feng's eminent institution. He also began to harbor a not-so-secret wish that after the thoroughly Confucian and uneducated Zhu Denong, his next companion be more like a Russian mathematician.

" 'The Life of Sofia Kovalevsky,' " Zhang Shenfu tells me in the summer of 1983, "let me explore a different kind of woman from a distance, in my imagination as it were." Sofia Kovalevsky had been unable to study mathematics at a university in czarist Russia and decided to pursue her education at the University of Heidelberg. Prevented from enrolling there as a single woman, she married in a ceremony that remained a mere formality for years. Forbidden to take her oral examination in person, Kovalevsky managed, nonetheless, to write one of the best theses ever presented in the Heidelberg mathematics department. Finally, unrecognized for her abilities in her home country, she found employment as a professor of mathematics at the University of Stockholm. The high point of her distinguished career came at the International Mathematics Meeting in Paris in 1900, where she gained supreme scholarly recognition for a paper on the "Proof of the Rotation of a Solid Around an Immutable Point."

From its opening words to its conclusion, Zhang Shenfu's biography of Sofia Kovalevsky makes it clear that the twenty-two-year-old author is as ready to challenge his contemporaries as his subject was in her day. Like the mathematical genius whom he writes about, Zhang Shenfu refuses to abide by the "common view that women are not as intelligent as men." Drawing on his own efforts to educate Zhu Denong and on his reading about Western female mathematicians from Hypathia to Sophie Germain, Zhang Shenfu argues that there is absolutely no difference in "nature" between men and women. In fact, he points out, "anyone who has observed the early training of boys and girls knows that the latter can do all the tasks that the former can do and do them more meticulously."[5]

In this winter of 1915, Zhang Shenfu's arguments against the prejudices of his contemporaries are still cast in an impersonal tone. Unlike his friend Liang Shuming, who was already beginning to confess inner turmoil in his work on

Zhang Shenfu
with his six-year-
old daughter
Alice before his
departure for
Europe in 1920.
(Courtesy of
Zhang Shenfu)

Buddhism, Zhang Shenfu writes about Kovalevsky as if her intelligence and accomplishments were a matter of abstract verity. Zhang's incipient feminism, unlike Liang's Buddhism, was not a matter of life or death. Rather, it was the result of a vague longing for a more intellectual companion. This was not yet a matter of passionate commitment.

Within the next three years, however, all that changed. Family arrangements came close to overwhelming the budding mathematician. Zhang Shenfu responded with rage and the full force of his rebellious intelligence. The event that shook Zhang out of daydreams about women like Sofia Kovalevsky was his second marriage in the winter of 1915–16. His life as a widower came to an end less than two years after it had begun. The way it ended left Zhang furious.

JUNE 15, 1981. "Throughout the spring of 1915, I had showed no opposition to the idea of remarriage. I knew my parents were right when they said my baby daughter needed a mother. At the same time I began to develop a strong attraction to a certain young woman whom I had seen several times on the train ride from Tianjin to Beijing. I was still conservative then, so I asked my parents to use the services of a matchmaker to contact the girl."

Sixty-six years after the event, Zhang Shenfu's face twists in anger: "Everything was arranged. I agreed and signed all the appropriate papers—only to find out that the bride was not the person I had seen on the train. I felt so cheated! So powerless! She turned out to be a totally uninteresting, passive creature. It was at this time that I started to read Bertrand Russell so avidly. His ideas about the freedom of marriage and of sex suddenly made so much sense to me. They saved my life."

More than the words he speaks, it is Zhang's fervor that competes with the summer heat around us. Then, suddenly, he laughs: "Because of that betrayal in 1915, I started to take Russell to heart. Here was salvation for me. There was nothing like Russell's thought on native ground. . . . Yes, you could say that I found salvation in Russell while Liang Shuming reached enlightenment through Buddhism. We were so young, but so different already."

More self-mocking laughter. Then another recollection from the eve of the betrayal: "Where I was writing about Sofia Kovalevsky, I let myself combine two of my new loves: women and mathematics. I remember all those daydreams on the train between Tianjin and Beijing. I would look at an interesting young woman and imagine her mind, her body, how she might share my life. Later, in the 1920s, I wrote a series of letters to such an imaginary lover."

The daydreams of Zhang Shenfu were unknown to his parents and to the matchmaker, who did not understand the power of the wishes growing inside the young widower. In 1915 they decided what would be best for the whole Zhang family—just as they had done with Zhu Denong in 1911. But this time Zhang Shenfu felt that his world had caved in.

Personal disillusionment turned into intellectual fury for Zhang Shenfu. Unlike his friend Liang Shuming, who had turned inward after the prelude of the revolution of 1911, Zhang took on the shortcomings of society. In contrast to his schoolmate from the Shuntian Academy, Zhang Shenfu turned against unreason in the world. Liang Shuming's despair made him angry at himself. As Liang recalled later: "Because the standards were so high, it was also easy to have contempt and disgust for myself for not having lived up to them. . . . When I fought myself into a state of confusion, to the point that I could not stand it any longer, then I desired only death."[6]

Zhang Shenfu never sank into such despair. He retained his hopes and fantasies even after the betrayal of 1915. He might have refused his second marriage the way Liang Shuming had with several offers after 1911. But Zhang Shenfu did not. He had no principled aversion to marriage, and he did have a young child to think about. So Zhang went ahead with the marriage and continued to rage: "That wife meant nothing to me. I only went through with the contract for the sake of filial duty. . . . Yes, we had two children, a boy and a girl. But as with their mother, I didn't care for them much. I found relief and interest somewhere else. In the world of books, of magazines. Out there in the world, in the world beyond the family compound, beyond China's border, I found encouragement for challenging adventures of the mind. There, I found Russell.

"To be sure, I had heard Russell's name even before the revolution of 1911.

After 1911 I learned more about the British mathematician as news of *Principia Mathematica* began to come through Beida. The first foreign book I ever bought with my own money was a copy of Russell's *The Problems of Philosophy*. This book came out in 1911 but was not available in China until 1914. At first, I picked it up out of abstract curiosity. I was already a lover of books and so this one was added to my collection with the aid of a Japanese bookseller in Beijing. But I did not read Russell for solace until after the shock of my second marriage. During the next three years, from 1916 to 1919, I read everything by Bertrand Russell that I could get my hands on—books, periodicals, anything. I began to see that my own tragedy was also the tragedy of all of China."

Like his friend Liang Shuming, Zhang Shenfu used personal despair as a magnifying glass. It served him in the analysis of the nation's spiritual malaise. Whereas his schoolmate chose to shut himself off from the world for a prolonged period of psychological self-interrogation, Zhang Shenfu stayed in the world of family, of schooling, of philosophy. Over time, he grew increasingly angry and increasingly convinced that logic held the key to the distinction between truth and lies.

"I had been the victim of error and came to realize that errors, like lies, were nothing but the consequence of faulty reasoning. If the mistaken assumption could be identified, there was some hope after all. By the time of the May Fourth movement of 1919, by the time I met Liu Qingyang, I had figured out that the traditional marriage system in China was just such a false presupposition. Like Russell, I became an enemy of marriage and a lover of logic."

Through mathematics, and then logic, Zhang Shenfu found the kind of healing that Liang Shuming had sought through Buddhism. Each young man had gained social recognition and academic status through his personal quest: Liang Shuming's articles on Buddhist epistemology and metaphysics attracted the attention of Cai Yuanpei, the man who assumed the presidency of Beijing University in 1917. Cai was so impressed that he invited Liang Shuming to join the faculty. By autumn 1917 Liang had accepted and began to teach a course on Indian philosophy.

That same autumn Zhang Shenfu, too, was recruited to teach logic at the preparatory school of Beijing University. Even before he graduated from the philosophy department, Zhang had also come to the attention of the new president. Cai Yuanpei was instrumental in Zhang's promotion as well. The narrow criteria of degrees were abandoned in the case of both Liang Shuming and Zhang Shenfu. By 1918 each was launched on a path that would be his alone: Liang was moving steadily from Indian philosophy toward Confucian thought. Zhang, having started in mathematics, moved further away from China through the study of logic and the practice of social criticism.

Zhang Shenfu and
Li Guangyu in
1917, while
students at the
National Beijing
University.
Though still in
Confucian garb,
both young men
had already
become involved
in revolutionary
politics. (Courtesy
of Zhang Shenfu)

At Beijing University

AUTUMN 1917. Zhang Shenfu's first formal portrait at Beijing University, taken in the company of his new friend, a budding scholar of Daoist texts, Li Guangyu. Liang Shuming, with his monkish reserve, seems far from the world of these stylish youths. Like other students at the National Beijing University at the time, Zhang and Li are dressed in long silk gowns. This customary sign of distinction set them apart from the laboring masses. Shunning the virile image of those who live by brawn, the two young men strike a slender, cultivated pose. By 1917 both Zhang Shenfu and Li Guangyu, like Liang Shuming, had had their brush with revolutionary politics. Yet, on this occasion, they faced the camera as traditional scholars.

Li Guangyu is dressed in a simple white gown. His hands are folded demurely in front; his eyes look straight ahead. Two years older than Zhang Shenfu, Li had been an active leader of middle school students in the revolt against the Manchu dynasty in 1911. In the half decade since his career as a revolutionary propagandist, Li Guangyu had gained considerable popularity among Beijing

University students for his essays about the Daoist philosopher Laozi.[7] Unlike his friend, Zhang Shenfu does not face the camera directly. He shows a three-quarter profile that accentuates his round, inquisitive face. He gazes off to the left. A dandy's manner is apparent in the colored silk gown. The black and white print sharpens Zhang's robe with its bold flower motif.

Zhang Shenfu, like Li Guangyu, also holds his hands in front, a pose that emphasizes the round belly beneath the flowery gown. To Confucian eyes, such a protusion must have appeared thoroughly proper. A gentleman, after all, did not strain himself with physical labor. At most, he practiced a mild form of *qigong*, a branch of martial arts meant to exercise one's inner organs and spiritual essence simultaneously. A round belly signaled prowess in breathing from the diaphragm.

To Western eyes, Zhang Shenfu appears slightly pregnant. And so he was, with Western ideas. At the age of twenty-four this young man was full of lofty notions about himself and held new ideas about how to save China. Within the university he found a small community of like-minded, iconoclastic intellectuals. In their company Zhang had begun to find his own voice, to make his distinct mark on the debates of the day.

By 1917 Zhang Shenfu had come to the attention of the dean of humanities, Chen Duxiu, who was an outspoken critic of Confucian mores and, later, a founder of the Chinese Communist Party. That same year, Chen was editor of *New Youth* magazine, the radical publication in which Zhang Shenfu made his debut as public advocate of a new Chinese culture.

OCTOBER 1918. Zhang Shenfu joins the national debate about the fate of Chinese culture with a markedly bookish letter to the editor. Entitled "A Plea for Reading Magazines," this essay comes as no surprise to those who know the young man personally.[8] The recently appointed instructor has been spending most of his days in the library stacks.

A voracious reader, Zhang Shenfu has unlimited access to the foreign language periodicals in the library. Unlike Liang Shuming, who is still steeped in Buddhist meditation and epistemology, Zhang finds his most important spiritual nourishment in this milieu. By 1918 Zhang can read English, French, and German. He is also teaching himself Japanese, Russian, and Polish—all in order to read more about his favorite subjects, logic and mathematics.

In the essay, he addresses his fellow comrades in the war against outmoded ways of learning. Like Chen Duxiu before him, Zhang Shenfu argues that China must start to save itself by changing its literary practice. For Zhang, in 1918, this means a change in reading habits: "In the past China did not have a periodical press. Our people, unfamiliar with magazines, can hardly be expected to know how to use them. But now times have changed. A periodical press is taking root in China, as witnessed by *New Youth* itself. Magazines are rapidly multiplying within China and even more so abroad. To know nothing of what is written in the periodical press is to know nothing of the present. And to be ignorant of the present is as good as killing the present.

"When we compare China's present culture to that of the West, how can we fail to be ashamed! Knowing that we do not measure up, we must rouse ourselves to catch up. It just won't do to be perfunctory in our knowledge, to just drift along with old certainties. Recently China has opened its doors politically and commercially. But as far as scholarship is concerned, it still maintains a closed mind. Even when schools set up new courses, what is discussed in them is the same old stuff. In geometry, for example, there is now available a new edition of a university text. This book came out in the West eight years ago. It is much better than the old one and readily available abroad. But in China, we continue to use the old one. This amounts to living off the refuse heap left by the others."

To equate Chinese learning with garbage was more than just a harsh metaphor. It was a hallmark of the kind of self-styled iconoclasm that led another *New Youth* contributor, Lu Xun, to identify Confucianism with cannibalism in his "Diary of a Madman." Like Lu Xun's story (also published in 1918), Zhang Shenfu's bitter words were meant to wound Confucian pride and thereby arouse nationalist sensibilities.

At the same time, however, Zhang tried to shore up the foundations of a traditional Chinese culture. Nowhere in this early essay does Zhang insist that Chinese tradition is to be condemned in its entirety. To have value, according to Zhang Shenfu, the Chinese culture must stay in touch with the world beyond China's borders. And reading magazines holds the key to such cosmopolitan knowledge:

"To seek new knowledge and to advance in keeping with the times—these are the twin goals, the twin slogans of our new culture movement. In today's world, one must be able to share ideas, to communicate with other scholars in the world. To do this, one must strike to obtain a global education, to acquire global knowledge, to adopt a global perspective, and to stand in a global context. But first and foremost, one must have personal familiarity with global issues. This is precisely what reading magazines can offer you.

"Knowledge obtained from magazines cannot help but be disorganized and fragmentary. It lacks coherence. Unlike scholars of the past, today's learned people do not concentrate their energy into one great book. Rather, as soon as they have a new finding, they publish it in a journal to spark discussion. Thus they constantly improve their knowledge. All that is needed, then, is the ability to make good use of this assorted knowledge for the benefit of the present and of the future."

Decades after he left Beijing University, Zhang remained the embodiment of the informed journal reader. Yet Zhang Shenfu also sensed that there was a lack of coherence in all that he knew. He often tried to take refuge in the thought that modern scholars need not concentrate on big books as long as they continue to experiment with new ideas. But such consolations did not last. Unlike his friend Liang Shuming, Zhang neither wrote one great book nor managed to sustain a global discourse with like-minded scholars. To the end of his life, he remained what he was in 1918, the author and reader of scattered magazine articles. Looking back over his academic career in our conversations, he managed to laugh even as he went on to criticize his own proclivity to diffuseness, to what classical Chinese scholarship had always warned against as za, broad-mindedness to the point of muddiness.

JUNE 10, 1981. Zhang Shenfu is going over his school years with me today. After each stage he ends the story with a self-mocking yet prideful chuckle. Zhang's eyes sparkle with mischief in the late afternoon sun: "I don't know why, but I never finished any part of my formal schooling. I was always skipping grades, skipping from one school to another. I never graduated middle school before I got into Beida's Preparatory School. I never finished my undergraduate education before I became an assistant professor of logic. Skipping from grade to grade, I jumped from subject to subject, from mathematics to philosophy, from logic to dialectical materialism."

A tired, regretful old man is dissecting his fragmented, novelty-ridden life this afternoon. He tries to weigh the significance of what he brought to the stormy world of Beijing University.

Near the Eye of the Storm

SPRING 1919. A photograph of Liang Shuming and Zhang Shenfu from their shared days at Beijing University. The circle of intimates has expanded. The positions of the two young men both ideologically and spatially is fixed for posterity. Again, as in the photograph with Zhu Xizhou taken shortly after Zhu Denong's death, Zhang Shenfu is on an outing in a Beijing park. He stands high on a rock, with his side to the camera. Elevated above three other companions, Zhang is sporting a white silk gown and Western glasses.

This Western-influenced dandy stands in the sharp contrast to the seated, almost crouching, Liang Shuming. The difference in their height and demeanor is striking. Liang, with his closely cropped hair, is also wearing a white gown. But the camera finds him low, modest, inward. Here is a young philosophy instructor already deeply interested in China's Confucian heritage, so unlike the long-haired, flamboyant Zhang Shenfu. Zhang was the "expert" among them—an expert in foreign-language periodicals, which he had just written

Zhang Shenfu on an outing in 1919 with friends from Beijing University. *Left to right*: Lei Guoneng, Li Dazhao, Liang Shuming, and Zhang Shenfu. (Courtesy of Zhang Shenfu)

about in "A Plea for Reading Magazines." Yet Zhang Shenfu and Liang Shuming form an intimate grouping of their own, a visual symbiosis of the friendship that would nurture them over the decades.

To the left of the pair is another duo, distinguished from the others by dark silk jackets and a more active political agenda. In the foreground stands Li Dazhao, head of the Beijing University Library, who was senior in both age and experience to the young men around him. After studying in Japan, Li returned to China in 1916 to advocate Marxism and, later, communism. Behind Li stands

Lei Guoneng, a Beida student majoring in political science who had befriended both Zhang Shenfu and Liang Shuming. By spring 1919 Lei was a veteran of student organizing, having mobilized fellow classmates a year earlier in a protest against Japanese aggression.

Lei Guoneng was also at the center of the May Fourth movement of 1919, an event that irrevocably changed the lives of all four men in the photograph. Each would understand it in his own way; each would become committed to its goals in his own fashion—with Li Dazhao and Zhang Shenfu moving into closer collaboration through the founding of the Chinese Communist Party in 1920–21.

Although the student movement and Party building lay in the future, all four already bear the imprint of their varied and enduring political passions. Each man confronts the camera with a serious, focused gaze. Even on this outing, there was no doubt that China was in grave distress and that these men were determined to take on the challenges of national salvation.

NOVEMBER 12, 1979. In the presence of the Communist Party cadres, who attend our first meeting at the Beijing National Library, Zhang Shenfu chooses to dwell on ill-fitting details concerning the student movement of 1919. Secure in his connectedness to the past, Zhang recalls the day of May 4, 1919, just as he experienced it. He describes himself as a marginal observer of a storm that consumed his friends and associates alike:

"I remember hearing about the meeting of May 3—the one at which impassioned schoolmates from Shandong had cut their wrists and written in blood a protest against Japanese claims on their home province. On the day of the demonstration, I came to work in the library's acquisition office, a place I liked to be because of my love of books. . . . In the late afternoon I passed by Li Dazhao's office to find out what had happened in Tiananmen Square. . . . Then—I can still see this clearly in my mind—Luo Jialun, one of the main leaders of the demonstration, came flying in. His clothes were all messed up, hair flying, eyes bulging. He recounted the events that had led up to the students' arrest. Li Dazhao and I listened eagerly, though we were surprised that so much had happened in such a short time. Between about 1:00 and 4:00 P.M., several thousand students had marched to the foreign legation quarter. Then they marched on to the house of President Cao Rulin, breaking in and setting it on fire."

DECEMBER 10, 1979. In his home now, Zhang Shenfu tells me another version of May Fourth—or rather one with a different epilogue: "I am always close to the center of events, but never fully consumed. I am what you might call a supportive bystander of revolution."

On May 4, 1919, as in October 1911, Zhang Shenfu was close to, but not at the center of, political upheaval. In 1911, when China got its first taste of republicanism through the armed rebellion of young military officers, when Liang Shuming was actively involved in gun smuggling, Zhang had been in the Hebei countryside getting married. Upon hearing news of the revolution, he was instinctively sympathetic and wrote essays to support it. In 1919, eight years later, a similar scenario was enacted. "I was never fully consumed by the passions of the masses. In this, too, I am a lot like Bertrand Russell. Supporting the cause of justice, but remaining logical, evenhanded at the same time."

In his own tale Zhang appears as a revolutionary who always held back a little. That little bit would suffice, repeatedly, to spark doubts. Doubts, in turn, led Zhang Shenfu to be a fellow traveler with a divided heart precisely when other political activists gave themselves fully to the revolutionary cause.

Zhang was not present when students wrote out their protests in blood on May 3, 1919. He knew that they felt outrage against China's betrayal at the Paris Peace Conference. He knew that they were vehemently opposed to the Versailles Peace Treaty, which the Chinese delegation was about to sign and which acknowledged Japan's special interests in the former German colony of Shandong.

Still, he kept his distance and focused on other matters. Zhang preferred the commotion around the new magazine *Weekly Critic* (which he and Beijing University faculty members Li Dazhao and Chen Duxiu had just founded) to the thrill of late-night student meetings:

"I always enjoyed intellectual debate the most. . . . Yes, that is what I joined the *New Tide* Society [a student-run group that published a journal at Beijing University]. It was founded by cultural radicals . . . men who never became Communist revolutionaries, men like Luo Jialun and Fu Sinian. I did not join them on the day of May 4, when these two led the march through police barriers in the foreign legation. I did, however, contribute several articles to their journal, all of them on subjects that interested me at the time: the history of mathematics, scientific philosophy, modern psychology.

"Now, Lei Guoneng, he was different. One of my best friends at Beida, he was always in the eye of the storm. Lei led nationalist demonstrations in 1918 and he was one of the founders of the Young China Association (a group, also started in 1918, that mobilized young intellectuals in the political work of national salvation). I joined the Young China Association too, but only after May Fourth. . . . All along, I had philosophical reservations about nationalism. Maybe this was because of the influence of Russell, who criticized provincial loyalties of all sorts. Maybe I held back a bit because of my friendship with Chen Duxiu. He, too, was bitterly opposed to mindless nationalism."

JUNE 9, 1919. Chen Duxiu, dean of humanities at Beijing University and one of the most active supporters of the May Fourth demonstrations, is publish-

ing a strongly worded warning against nationalism. Three days before his arrest
and imprisonment for the distribution of antigovernment leaflets, Chen is telling students that "nationalism is chiefly an emotional response. It can drive
people to extreme, irrational behavior. . . . Nationalism is just another excuse
for harming people, making them blind, mad enough to sacrifice themselves
wantonly."[9]

JANUARY 15, 1920. Six months after Chen Duxiu's warnings, Zhang
Shenfu publishes a translation of Bertrand Russell's essay "The State" for the
journal of the Young China Association. Zhang's work is also motivated by fear
that Chinese students will be swept up by an excess of patriotic passion. Through
the words of Russell, who was jailed for his resistance to war in Europe (on the
grounds that it was fueled by petty nationalisms), Zhang is now addressing
China's young people. His introduction to Russell's essay leaves no doubt that
the state—any state—"is nothing but an instrument of oppression whose chief
aim is to suppress the liberty of citizens. It deadens critical thought in the name
of outwardly imposed loyalties."

Then, using Russell's words, Zhang reminds China's students that self-
liberation, as opposed to politically induced institutional change, should be the
goal of their movement. Political activism, though necessary, must not replace
critical thought. If state-imposed loyalties can deaden thought, so can patriotic
passion. In Zhang's view, neither is as necessary in the present moment as
"new thought." This, he adds, "is the only force that can upset inherited values
and slavish loyalties."[10]

MAY 1919. New thought is an old cause for Zhang Shenfu. On the eve of the
May Fourth movement *New Youth* magazine published his subversive essay
entitled "Dangerous Thought," in which he celebrates the iconoclastic spirit
brewing at Beijing University. Days before students break through words and
metal barricades, Zhang Shenfu asks:

"You think that there is such a thing as safe thought? There is no thought
that is not dangerous. All thinking disturbs, revolutionizes, and destroys. It is
merciless toward established systems, toward privileges, class distinctions, and
inherited customs. The realm of thinking—not just that of new thought that
you conservatives curse and blame for today's trouble—is limitless. It stands
above death, suffering, poverty, illness, and fate. Nothing can hinder and en-
slave it. Thought is bound to upset you, you who would enforce worn-out ideas
on social inferiors.

"If proletarians were to think freely and critically, the rich would get upset.
If soldiers were to think freely, military discipline all around the world would
fall apart. If youth were to think freely, sexual desire would sweep away all
traditional morality. You curse thought, you resist thought. . . . But even in the

process of resisting thought, you are forced to think. The future belongs to those who dare to think."[11]

Once he had identified himself as one who "dares to think," Zhang Shenfu became convinced that men like him were the true saviors, the true heroes of China.

MAY 18, 1919. Zhang Shenfu's old school friend Liang Shuming is much less impressed by the airs of the "heroes" of May 4. Two weeks after the demonstration in Tiananmen Square, he publishes a critique of student arrogance and unlawfulness in the *Weekly Critic*.

Temperamentally, Liang Shuming had found little common ground with the vehement iconoclasm of the new culture movement. Even as Zhang Shenfu wrote essays about free love, the evils of the state, and the history of Western mathematics, Liang sought to organize a Study Confucius Society for Beijing University students and faculty. Though not opposed to the new cultural movement, Liang was moved by something else, something more intimate, more troublesome: the shortcomings of Chinese students.

In the wake of the May Fourth demonstration, Liang Shuming, unlike Zhang Shenfu, is troubled by what he perceives as the "selfishness" of student demonstrators. Whereas Zhang celebrates the danger of all thought, Liang bemoans the erosion of ethical norms that led young people to take the law into their own hands: "Many people may not agree with me. If so, there is something amiss here. For ten thousand years we, the Chinese people, have thought only of benefit for 'myself,' never for others. We have either held our head too high or bowed down too low. We have no sense of law, of courts. . . . This is our national shortcoming."[12]

In summer 1919, Liang Shuming was already on his way to becoming a self-styled Confucian sage. Although he did not publicly renounce Buddhism until 1921, he had begun to take an active interest in China's intellectual heritage and to dissect its virtues and shortcomings.

Buddhism would remain Liang's inner path toward spiritual self-cultivation. Confucianism, on the other hand, linked him to the society that Liang Shuming —like Zhang Shenfu and other May Fourth activists—believed was in need of salvation. On his side of the fence, Zhang Shenfu also began an intellectual evolution, which by 1921 led him to declare himself a Communist. Zhang's path, in contrast to Liang Shuming's, took him deeper into the thickets of Western thought. Eventually it led Zhang to study abroad.

But in the months following the student demonstration of May 4, 1919, the two friends remained in close touch. As in the photograph taken during their spring outing, whether seated or standing, whether inspired by Chinese texts or Western texts, the two young scholars were concerned with the same problem:

the fate of Chinese culture. To both of them the students' political upheaval signaled an eruption of opportunity. And danger. Their determination to read the event of May 4 in light of a deeper cultural crisis set Zhang Shenfu and Liang Shuming apart from activists consumed by the passions of patriotic mobilization.

Single-minded political activists were busy organizing street corner lectures and urban strikes. They had little time, or interest, in the slow-paced project of cultural criticism. Politics, in their eyes, was not a philosophical problem but a shortcut to national salvation. They were not about to stop and wonder about the blemish of "selfishness" festering inside themselves, or in others. Zhang Shenfu and Liang Shuming did just that: blemishes of the spirit were what they cared about and wanted to expose, above all.

JULY 13, 1919. The *Weekly Critic* is publishing the first of a two-part essay entitled "Freedom and Order" by Zhang Shenfu.[13] In this piece, Zhang makes an effort to summarize his reflections on the recent political upheaval. He never mentions the actual event of May 4, though he puts forth a heartfelt plea for an ongoing commitment to self-emancipation. Compared to other contributions to the magazine that praised the social revolution ignited by the students' movement, Zhang Shenfu's plea for inner freedom strikes an odd note indeed: "Everyone seems to be talking about the importance of 'order' these days. Government politicians are constantly warning us about the dangers of too much freedom. But there is nothing more precious, more rare than this freedom. Look around. Who talks loudest about law and order? Those who want to use these to satisfy the needs of the few against the rights of the many. Freedom, on the other hand, is nobody's to give or to use. It is out there in the world of nature and cannot be realized except through self-emancipation.

"Descartes, with his notion of 'methodological doubt,' understood freedom. Russell, one of the greatest modern mathematicians, understands freedom. Confucius understood freedom when he wrote about *wu wo* [not I]. He too warned against the danger of taking ourselves as the measure of all things. So, all those who understand freedom tell us there is no way but to let nature speak to us directly. We must stop worrying about order and begin the difficult task of self-emancipation.

"When you fight for freedom, the first step is to liberate yourself. Our minds and our spirits must be made more free. All psychological barriers must be removed and all intellectual chains broken in the process. Evils of the past must be destroyed. Otherwise they will come back to haunt us. There must be inner freedom before outward freedom can have any meaning at all. In this struggle, no authorities can stymie us, no tradition can hold us back, no ancients can restrict us, no centuries can limit our view."

Zhang Shenfu's words in summer 1919 fell on deaf ears. Few readers—even of the relatively cosmopolitan *Weekly Critic*—understood his jumble of references stretching from Confucius through Russell. Even fewer had time to ponder the intricacies of inner freedom at a time when the wave of social revolution was beginning to crest.

Certainly the student activists, who were just getting a taste of power in the battle with the warlord government, were not much interested in inner freedom. Cultural conservatives, who comprised the majority of the faculty at Beijing University and who wrote endless essays about the dangers of too much freedom in the classroom, in marriage, and in local elections, were not about to embrace the cause of Zhang Shenfu. Pragmatic revolutionaries like Sun Yatsen and the young Mao Zedong, busy conceiving new ways to harness the social awakening of the student movement, had little interest in Zhang's philosophical ruminations about self-emancipation.

Zhang Shenfu was out of tune, though not quite out of step. He sensed and developed some common ground with political revolutionaries such as Li Dazhao and Chen Duxiu. And yet, even as Zhang joined them in various organizational efforts that culminated in the birth of the Chinese Communist Party, he never gave up his own vision of what the movement should be about: liberation from within.

Zhang continued to pursue this goal through reading, through that habit of broad-minded inquiry that he had urged upon his countrymen the year before the May Fourth movement. In 1919 Zhang, then twenty-six, was a twice-married and still-frustrated young man. Abstract contemplation about freedom had not yet ignited his own love of life. Though in public he fulminated against the hypocrisy of arranged marriages, he did little to challenge those arrangements at home.

MAY 12, 1980. The spring warmth lightens our conversation in Zhang's sitting room on Wang Fu Cang Lane. Today Zhang Shenfu drifts back to his days at Beida, especially 1919: "Before May Fourth, my schoolmates had a nickname for me—*Daode jun*, meaning 'moral gentleman.' It was Luo Jialun who coined it, as a pun on a Daoist text, the *Dao de jing*, you know. It was quite apt. Unlike most of my friends, I did not have a girlfriend until after May Fourth."

"Girlfriend [*nu pengyou*] was a notion that always had a Western ring in my ears. There was nothing like it in traditional China. In the Confucian world of my father, men had concubines and mistresses, but never a girlfriend. May Fourth, yes, May Fourth is when I finally became free to find girlfriends. You might say that I finally became a man during May Fourth."

2

LIBERTINE AND

LIBERATIONIST

Yes, I think marriage should be abolished. I believe in sexual freedom, controlled by such temperance as sensible people exercise in regard to eating and drinking.
—Bertrand Russell to Zhang Shenfu, November 10, 1920

PARIS, MAY 20, 1985. I have trouble moving on with my father's book. His notes are filled with endless stories about girlfriends, as if all he did was move from one conquest to the next, as if women were flowers in a garden, waiting for him to pick them. In passages that survive from a creative writing class for the elderly in Miami, my father describes his promenades in a park along the river in his hometown of Timisoara, Romania. This story irritates me. It grates even more because it is confirmed by older women in Miami who remember my father from those days. They tell me how on Sunday afternoons they used to wait along the promenade for a glance from my father, "the best-looking guy around."

In my father's scattered notes I also find tales of his first love affair, with a Gentile seamstress-model. He goes on about the first time she brought a nightgown on an outing with him—a wordless sign that she was ready for sex.

Why am I wasting part of each week in my Paris studio on my father's amorous fantasies? There is so much to be done with the book on Zhang Shenfu. But when I turn to Zhang's essays, to his narratives, to his photographs, I realize that his story echoes my father's. Here, too, eros overflows the banks of politics, of philosophy—often in the least expected ways. And yet, making sense of Zhang's relationship with women is somehow easier. I have more details. And I countenance them with more equanimity. If I can understand Zhang, perhaps I shall be able to understand my father as well.

PARIS, OCTOBER 1922. A handwritten, mimeographed publication by the little circle of Chinese Communists in France carries a lead article by Zhang Shenfu. The magazine is called *Shaonian* and bears the French subtitle *La Jeunesse*.[1] Zhang's essay is entitled "An Unproblematic Solution to the Man-Woman Problem," a topic that by now is an old theme in the writing of May Fourth radicals.[2] What is new is the Parisian setting and the details of Zhang's argument.

In Europe, other Chinese Communists such as Zhou Enlai, Deng Xiaoping, and Zhao Shiyan have other things in mind. Most of their essays discuss how to organize Chinese workers and students in France. They dwell on Marxist theory or the activities of other Communist youth groups in Germany and Russia. Zhang alone appears interested in sex. He is determined to remind his comrades that social revolution will mean nothing unless it is accompanied —grounded, really—in a revolution of consciousness. This revolution must begin in the most basic ways that men and women relate to one another.

From the opening words of the article, Zhang seeks to link his concern with sex with the materialist assumptions of his comrades: "Food and sex are both basic human needs. The first is not considered divine or dirty, so why should the latter be?"

This rhetorical question is followed by a lengthy argument that draws in everything from Freud to Russell to show how sex is the necessary starting point of all human enterprises. If repressed, Zhang Shenfu argues, sex will subvert the loftiest undertaking, even if it is clothed in the language of political revolution or romantic love. The only solution—simple and unproblematic in Zhang's mind—is to acknowledge sex, to seek sexual gratification, and only then to proceed to social projects beyond personal, physical fulfillment: "In the early stages of a relationship between members of the opposite sex, sexual desire will be satisfied through the most direct means: intercourse. But this cannot be perpetuated indefinitely. To sustain a long-term relationship, some part of sexual desire must be directed to a more encompassing enterprise. This requires not only that the partners love each other but that they be devoted to a larger whole. As a portion of desire is thus sublimated, sexual intercourse will become less important. . . . When these goals are achieved, the question of the relationship between the sexes will cease to be a problem. At that point, marriage as an institution will become superfluous, and the fallacious theory of romantic love will have collapsed of its own weight."

MAY 25, 1985. Food and sex, sex as food—I now recognize this as a constant theme in my conversations with Zhang Shenfu. He held on to this basic equation to the end of his life. But I still find it difficult to accept its naked materialism. I used to be embarrassed when Zhang talked about sex as food on Wang Fu Cang Lane. Now I face my discomfort alone.

For his views about sex, Zhang Shenfu liked to find support in Confucius. He often told me that "the Sage had known the importance of satisfying physical needs before any spiritual undertaking." More often, though, Zhang liked to trace his convictions about sex and food to Russell, the mathematical genius who also claimed to be an expert on sex, marriage, women's liberation, child education, ethics, and world peace. In his personal life, Russell married four times, divorced three times (twice with great bitterness), and took pride in a series of celebrated love affairs in between.[3]

Zhang used everything that Russell wrote about women—and did with them—to buttress his own belief that sex is a powerful, positive force in social life. Convinced that sex had been overlooked by China's social revolutionaries, Zhang saw his mission as follows: first, he set out to make a coherent argument for sexual liberation, dwelling on its benefits for women in particular; second, he was determined to reap the fruits of his own advocacy. After 1919 Zhang Shenfu sought to love as freely—and often as callously—as was possible in China's revolutionary times. The inevitable contradictions between what he wrote and what he did seemed to bother him very little.

To me, his writings about women and sex pose an irritating question: How could this self-styled, articulate feminist entangle himself in so many distracting amorous knots?

Perhaps the knots are more telling than the words. Perhaps, like Bertrand Russell's feminism, they represent two sides of a coin. Others before me who have tried to solve the dilemma of Russell's feminism have fared no better. Brian Harrison, in a 1984 article for the journal *Russell*, had to resort to newfangled terms like "false consciousness" to answer his own question concerning why Russell wrote about women so well and loved them so poorly: "A feminist allegiance makes such stringent demands on the male who wants his conduct to match his convictions that many male feminists will fall by the wayside; their false consciousness will then extend beyond the alleged betrayal of their sex into a concomitant betrayal of their feminist beliefs."[4]

Fateful Encounter

NOVEMBER 10, 1920. Bertrand Russell, the world-famous author of *Principia Mathematica*, is in the second month of his year-long journey to China. Having arrived in the capital after a lecture tour in the provinces, he invites to tea one of his most enthusiastic admirers: Zhang Shenfu, a young philosophy instructor at National Beijing University.

On the stationery of the Continental Hotel, Russell writes: "I thank you for your letter and enclosures. Your bibliography of my works to date is quite extraordinarily accurate and complete. Thank you also for your kind words as to myself, which took me by surprise. Could you come here at 4:30 tomorrow (Thursday) or Friday, if Thursday is impossible? Then I would give you fuller answers to your questions. If neither of these days is possible, please suggest another day."[5]

Zhang Shenfu had enclosed in his letter a recently compiled bibliography of

Bertrand Russell and Dora Black in front of Beijing University, November 1920. Zhang Shenfu is at the far right. (Copyright Features International)

Russell's works that he had edited and annotated for *New Youth* magazine. Russell's notes attached to the letter of November 10, 1920, show that Zhang's questions to the British visitor ranged from the relationship between philosophy and science—especially philosophy as it affected physics and biology—to the problem of love and marriage. Russell appears surprised by Zhang's high regard for him, because, as he adds, "I heard that you are Bolshevik and disapprove of my criticism of Soviet Russia."

CIRCA NOVEMBER 1920. One photograph survives from the time of Russell's tea invitation. It shows both Russell and Zhang Shenfu in a formal portrait taken at the entrance of the Beijing University Library.[6] It also suggests—unwittingly, no doubt—the distance between Zhang Shenfu and Bertrand Russell. Russell is the focal point of the photograph, while Zhang stands far removed, almost out of the picture. Russell and his companion, Dora Black, pose stiffly and formally. Behind them are the flags that decorate the library entrance.

Russell, the teacher-preacher, holds a book in hand. His shock of white hair and proudly carried height set him apart from his Chinese colleagues. Next to Russell, yet as if in a world of her own, stands Dora. With braids coiled upon her head she is rigid in her white dress and laced-up walking shoes. No concession to feminine grace here. At the far right is Zhang Shenfu. In Western suit and up-to-date bow tie (he is the only one of the Chinese scholars to sport the latest fashion) he poses with glasses and long, carefully parted hair. There is no hint in the photograph of Zhang's intimate, intense reaction to Bertrand Russell, the man on center stage.

NOVEMBER 11, 1920. The forty-eight-year-old British philosopher and his twenty-seven-year-old Chinese admirer hold their first extended conversation alone (they had met earlier at ceremonial dinners and lectures shortly after Russell arrived in Shanghai). Russell could not have missed the personal longing behind Zhang Shenfu's questions about love and marriage. Logic and mathematics, about which Zhang appeared so well informed, were passions of the mind. Other, less intellectual passions, mentioned in Russell's letter to Zhang Shenfu the day before, were more troublesome. These Russell sought to clarify when he repeated to Zhang his conviction that sexual freedom should be managed with only such "temperance as sensible people exercise in eating and drinking".[7]

Twice married and bitterly frustrated, the younger man now faced Russell with hope and envy: hope, because Zhang Shenfu was also convinced that sexual freedom was within his grasp; envy, because Russell, unlike Zhang, had already claimed that freedom for himself.

At the end of tea Russell introduced Zhang Shenfu to Dora Black, his lover who was accompanying him on this extended adventure in China. Zhang had heard Dora's lectures in public. In private he sensed the intimacy between Russell and her, which he wanted to believe was fed by the spring of freely given, freely taken sex. The next day Zhang Shenfu wrote an irate letter to the editor of *Chenbao*, North China's major newspaper, quarreling with the "hypocrisy" of an article about Russell that referred to Dora Black as "Mrs. Russell."[8]

NOVEMBER 13, 1920. Others among Russell's hosts in China had tried to gloss over the "immorality" of this unmarried couple. Newspaper reports had described Russell's relationship to Dora as a "friendship between teacher and student"—in an effort to make sense of it in familiar, Confucian terms. This infuriated Zhang Shenfu. In his letter to *Chenbao*, he took pains to explain that Russell and Dora were linked by nothing but love (*lianai*):

"This is the logical outgrowth of the ideas Mr. Russell already developed in his book *Paths to Freedom*. Theirs is a mutual, equal relationship. If Miss Black had not come to China, Russell would not have come either. This is proof not only of their closeness as a couple but, more generally, of the importance of the man-woman relationship in human life. Miss Black is very intelligent, vivacious, brave, and ambitious. She is also a very wonderful helpmate in Russell's work. One can tell this by seeing them together. Wherever Russell is, there is his lover. Whenever Russell explains his ideas, there is always Miss Black, who is a great help in elucidating them."

Was Zhang Shenfu simply describing or embroidering upon his impressions at tea the day before? He certainly did not miss any chance to defend Russell in public—especially when defending Russell gave him an opportunity to explain his own views. To write about Russell's personal conduct was to strike one more blow in the battle over sexual freedom in China. But there was more than public bravura here. Zhang Shenfu was also beginning to identify with Russell. He was convincing himself that a woman such as Dora Black was waiting for him, too.

In the decade following the November 13, 1920, letter to the editor of *Chenbao*, Zhang Shenfu would read and elaborate upon what Russell had written about marriage and morals. He was also tireless in the pursuit of his own sexual freedom—a pursuit that began in November 1920, when Zhang became attracted to Liu Qingyang, an outspoken student activist from Tianjin who would become his lover and common-law wife.

In autumn 1920, Zhang was poised to explore in his own life the ideas that he had discussed with Russell over tea. Bertrand Russell used words that Zhang already knew in his heart: "From a psychological standpoint the desire for sex is precisely analogous to the desire for food and drink. Moreover, as in the case of food and drink, the desire is enormously stimulated by prohibition. . . . Nothing but freedom will prevent this undue obsession with sex. But even freedom will not have this effect unless it has become habitual and has been associated with wise education as regards sexual matters."[9]

Zhang had begun to explore the implications of these ideas a year before he had tea with the British philosopher, a year before he began the love affair with Liu Qingyang. Russell's impact on Zhang's life was dramatic precisely because Zhang had readied himself for Russell's ideas. Zhang Shenfu had thirsted for, read about, and written on sexual freedom before he ever met Russell or Dora or the beautiful young woman from Tianjin. His admiration for Russell was rooted in a self-serving discipleship nurtured by Zhang's personal frustration and public righteousness.

FEBRUARY 2, 1919. Zhang Shenfu pours out his pent-up anguish about arranged marriage in an essay for the *Weekly Critic*.[10] Entitled "Marriage and Women"—a subject familiar to many of the young men of the May Fourth era—Zhang's essay is distinguished by psychological inwardness. While others are raging against the social injustice of arranged marriages and woman-bartering practices, Zhang writes about the inner deformity of those who are willing to participate in the cruelties of China's traditional customs. His bitterest words are addressed to women. He asks them why they avoid the challenge of autonomy, why they forsake maturity as human beings for the suffocating security of marriage: "Why can't you take care of yourselves? Why must you starve as soon as a man leaves you? Why won't you develop your own talents? Why do you continue to let someone else eat the food out of your own mouth? Chinese women, why do you let yourselves be trampled on?"

This outburst signals the suppressed impatience of a young man who had fought for the right to educate his first wife, who had acclaimed the talents of Sofia Kovalevsky, and who was unreconciled to the burden of his second marriage. But this is still a muffled cry. Aware of his filial responsibilities, Zhang Shenfu could not simply shove his second wife out of his parents' home. She had already borne him two children. Divorce was out of the question in his literati household. For the moment, Zhang Shenfu could only urge Chinese women to seek their own spiritual autonomy and economic independence.

FEBRUARY 9, 1919. In the *Weekly Critic* of the following week Zhang Shenfu publishes a follow-up article on the marriage problem.[11] This time Zhang addresses men in an attempt to persuade them that marriage is the most selfish, irrational, uneconomical, and uncivilized solution to the problem of desire and love. Whereas the plea addressed to women was short and emotional, this is a longer, more philosophical indictment of the arranged marriages that keep both men and women in a state of emotional immaturity. Accusing most of his male contemporaries—and himself, by extension—of entering into marriage blindly, Zhang concludes: "When will you stop being a passive agent in the hands of fate? When will you stop sleepwalking? When will you cease being a slave of history, without an iota of self-awareness? . . . How do you dare call yourself a rational being?"

MARCH 1919. Zhang Shenfu enters further into the current debate about the man-woman problem. His contribution this time is a long article on this subject in the main forum of progressive intellectuals, *New Youth*—edited by the same men he worked with on the *Weekly Critic*, Chen Duxiu and Li Dazhao.[12] Zhang's was neither the first nor the last essay in *New Youth* to put forth a vision of how men and women should refashion their relationships at the dawn of this "new culture." Some essayists, armed with ideas from Karl Marx and Friedrich Engels, called for the wholesale demolition of the Confucian family system. Some *New Youth* writers had just finished reading Ibsen's "Doll's House" and were much impressed by Nora's final rejection of wifely and motherly duties when she says, "I have other duties equally sacred. . . . Duties to myself."[13]

Still other young men wrote about their own predicaments as victims of the system of arranged marriage. And there were some budding social revolutionaries who decried the rash of female suicides as a symptom of women's inability to wrest the freedom of education and of marriage. Mao Zedong was typical of the young men who became outraged on behalf of women and pointed the finger at society. He believed social revolution was the starting point for psychological emancipation.

This was not the case for Zhang Shenfu, who entered the man-woman debate empowered with Bertrand Russell's ideas and with a growing personal conviction that freedom was a matter of inner emancipation. It can only begin in the self's own realization that acquiescence to bondage must stop, said Zhang. Psychological revolution, then, is the place to start, and it is rooted in the affirmation of desire—not in will, as for Mao. Following Russell's arguments, Zhang declared that love is nothing but the natural, spontaneous development of sexual desire between men and women.

Everything that thwarts this feeling, Zhang Shenfu argues, is irrational and inhuman. Arranged marriage is the ultimate evil, because it forces men and women to feign emotions for each other that no longer exist or, worse, never did. Building on Russell's attacks on Victorian marriage, Zhang suggests an alternative to the suffocating, hypocritical Chinese arrangement (with which he was so familiar). The alternative is a free, if temporary, union of the sexes. Without calling it "trial marriage," Zhang describes this union as the only way out of the burdensome compulsion to act out the Confucian roles of husband and wife.

More than a year before he met Russell and Dora Black, Zhang wrote: "A man and a woman should be able to live together regardless of socially sanctioned titles such as Mr. and Mrs. If there is no love between them, they should be able to leave each other freely. This is as natural as the change in weather. It certainly is nothing to be ashamed of. . . . As Russell says, "Divorce is the best way to avoid the failure of marriage."[14]

OCTOBER 1919. Five months have passed since the May Fourth demonstration in Tiananmen Square. China is still filled with the excitement of patriotic

Zhang Shenfu in Western garb among fellow activists of the Young China Association. *Left to right*: Su Jiarong, Meng Fuchun, Shen Yi, Zhang Shenfu, Xu Yanzhi. (Courtesy of Zhang Shenfu)

strikes by merchants and workers who supported the May Fourth movement. Students are on the street corners of major cities preaching the gospel of new culture: more democratic politics, more freedom in marriage, more attention to women's liberation. Their numbers and voices, however, are weak in comparison with those of the conservatives who attack them.

But the May Fourth veterans know themselves to be the voice of the future. Their national organization, the Young China Association, is a living net that contains and nurtures their idealistic proposals for national regeneration. The October issue of their journal, *Young China*, is dedicated to the problem of women's liberation. This special issue contains contributions from famous professors at Beijing University, Li Dazhao and Hu Shi among them. It also features essays by representatives of the students' generation; Kang Baiqing and Zhang Shenfu, members of *New Tide*, are most prominent.

Again Zhang's essay "The Great Unfairness of Women's Liberation" strikes a discordant note.[15] Again he takes issue with a position that his comrades and friends think is the beacon of hope. Zhang dissects women's liberation with the knife of cool reason. Behind all of the supportive slogans for women's liberation, Zhang argues, are young men giving themselves virtuous airs and young women not yet ready to mobilize for their own emancipation.

Zhang Shenfu and Liu Qingyang in 1920 on the eve of their departure for Europe. *Far left*, Chen Yusheng, the patriotic activist who helped found the Young China Association; *second from left*, Liu Qingyang, leaning on the shoulder of her Hunanese friend Wang Weiyu, who accompanied them on the boat to Marseilles; *far right*, Zhang Shenfu, standing next to Cheng's wife and daughter. (Courtesy of Zhang Shenfu)

Zhang Shenfu intends to shock his readers into critical self-awareness and finds the words to achieve this goal: "The very idea of women's liberation is wrong. Those who respect others don't go around liberating someone else. Men who talk about women's liberation all the time reveal that fact that they are full of unequal ideas. 'Women's liberation' is an insult to women. The only kind of liberation is self-liberation."

Was Zhang Shenfu referring to himself here? Yes and no. He was, first and foremost, addressing fellow male feminists in the new culture camp. The most enthusiastic among them had risen to defend women with a fervor that belied the fact that they were part of the problem faced by women. All too frequently forgetting their own role in the dilemma, men went on to design social solutions to women's personal problems.

What was needed, in Zhang's view, was a quieter, slower, more difficult "inner revolution," which had to start with women themselves. They had to find their own voices, to talk back to society. They had to want to take the risk of personal autonomy and social action. And by October 1919 Zhang knew this was possible—not just theoretically because Bertrand Russell had said so, but because he was already taken with the fiery activist Liu Qingyang.

CIRCA OCTOBER 1920. The first photograph of Zhang Shenfu and Liu Qingyang together provides an odd contrast to the group photograph of Russell and Zhang Shenfu taken in Beijing.[16] Here, too, Zhang stands off to the far right. In this photograph, however, taken only a month earlier than the one with Russell, Zhang is sporting a Chinese silk jacket over a long robe. His long hair is carefully groomed and parted Western style. His foreign-looking horned-rimmed glasses strike a discordant note in this thoroughly Chinese setting. At the far left stands Zhang Shenfu's host for this occasion, Chen Yusheng, the activist from Beida who along with Li Dazhao (and other students including Lei Guoneng) had been the moving force behind the founding of the Young China Association in 1918.

Between the two men in dark silk jackets stand four women in white silk jackets and dark skirts. They look like sisters—which they were in political action. Liu Qingyang, the most prominent activist among them, stands next to Chen. She is, by this time, a member of the Young China Association. She has already proved valuable as a public speaker and fund raiser. In fact, Liu Qingyang is so well known that she is the first member of Mao Zedong's "New People's Society" to be recruited outside of his native province of Hunan.[17]

An embodiment of China's new woman, Liu Qingyang is no Dora Black. Her striking, sensuous beauty is displayed without self-consciousness. She stands in a world of her own making, leaning against another woman, a school friend —who, Zhang recalls, "attracted me first, before Liu Qingyang." In the company of women, Liu has already found and tested her voice on a variety of issues, ranging from national salvation to women's liberation. She has chaired large meetings about the May Fourth incident, starting with a gathering of six hundred on May 25 in Tianjin. She has lectured on street corners in Beijing. She has been arrested by the warlord government for being a troublemaker, while at the same time the newspapers in her hometown defended her as "a pure-minded patriot."[18]

Now, after a year of intense organizing for the student movement, Liu Qingyang was preparing to leave for France. She was ready to see what lay beyond the borders of the native land she had defended with fierce passion for more than a decade.

Though he stands apart, as in the November 1920 photograph with Russell, Zhang Shenfu is already intimately connected to Liu Qingyang. With Russell, Zhang shared philosophical interests and a passion for sexual freedom. With Liu Qingyang, Zhang is linked by a common dedication to the cause of national salvation. Sexual desire followed, and was quenched, not long after this October photograph.

Woman Warrior

JUNE 10 1981. Zhang Shenfu is talking about Liu Qingyang once again. Our conversations during my return trip give him a chance to recall many times the woman who held center stage in his affections. Even after straying from her, even after loving and marrying other women, Zhang still thinks of Liu Qingyang as the most important woman he discovered, educated, and launched onto the path of revolution.

Today he leans his head back and once again lets the details of his life and quarrels with Liu float up out of a politically clouded past. He seems to be riding the crest of a memory wave that gives him great pleasure. She is always there with him, like the foam—an ever-present companion during his turbulent life. Their roles remain fixed in his mind: she is the heart, he the brain. He leads, she follows.

Yet the details he gives me today call into question the very picture he tries to engrave in his mind: "We have been living together since 1920. It was she, you know, who started the affair on the boat to France. After that she did pretty much what I told her to. She joined the Communist Party upon my recommendation. She cooked pork for me even though she was Moslem. . . . When we came home from Europe, she lived with my family even though I had another wife at the time. She was more of a concubine at first. But we were both above such notions. . . . I wrote most of her speeches. She could not think very clearly. But she was a fiery, convincing public speaker."

JUNE 15, 1981. It is time to look for the historical Liu Qingyang. Zhang keeps circling back to this one woman. Of all the people who crossed his life, she is the preeminent figure, not just the lover and wife who lasted the longest of the four (from 1921 to 1948). Even in his self-serving recollections, she has a presence all her own. Her political career parallels and intersects Zhang's but follows its distinctive rhythms. A friend in the Beijing University Library helps me locate Liu Qingyang's obituary in the *People's Daily*.[19]

It is dated August 3, 1979. On the back page, I find a picture of Liu Qingyang as she was after "liberation," after 1949 and the breakup of her relationship with Zhang Shenfu. I search the small, faded newspaper image for a hint of what she was really like, apart from Zhang's words. The image is mute, formal, almost dull. A stern-looking woman, greying hair pulled tight around her face, looks out at the camera in a conservative (but Western) suit. There is nothing here to distinguish Liu Qingyang from the other officials of the Wom-

Liu Qingyang's memorial photograph as it appeared in the official obituary in the *People's Daily,* August 3, 1979.

en's Bureau—the Party-run organization in which women activists have been sequestered ever since the 1920s.

The obituary is as conventional as the photograph. It is not even about Liu's life or death. Rather, it dwells on her political rehabilitation:

"Today, at Babao Shan cemetery a ceremony was conducted in commemoration of comrade Liu Qingyang, a member of the People's Congress, vice president of the Chinese Red Cross and a member of the standing committee of the Chinese Democratic League. Comrade Liu died in Beijing on July 19, 1977, at the age of eighty-three, after cruel treatment by the Gang of Four. . . . Flowers were sent by comrades Deng Xiaoping, Song Qingling, Deng Yingchao. . . . Comrade Liu went to Paris in 1920, where she joined the Chinese Communist Party. . . . She was active in the war of resistance to Japan. After the war, she was active in the democratic movement and went to the liberated areas in 1948. After liberation she was active in democratic circles and women's work."

The only words in the obituary that capture the spirit of Liu Qingyang are credited to Kang Keqing, another prominent woman activist and widow of the famous military leader Zhu De: "Liu Qingyang's whole life was a life of revolution. She was bright and honest, open-hearted and broad-minded, extremely responsible in her work, modest and long-suffering in her demeanor, full of vitality. She carried out earnestly each directive and policy of the Party. She made a considerable contribution to developing the revolutionary united front and struggled for women's liberation."

All these are well-worn phrases used to praise women who have been long-time fellow travelers of revolution. The only conventional phrase missing here is "loyal daughter of the Communist Party"—withheld in Liu's case because she drifted away from the Party in 1927 and did not rejoin formally until 1961. But she is still presented as an unflinching follower of the Communist line. Hence, she deserves burial in the official cemetery at Baoshao Shan and rehabilitation in the pages of the *People's Daily*.

There is nothing in these paragraphs about the inner life of the woman who set off with Zhang Shenfu in 1920. The formulaic phrases—such as "modest and long-suffering"—do not leave room for the fur-wrapped Communist who appears in photographs with Zhang and Zhou Enlai in Germany in 1922. Such descriptions as "upright and honest" make Liu seem like an open book, readable by all.

There is no mention here of Liu Qingyang's writings on women and sex; nothing about the children she bore or the pain she suffered in the course of political agitation; no mention either of her complicated relationship with Zhang Shenfu. The conclusion—that she followed the Party's directives and policies —though important in vindicating her in the official annals of revolution, leaves out too much about the unique individual who shaped her own political commitments.

I must therefore continue to look for Liu Qingyang. I no longer search for the historical Liu but for the woman who has been read out of history. I am looking for the independent-minded woman squeezed out of the public record and out of Zhang's recollections. Both prefer to remember Liu as a follower. I am trying to find something about the impassioned girl who started student organizations in Tianjin. I am looking for the fiery orator who stirred crowds in Beijing. I am seeking the woman who stormed into Zhang's life the year after the May Fourth movement.

AUGUST 24, 1986. After a long wait, I have been granted an interview with Liu Fangqing, the younger daughter of Zhang Shenfu and Liu Qingyang. After five years of being told that I cannot, must not, see her—because "she is too high up in the Marxism–Leninism–Mao Zedong Thought Institute"—we meet.

Ever since I started going to Zhang's house in 1979, his current wife has been insisting that Liu Fangqing is a "heartless daughter" who wanted nothing to do with Zhang Shenfu in order to protect her own political position and that of her mother. But Zhang Shenfu's death appears to have loosened old affections and lessened political anxieties.

A middle-aged woman greets me at the door. Her face is the image of both her parents: she has Liu Qingyang's sensuous mouth and Zhang Shenfu's sharp, almost hooked nose. Liu Fangqing is eager to start talking about her parents. Both are dead and both have been rehabilitated in the Party's history. Zhang is now inscribed in the annals as an "old friend of the Party," as a "loyal, respon-

Liu Fangqing, Zhang Shenfu's daughter, during our interview at her home in 1986.
(V. Schwarcz)

sible comrade." This year, Zhang Shenfu is getting more attention than Liu Qingyang. His interviews concerning Zhou Enlai are widely quoted, and his scholarly books are being reissued. Liu Qingyang, on the other hand, has just begun to be noticed and written about. This is an odd fate for the partner who tried much harder to be politically correct.

During our three-hour conversation, Liu Fangqing gives me many details about the political life of Zhang Shenfu and Liu Qingyang. I finally learn the full story of their tensions and their divergent points of view during the split of 1948. In the end the daughter's tale confirms the image of the mother that appears in the *People's Daily*. She, too, recalls Liu Qingyang as a loyal, ardent follower: "My mother was put in jail from February 1968 to May 1975. In 1974, I was informed by the committee in charge of her case that I could visit her. . . . After so many years of accusations, she was a little bit numb. But when she saw me, her face came alive. She did not ask about the situation at home. She only talked about the two things that mattered to her.

"My mother said to me: 'Fangqing, you must remember that I have been loyal to the revolution all my life. All my life I have followed the Communist

Zhang Shenfu's lover, Liu Qingyang, in 1906, striking a martial arts pose in her parents' courtyard in Tianjin. (Courtesy of Liu Fangqing)

Party. I love the leaders of our Party and Chairman Mao with my whole heart. I love Premier Zhou. Another thing I want you to know is that I am worried about Premier Zhou. I have a feeling that some terrible pressure is being applied to him. I just feel this.'[20]

"The rules for visitation do not allow talk about politics, so I told her to be careful. Still, she insisted on telling me this."

The Party's loyal follower thus lives on, even in the daughter's recollection. Although Liu Qingyang broke the rules for family visits by talking about politics, although she presumed to speak about the personal anguish of China's premier, she is still remembered most kindly for her love of the Party, of Chairman Mao, and of Zhou Enlai.

I listen to the loves of Liu Qingyang with puzzlement. The only one that makes sense to me is the affection for Zhou—her old friend from Tianjin with whom she also shared several years in Europe. The other loves seemed extraneous. Perhaps these are code words for her ardent patriotism. Nonetheless, I have no reason to doubt the daughter's story about the jail visit.

At the end of our conversation, Liu Fangqing brings out a box of old photographs. The first one fascinates me, and I ask for it unabashedly. Here, finally, is an unexpected glimpse of the Liu Qingyang before she became Zhang Shenfu's lover, before she became a cadre in the Communist movement. Here, finally, an image that provides some tension with the official portrait in the *People's Daily*.

CIRCA AUTUMN 1906. A twelve-year-old girl holding a sword in her right hand strikes a martial arts pose in her family's courtyard. Her knees are curved inward for strength and balance; her left hand is frozen close to her forehead, the fingers pointed in the formal attack position.

Here Liu Qingyang looks the part of the legendary woman warrior who led peasant masses in rebellion against foreign invaders. But she has a presence all her own, even as she evokes the myth of Hua Mulan, the girl who dressed up as a boy and trained to do valiant feats for the nation. A sensuous femininity radiates around Liu in spite of her intense concentration. She seems to be practicing martial arts for pleasure first and foremost.

Liu Qingyang's daughter, Liu Fangqing, looks at the photograph eighty years later, nodding: "Oh yes, she was so good at every kind of martial arts. She trained herself for physical activity from early youth and so maintained her strength until old age, even in jail."

It is not the physical strength of the girl in the photograph that moves me but her forceful will, the inner passion. This is what I think links her to the woman who became Zhang Shenfu's lover and later served the Chinese Communist Party with a fierce kind of loyalty. An incident from the daughter's story about Liu Qingyang's youth confirms this impression of a girl moved to serve the nation in a way all her own:

"By 1906 my mother was already active in the patriotic movement. A campaign was underway in Tianjin to raise funds to strengthen the Chinese Navy. She took part in the campaign by collecting money in the neighborhood. She asked people to skip breakfast and contribute the savings to the campaign. On one street corner she took out her own purse and emptied all its contents in the collection box without a second thought. This act of generosity made a deep impression on those who observed it. Later, my mother's gesture was talked about and written up in newspapers as an exemplary act—a young school girl offering her purse for the nation."

To be in the public eye as an autonomous actor was no mean achievement for a twelve-year-old girl in Liu Qingyang's time. How did she get there? Again the public record credits someone other than Liu herself. In a recent essay on Liu Qingyang edited by the Women's Bureau, I find a passage that attributes her patriotic passion to her oldest brother, Liu Mengyang. This sibling entered the world of Tianjin journalism early and is assumed to have been responsible for the attention given to his sister's actions in 1906.

Liu Mengyang is also credited with showing his sister a picture of Qiu Jin, the female revolutionary executed by the Manchu dynasty. Liu Qingyang, the Party-sponsored narrative concludes, "vowed to follow her brother's advice and became a patriotic revolutionary on the model of Qiu Jin."[21] The picture that Liu Mengyang showed his youngest sister was, indeed, that of a hero. Qiu Jin—a mannish woman who liked to dress in the costume of a Japanese male, complete with a small dagger—was ready for rebellion, secret society plots, and even assassination assignments. Liu Qingyang, on the other hand, wore her femininity with ease. What did she really think about Qiu Jin? The voice of public memory is silent here.

So I seek other paths through Liu Qingyang's photographs, around the edges of her daughter's talk: in contrast to Qiu Jin, Liu Qingyang appears to have kept away from violent politics whenever possible. Perhaps, unlike Qiu Jin, Liu Qingyang could afford to. The world had changed between Qiu Jin's birth in the 1870s and Liu Qingyang's in the 1890s. By the time Liu came of age, Chinese women had more choices concerning demeanor and commitment. There is no doubt that Liu Qingyang took advantage of those choices and cultivated her demeanor—specifically, her body and her voice—in a way that was indebted to her brother and Qiu Jin. But the cadence was all her own.

AUGUST 24, 1986. Liu Qingyang's daughter is walking me through her mother's childhood. With the 1906 photograph in hand, she reaches back to her grandparents' world: "Born in 1894, Liu Qingyang was the youngest daughter of a merchant Moslem family in Tianjin.[22] This meant that she was spared some of the most burdensome expectations that fell on the daughters of strictly Confucian gentry. She had four older brothers and two older sisters, all of whom doted on her. She also received a good education. As Moslems, the family did not believe in the Confucian idea that lack of talent is a virtue in a woman.

"Her martial arts training was but one sign of this. When Liu Qingyang was ready for school, my grandparents sent her to the best institution for women in Tianjin. This was a boarding school for girls run by a Moslem woman named Madame Yan. Liu Qingyang attended Madame Yan's school from 1905 to 1909. In 1909 she passed the examinations for Tianjin Women's Teacher's College, a place that nourished her organizational talents and patriotic passions."

I listen with two chronologies in mind—Liu's and Zhang Shenfu's. In 1911, when Zhang Shenfu was called home to be married, the seventeen-year-old Liu Qingyang was already actively involved in the revolution. She joined Sun Yatsen's organization, the Tong Meng Hui. For this, the daughter gives credit to a male geography teacher, Bai Yayu: "Bai was an important cadre in Sun's revolutionary group. He invited Liu Qingyang to his home often. Through talk of history and geography, he implanted in her sympathy for China's suffering and for the need for revolutionary action."

"Did Liu Qingyang have ideas, ideals of her own?" I ask, not willing to let my own questions be drowned out in this narrative of Liu's male mentors.

"Oh yes, of course," the daughter smiles. She, too, is looking for the other side of her mother. By 1912 not only was Liu Qingyang a member of Sun Yatsen and Bai Yayu's revolutionary organization, but she was planning to start a school of her own. With financial support from her brother she opened the Datong School for Girls in 1914.

"Although the school lasted for only one year (it collapsed financially), this enterprise showed her determination and ability to strike out on her own. She could always convince others to support her cause—which, in 1914, centered on women's emancipation. By 1915 she was active in the Association for Women's Rights and other groups that promoted women participation in politics."

In 1915 Zhang had been cheated into his second marriage. In 1916, the daughter tells me, Liu Qingyang broke off a marriage arranged by her father before his death in 1901. While Zhang still followed custom, used go-betweens, and agreed to his family's arrangements, Liu was already breaking new ground. Zhang was still swayed by his duties as son and father to a little girl. Liu Qingyang, freed by her father's early death, enlisted her brothers' support in the fight for freedom.

Liu Qingyang's daughter laughs as she recalls her mother's independent-minded character: "My mother was always so strong-willed, so sure of what she wanted or did not want. In 1916 the family of her arranged suitor came to ask the Liu household to fulfill the contract. Liu Qingyang refused. Her mother did not care whether she went through with the contract, and the oldest brother was thoroughly on her side. My mother then came up with an idea: she would test the suitor herself—they would both write papers on a topic of her choosing. If his paper was better than hers, she would marry him. The suitor became very upset. Liu Qingyang's brother managed to calm him and persuade him to cancel the marriage. So she became free to throw herself into full-time teaching and patriotic activism."

The woman warrior putting a suitor to the test—this is the image that lingers as Liu Fangqing holds the 1906 photograph in her hand. The test was not in sword techniques but in words, the medium that Liu Qingyang had mastered even before meeting Zhang Shenfu in 1919.

By 1920 their concerns converged. Liu was a prominent speaker, especially in street demonstrations; Zhang spun essays about freedom and order, women and marriage, Bertrand Russell and Auguste Rodin. Their meeting was all but fated by the explosive patriotism of the day.

I ask the daughter more about Liu Qingyang's patriotism. What was unique about it? How is it related to the geographical and historical circumstances of her birth? Clearly Liu was a young woman thirsting to make her mark in the

Liu Qingyang in
1920 as a
member of the
Enlightenment
Society in Tianjin,
after she had
already achieved
fame as an
activist and orator
during the May
Fourth movement
of 1919.
(Courtesy of Liu
Fangqing)

world. Having been born in Tianjin, she had seen foreign troops invade her city
in 1900 (to quell the Boxer rebellion):

"In 1900 the Liu family business—they were merchants of beef for the
Moslem community—collapsed. This, too, affected my mother's patriotism.
At this time, Tianjin was carved up among various foreign powers with special
interests. It became a city full of foreigners, more like Shanghai than Beijing.
As a young girl, Liu Qingyang identified with her city and with her country's
plight. And she found kindred spirits. At first, her brothers supported her.
Later, schoolmates and students from Madame Yan's School, where she taught
from 1916 to 1919, supported her. In 1919 she, along with Zhou Enlai's future
wife, Deng Yingchao, joined Zhou's Enlightenment Society. To signal the break
with old family loyalties, members of the society used numbers as their pen
names. My mother's was '25'—a pen name she continued to use even after
she joined the Communist Party in 1920."

Back in my room, I reread the manifesto of the Enlightenment Society. It is
composed of impassioned, vague words that sound no different from the hopes
of other May Fourth students: "We have made up our minds to search for
enlightenment. We hope that other people in our society will also become
determined to march toward enlightenment."[23] But what is obscure to me today
must have been like music to the ears of a cultural radical like Zhang Shenfu.

He, too, supported the students' political activism, but always with a concern for enlightenment. No wonder that he was so taken when such ideas were put forth by an attractive young teacher from Tianjin.

Zhang Shenfu had heard about Liu Qingyang even before she joined the demonstrations in Beijing in the summer of 1919. He got to know her better over the following year as she rose in prominence within the Young China Association. From older friends at Beida, such as Li Dazhao and Chen Duxiu, he heard that the young woman from Tianjin was such an effective public speaker that she had been sent to Southeast Asia in the winter of 1919–20 to raise money for the student movement among overseas Chinese.

JUNE 15, 1981. In a formal memoir for Party archives, Zhang Shenfu recalls how he asked Liu Qingyang to join the Communist cell in Beijing: "In the fall of 1920, the first person I approached to join the Communist cell was Liu Qingyang. She was known to me and Li Dazhao, and she had just returned from raising money for the student movement among overseas Chinese in Southeast Asia. But she refused. So we recruited another May Fourth student activist, Zhang Guotao."[24]

In 1920 the girl with the sword, the young woman who had tested her suitor, was still not a joiner. She still followed the beat of a different drum. Liu Qingyang retained her independence even after she joined the Communist Party in Paris in 1921; even after she became prominent in the Party's Women's Bureau in the 1920s; even after she gained national prominence during the anti-Japanese mobilization of the 1930s; and even after she assumed a leadership role in the pro-Communist Democratic League in the 1940s. She was a patriot who tried to serve the nation according to her own vision and temperament.

But the revolution she joined proved inimical to independent-minded women. Some were tamed, others ostracized. Liu Qingyang was subject to both strategies. After her death, obituaries wove her political career into the larger tapestry of the Communist movement. The vivid threads that were her choices and her passions became muted in the encompassing story of women pioneers and martyrs. The verdict—the "positive judgment"—of the *People's Daily* in August 1979 still stands today. It is restated in an official biography of Liu Qingyang: "Liu Qingyang's whole life is a revolutionary life."[25] Revolutionary remains synonymous with loyalty to the Party line.

In the public annals of the Communist revolution, the discrete details of Liu Qingyang's life—such as her marriage to Zhang Shenfu and her prolonged withdrawal from politics between 1927 and 1935—are overlooked in favor of her service to the Party and the nation. What matters here is the exemplary cadre, not what made Liu Qingyang a unique woman.

Among contemporaries in the Communist movement, Liu's distinctive manner proved to be an irritant. Peng Shuzhi, one of the young men active in the founding of the Chinese Communist Party, showed his displeasure early. In the summer of 1924 he and Liu had visited Moscow as members of the Chinese Communist Party delegation to the Fifth Congress of the Communist International (Comintern). Peng Shuzhi never forgot his impression from that summer. To be with Liu Qingyang was to suffer a constant thorn in his side. Fifty-nine years later he still called her "sheer hell."

PARIS, MAY 30, 1985. I have found Peng Shuzhi's memoirs in French.[26] Written in exile and edited by his daughter and Parisian son-in-law, Peng's recollections are intended to settle scores with the Chinese Communist Party. The text is colored by the bitterness of an old man who became a follower of Trotsky and believed that "real Communism" was betrayed in his native land.

Liu Qingyang appears in this vengeful memoir for a brief but vivid moment. I read Peng's words in French and imagine Liu Qingyang's ironical smile if she heard this. Or would she fly into a fit of rage instead? But why bother? The text reveals nothing that Liu Qingyang did not know before—that her Communist comrades were as prejudiced as the conservative warlords she had learned to battle during her Tianjin girlhood:

"It was Chen Duxiu who wanted Liu Qingyang to go to Moscow," Peng Shuzhi writes, "to represent the Chinese Communist Party along with Li Dazhao, Zhang Tailei, and a railway worker, Tang. Chen's reason was twofold: first, he prized the aura surrounding Liu from the May Fourth movement; second, he thought it a good idea that the Chinese delegation to the Fifth Congress of the Comintern include at least one woman. A good idea? I have nothing to say about this. What I do know is that if we had to have a woman at all, our choice should have fallen on someone other than Liu Qingyang.

"In 1923, during the few weeks that Liu Qingyang and Zhang Shenfu (her husband) spent in Moscow, following their stay in Germany," Peng Shuzhi concludes, "I realized that she had learned absolutely nothing in Berlin. Her general cultural level and her political understanding were extremely low. She seemed more concerned with her own glory and well-being than with the future of the revolution.

"I figured this out in more detail during the month I was with her as a codelegate to the Fifth Congress of the Comintern. I finally saw that she was an endless talker with no other purpose than to make herself known and valued. The railway worker Tang, a man of the north whose manners were hardly refined, could not stand Liu Qingyang. What hell to be with her!"(367–68).

Peng Shuzhi condemns Liu Qingyang for being insensitive to proletarians. He calls her vain and self-seeking—both commonplace charges by men who are irritated by renowned women. Peng cannot forgive or overlook the aura of glory that surrounded Liu Qingyang after the May Fourth movement of 1919. His memoir provides unwitting testimony to her prominence in student circles at the time. She stood out by sheer force of personality. In revolutionary China—as in traditional China—this would count against her.

Militant among the Shades

FEBRUARY 8, 1989. How to untangle the stories of Zhang Shenfu and Liu Qingyang, which cross so often over the twenty-eight years of their common-law marriage? They even mirror each other in the distortions and omissions that mark their biographies in the official annals of the Communist Party. And yet their stories are fundamentally different. I know Zhang Shenfu's story better. His conversations with me are detailed and self-serving, exemplifying a man's point of view.

I continue to try to excavate writings by and photographs of Liu Qingyang that would reveal her life in her own terms. Yet I cannot bring Liu to life with the nuances that fill out my picture of Zhang Shenfu. A few photographs and her daughter's cautious words are my limited stepping stones in this journey. I use these to look beyond the public persona of the loyal follower of Communism. At the same time I am hampered by a nagging question: What made Liu Qingyang so vulnerable to Zhang Shenfu and to other male authorities? A Moslem, she chose to eat pork after she became Zhang's lover. Even at the end of her life, even from jail, she continued to talk about her love for Chairman Mao and Premier Zhou. Why?

I cringe from the most obvious answer: her vulnerability lies in her sex. But this conjecture haunts me nonetheless. I search, again, the face of the girl with the sword. Around the edges of the photograph I sense the frail vanity of a young woman not yet tested by love or political dogma. By the time Liu Qingyang met Zhang Shenfu in 1919, she had mastered a great deal. Swords and words were one thing; sex was something else altogether. No amount of personality and idealism could have prepared Liu Qingyang for the passions, the responsibilities, and the humiliations she encountered after she became Zhang Shenfu's lover in 1920.

BERLIN, CIRCA 1922. Another photograph, another time, another world: eight young Chinese intellectuals gather for a formal portrait, seven men and Liu Qingyang. She occupies the middle foreground like a decorator's center-piece. Carefully posed, Liu leans toward Zhang Shenfu, who sits next to her. She is wearing an attractive European dress graced by pearls—evidence of the impeccable taste that shows up in a slightly later photograph with Zhou Enlai, who also had a penchant for embracing Continental mannerisms.

Zhang Shenfu's knees touch hers as a muted gesture of possession, as if to

Liu Qingyang and Zhang Shenfu (seated, *right*) with Chinese students in Berlin (1922). Standing between them is Zhang Bojun. (Courtesy of Zhang Shenfu)

say: "She is mine. I am the only man in this group to have a constant female companion. I am the only one who has regular access to sex." Zhang's face is turned to the camera, straight on, arrogant. He is the best dressed among the seven young men. He strikes the pose of a forceful, good-looking man, a counterpoint to Liu Qingyang's frail beauty.

The woman at Zhang's side is no longer the girl in the martial arts costume. She does not even look like the young woman who on the eve of her departure from China in 1920 posed for a solo photograph in a traditional Chinese skirt and embroidered tunic. That young woman faced the camera with strong, determined eyes. She was the one accustomed to public attention during the May Fourth movement.

In Europe, however, Liu Qingyang became not just a Communist but also a mother, all within one year. Vulnerability is now written all over her face. Before she boarded the boat to France on November 23, 1920, Liu was a virgin—as Zhang Shenfu boasted in our conversation. Zhang, by contrast, was a twice-married man who had fathered three children, the last two with a woman he found thoroughly uninteresting and burdensome. By 1923, also, Zhang Shenfu was the self-styled leader of Chinese Communists in Europe.

The public record of Liu Qingyang's life has little to say about the affair that began on the boat to France and nothing about how she felt when she became involved with a married man. Her official biography does not talk about her pregnancy and the birth of a son in the first year of her sojourn in Europe. It is mute on the subject of her giving up the infant to a French nanny in order to follow Zhang Shenfu and Zhou Enlai from Paris to Berlin.

The whole European experience is reduced to a few sentences: "On the boat to France, Zhang Shenfu introduced to Liu Qingyang the circumstances of the Russian Revolution. He imparted to her basic knowledge about Communist theory and raised her understanding of the Socialist revolution and Marxism. On December 27 the boat landed in Marseilles, after 35 days at sea. Liu Qingyang went to Paris. In January 1921 she married Zhang Shenfu. In February she was introduced by Zhang Shenfu into the Paris cell of the Chinese Communist Party. During 1921–22 she made a permanent contribution to development of the Chinese Communist Party. In 1923 she came back to China with Zhang Shenfu through the homeland of the October Revolution—Soviet Russia. After three years away, she came back to a calamity-ridden China."[27]

This amnesia-laden history of Liu Qingyang's journey in Europe stands in contrast to the German photograph. The biography insists, prudishly, that Liu Qingyang "married" Zhang Shenfu. In fact, there is no evidence of a ceremony in Paris, or later. Zhang and Liu did become intimate companions and stayed together in a common-law arrangement until 1948. But there is nothing in the written documents of the period, in the daughter's recollection, or in the conversations with Zhang Shenfu to suggest a formal marriage contract between the two.

According to the daughter's account, Liu Qingyang joined Zhang's life as it was. She treated his children as part of her family and even trusted his legal wife to take care of their little son when they returned from Europe in 1923.

The published biography uses vague words to describe Liu Qingyang's contributions to the building of the Chinese Communist Party in Europe. These generalities and a few stylish photographs are all that remain from Liu's years in Europe—in contrast to the wealth of Zhang Shenfu's essays on Russell, Freud, Marx, and Trotsky. Zhang also left a record of his views about sex in the article "An Unproblematic Solution to the Man-Woman Problem."

In that 1922 essay, Zhang Shenfu began an assault on romantic love that became increasingly strident in the late 1920s. Zhang railed against traditional marriages and romantic love because he could afford to. He had the time, the freedom, and the attention of interested comrades. Liu Qingyang had satisfied him sexually and released him for "more encompassing," more revolutionary activities. I have no account of her concerns—immediate or global. Her presence next to Zhang in the Berlin photographs suggests a shared point of view. But it is hard to imagine Liu Qingyang attacking romantic love, and harder still to fathom how she coped with being pregnant, giving birth, leaving her infant —all in strange countries and foreign tongues.

MARCH 6, 1924. Back in China, Liu Qingyang's voice is heard again. Maybe she has been freed by the death of her son shortly after the return through Moscow in 1923. Maybe the scarcity of female Communists on native ground is firing Liu's old passion for social action. Maybe Zhang's intimacy with the Communist Party's top leadership is providing her with more public visibility.

In 1924, after a stint in the Canton-based Women's Bureau, Liu Qingyang returns to Tianjin as editor of a newspaper called *Women's Daily*. This provides her with a forum for a series of essays on a wide variety of subjects, ranging from women's sexuality to Lenin's death.

Today's article, entitled "Purity and Chastity," opens with an impassioned attack on the double standard of sexual morality: "One-sided chastity! This is really an inhuman, crushing view of human sexuality! It is an odious old custom that deprives people of their freedom!"[28]

After this cri de coeur, Liu Qingyang proceeds to attack China's traditional marriage customs for the unfair burden that they placed on women. Here, as in earlier May Fourth essays, the focus is on widows who cannot remarry because of the one-sided expectations of lifelong chastity. Liu Qingyang takes this critique one step further. Beginning with a description of the tragic fate of a young widow who had been infected with syphilis by the uninhibited exploits of her husband, Liu goes on to the subject of women's emancipation in general. Here, Liu Qingyang unmasks the hypocrisy imbedded in the "ethical" standards that apply to only half of humanity. These standards, she argues, are both hollow and deadly: "Men and women are both human. Both have natural sexual urges. But if a man seeks other sexual liaisons before and after marriage, it is considered a mere appetite. If a woman so much as looks at another man she is deemed shameless, beyond the pale! Male-controlled societies have always licensed chastity for women and freedom for men.

"When my turn comes to go down among the spirits of the dead, I will go on propagating women's revolution. I am going to wake up all those wives already dead, all those who had followed their husbands into hell. I am going to harangue them until they call off their unfair marriages. But then, to hear such unscientific talk in the twentieth century can only lead you to burst out laughing no doubt."

A feminist in hell—this is the bitter self-description that Liu Qingyang offers of herself in 1924. By that time, she, too, had broken with conventional marriage taboos. She was living with a married man while quarreling with the one-sided ethics of Chinese society.

MARCH 7, 1924. The second part of "Purity and Chastity" goes on to assail traditional Chinese mores for promoting what Liu Qingyang calls ethical deformity.[29] Liu provides a long list of injuries, of crimes against women that are currently condoned in the name of chastity. Her argument is grounded in a strong belief (shaped by Zhang Shenfu) that human nature is primarily sexual: "Sexual activity is a necessary manifestation of being alive. It cannot be controlled by reason, much less by setting wrongheaded, negative restrictions that in the name of virtue are applicable to women alone."

In this essay Liu still talks about widows, who are the most visible prisoners in the citadel of chastity. But she insists that "all women, like men, are sexual beings. They have merely been deformed by male notions of one-sided chastity."

MARCH 8, 1924. In the conclusion to the essay on purity and chastity, Liu Qingyang addresses educated women—her own kind.[30] Here, too, she writes with the pathos of one still imprisoned by male notions of morality. To bolster the spirits of those prisoners, Liu points to modern American and European customs of love and marriage: "Maybe my examples will challenge what is held as 'natural' in China. Maybe love freely chosen will, in time, dictate its own ethic of chastity and fidelity. That means the end of one-sided morality, of ethics for women alone. Surely, both men and women might choose to stay together if they were free to choose whom they love."

Liu Qingyang's words were meant to stretch the parameters of what was deemed decent and proper in the world around her. Her attacks on one-sided chastity ran against the grain of what the vast majority of Chinese women thought about love and sexuality. Even the Communist Party—supposedly beyond feudal and bourgeois morality—was not particularly interested in love and sex in 1924. Rather, it concentrated on organizing women workers and strengthening its alliance with the Nationalist Party, or Guomindang (GMD).

Zhang Shenfu—still in Canton while Liu Qingyang wrote the essays on purity and chastity in Tianjin—must have been amused when he read them. Liu's writing style was more impassioned, more subjective than his. He, too, had written about women, marriage, and sex during the May Fourth movement and in Paris. But Zhang never considered himself a partisan of love, American, European, or Chinese style. Romance was, in his view, nothing but a newfangled trap for men, and women.

SEPTEMBER 26, 1924. Liu Qingyang publishes her strongest defense of women who defy morality to follow their natural sexual instincts. In a terse piece entitled "Alas! the Truth Seekers!" she addresses fellow revolutionaries who are attacking a certain young woman who has just returned from Europe.[31] Discovering that the young Chinese man who has become her lover abroad has a wife and family at home, she promptly leaves him. Radical newspapers insist on calling the young woman immoral.

In her defense of the girl's immorality, Liu Qingyang comes close to speaking about herself as the lover of a man with a wife and children. She defends the other young woman as if she was explaining her own actions: "Not to pay any attention to sexual desire is unrealistic, for men and women alike. To hold up ethical ideals that are too far from reality is not possible under any circumstances. So I believe that people's actions should originate in feeling [passion and desire] and end with reason."

To make this point more striking Liu uses the German philosophical words for *is* and *ought* (*sein* and *sollen*)—an indication of what she had learned in Europe. Here, she transgresses on Zhang Shenfu's territory. Liu Qingyang uses his ideas about reason and rationality to make her own point about the unfair expectations that face women even in the revolutionary camp.

AUGUST 24, 1983. A small photograph taken on March 8, 1925, points out Liu Qingyang's considerable visibility during the first International Women's Day celebration in China. Her daughter Liu Fangqing gives me the snapshot sixty years later, along with the summary of Liu Qingyang's speech on that day: "The Chinese Communist Party was leading this celebration, and my mother was the main speaker at the Beijing meeting. She got sick because she put so much effort into the preparation and delivery of that speech. She was also pregnant. Of course, Liu Qingyang's speech emphasized the role of women in the Chinese revolution. Male leaders such as Li Dazhao attended and were much impressed by her speech. When my mother became ill, her care was entrusted to Madame Borodin, the wife of the chief Comintern leader in China at the time."

The photograph Liu Fangqing shows me reveals a sunlit corridor marked by the shadows of trees and flowers. At the end of the corridor stand two women: a heavyset Russian woman in a loose, ungainly dress and Liu Qingyang, neatly coifed and dressed in a pregnancy smock. "Mother had made so many sacrifices before my older sister was born in 1928," the daughter continues. "She had several miscarriages, all because of her work for the revolution. This child, too, was lost."

"A high price for revolutionary activism," I want to add, but I refrain from saying it aloud. Instead, I ask about Liu Qingyang's work with Li Dazhao —work that went on until Li's death in spring 1927. The daughter takes great pride in describing the highlights of Liu Qingyang's political career. The climax came after Li Dazhao's death, when Liu Qingyang became head of the Women's Bureau in Wuhan during the summer of 1927. Liu's days in the high command were limited by the crushing defeat of the revolutionary forces in the fall of 1927.

"By August 1927 mother left Wuhan for Shanghai. In June 1928, taking along her recently born, three-month-old daughter—my sister Liu Fangming —she returned to Tianjin. There her political activity stopped until she joined the National Salvation Association during the anti-Japanese War."

Zhang Shenfu and
Liu Qingyang in
1935 outside their
home on the
Qinghua Univer-
sity campus. Liu
Fangming (b. 1928)
stands between her
parents; Liu Fangqing
(b. 1930) is seated.
(Courtesy of
Liu Fangqing)

"What led Liu Qingyang to withdraw from Communist politics?" I ask directly; "Zhang Shenfu had left the Party much earlier, in January 1924. Were politics too dangerous for a young mother during Jiang Kaishek's White Terror?" In the silence that stretches between us, I go on in my mind: What happened to the woman warrior, the girl in the martial arts costume? What happened to the agitator among the shades in hell?

"She had a family of her own by then," Liu Qingyang's daughter's murmurs, as if she heard my questions. "Here, look at these family photographs of us all in 1935."

CIRCA SUMMER 1935. "The Professor's Family," Liu Fangqing's title for the photograph between us, shows an image that is far removed from the Communists' revolution. Zhang Shenfu, dressed in Western jacket and white pants, stands next to Liu Qingyang, who wears a traditional Chinese gown. With one hand, Liu holds a summer fan. Her other hand is draped over her oldest daughter, Liu Fangming. The younger girl, Fangqing, sits at her mother's feet embracing a large Western-style doll. The group poses informally in front of their house on the Qinghua University campus, one of the most prestigious universities in the nation. Zhang Shenfu was among its senior lecturers in philosophy.

For this one moment, in summer 1935, the world appears at a standstill. Liu Qingyang appears content as mother and wife. Zhang's second wife had died by this time, and Liu had, for a time, the role of official consort. Her children embroidered the role with the details of real life.

But the "Professor's Family" tableau was short-lived. By 1935 the Japanese were already encroaching upon North China, an advance that economically threatened the family's domestic tranquility. In addition Zhang was filled with unease about marital life. In 1935 he was poised to betray his wife. Liu Qingyang was readying for yet another wave of patriotic political activism. In this photograph neither seems aware that the end of their harmonious academic family is in sight.

An Enemy of Love

The sojourn in Europe had given Zhang Shenfu the gift of time. Away from China's pressing social problems, he had developed his inquiry into the man-woman problem beyond the May Fourth attack on the institution of arranged marriage. In Europe, Zhang hit upon what he thought was the most pernicious enemy of personal freedom: the notion of romantic love.

It was an oddly "modern delusion" that Zhang Shenfu began to attack in 1922. Traditional Chinese culture did not value romantic love. Instead, it emphasized mutually beneficial arrangements between families. Zhang, however, had psychological questions of his own, which led him to look beyond Chinese tradition. He felt it important to attack the notion of love in the 1920s and 1930s even when other radicals, especially Communists, insisted that social revolution come first. One such young Communist, Yun Daiying, a labor organizer from Mao's home province of Hunan, went so far as to say that all talk of psychological emancipation was nothing but self-indulgence.

MARCH 7, 1925. Yun Daiying takes on self-styled male feminists like Zhang Shenfu in an article timed to coincide with International Women's Day. The essay, entitled "The Women's Movement," is published in a special issue of the Communist Party journal, *China Youth*.[32] Yun accuses male feminists of indulging in a hedonistic life-style. Worst of all, he writes, they seek only their own liberation, the expression of their own "spirit of individualism." Those —like Zhang Shenfu—who get carried away with ideas of personal freedom become ideologically muddled, "with all ideas of society emptied out of their minds."

Zhang Shenfu, in contrast to Yun Daiying, had left the Party in January 1925. His taste in books, clothes, and women bore the unmistakable imprint of what Yun Daiying described as hedonism. In the eyes of social revolutionaries, Zhang was living proof that the search for psychological and sexual freedom makes all ideas about society fly out of one's mind.

This, however, was proof only if ideas of society were limited to Communism. But Zhang was pursuing a different agenda. He championed a more encompassing social revolution—one that would not sever class revolution from psychological self-emancipation. Throughout the 1920s, Zhang Shenfu continued to insist that a revolution which merely rearranged institutions and classes was doomed to failure. Furthermore, he never abandoned his May Fourth convictions that women were at the front line of the battle between social and personal freedom.

During the 1920s Zhang Shenfu's ideas developed in tandem with his relationship to Liu Qingyang. In 1921 she had joined him in the Communist Party in Paris and then had followed him to Germany and back to China. After 1925, though no longer a member of the Party, Zhang Shenfu stayed with Liu, even when her activism exposed both of them to repression from the warlord and Nationalist regimes.

In 1927 Zhang Shenfu joined Liu Qingyang when she and Li Dazhao took refuge in the Soviet embassy in Beijing. That summer he followed her to Wuhan, where she headed the Party's Women's Bureau. Zhang Shenfu followed, but questioned, the Party's narrow view of social revolution. Even in the midst of the White Terror that followed the breakdown of the United Front between the Communist and the Nationalist Parties in 1927–28, Zhang Shenfu explored the "psychology of dependency" that chained men and women alike.

MARCH 10, 1928. Communist hopes for revolution appear crushed as activists retreat into the urban underground and the countryside. Liu Qingyang is about to give birth to her first child in Shanghai. Zhang Shenfu teaches there at Continental University and makes ends meet with translations of modern Western philosophy.

But he also continues to do other kinds of writing. On this day in March, he completes an essay entitled "The Art of Sex and Sexual Freedom." In it, Zhang is storming an old citadel: Chinese prudishness about freely enjoyed sexual intimacy.

Others had breached the walls before Zhang Shenfu. During the 1920s a veritable frenzy of research and publishing about sexuality took place. One of the most important works was Yu Feibin's *The Hygiene of Sexual Desire (Xingyu de weisheng)*, followed closely by Cheng Hao's *Human Sexuality (Renlei de xing shenghuo)*.[33] Both books praised the benefits of a more liberal attitude toward sexual intercourse. But their tone was medical and anthropological. Flesh-and-blood men—and especially women—had been left out of the story altogether.

By contrast, Zhang's brief contribution is personal. It brings the subject of sex closer to home. It is the first of three articles dealing directly with the subject of women, love, and sex—and his first essay since the one written in 1922 in Paris. In this opening piece, his argument is straightforward: the art of sex (*xing de yishu*) is the basic precondition for sexual freedom (*xing de ziyou*): "To think about how and why one engages in sex is one of the important tasks for us today. The act of sex must finally come off the dusty shelves of pornography into the brisk, open air of the revolution."[34]

Here, Zhang repeats his old belief that sexual emancipation is the most basic form of social practice. And again, as often before, he starts with the predicament of women. In 1919 Zhang had asked women to liberate themselves. He had also acknowledged what Liu Qingyang detailed with bitterness in her 1924 essays—that sexual mores weighed very differently on Chinese men and Chinese women.

Nonetheless, in 1928, Zhang Shenfu presses one step ahead. He asks: What would it take for women to have the same kind of freedom in sexual intimacy as men? What would women do if they were liberated from externally imposed prohibitions? Zhang Shenfu's answer is bleak: women, he suggests, would retreat into a new prison, the prison of lianai, of romantic love.

The opposite of romantic love is a vision of intimacy unencumbered by duty and anxious self-preservation. Where others wrote about sex in a language burdened by medical and anthropological notions, Zhang Shenfu concludes with a celebration of artful sex: "There cannot be love except where there is art. There cannot be love but where freedom prevails. Therefore, I believe in sexual freedom and oppose all notions of romantic love. In my view, to be romantically attached is to be inseparably bound. This situation is totally incompatible with sexual freedom. Sexual freedom exists only where there is affection without attachment. If you are sticking to one another like glue or lacquer, what's the point of talking about freedom at all" (218).

AUTUMN 1930. Zhang Shenfu is completing his first book, a collection of essays entitled *Thought as Such (Suosi)*. Liu Qingyang is pregnant again. Material security and social respectability are finally in sight for the forty-seven-year-old philosopher who has just witnessed a decade of frantic and often disillusioning political activism. Now that the Nationalists have the upper hand, Zhang Shenfu persists on writing about social revolution.

In autumn 1930 he completes an essay entitled "Women and Revolution."[35] Just when the terms *women's liberation* and *revolution* are being purged from public vocabulary, Zhang decides to recall in detail each of his previous articles on these subjects, starting with his May Fourth articles about marriage and the man-woman problem: "My articles managed to arouse very effectively sympathy for women—this most oppressed part of our society" (220).

Once he establishes his credentials for speaking to and about women, Zhang Shenfu goes on to restate his call for a "revolution in human nature," which he terms alternately *ziran geming* (revolution in nature) and *xingge geming* (revolution in temperament). In this 1930 essay Zhang defends his conviction that a "revolution in human nature" is more difficult and more important than social revolution. Using concepts from mathematical logic, Zhang describes social revolution as the "necessary but not sufficient cause for ending the predicament of Chinese women. This final goal will be achieved only when women examine and overcome their own subjugation."

"Why has the subjugation of women lasted longer than any other form of social repression?" Zhang goes on to ask. "Why have women been deemed inferior for so long?" His answer is a mixture of anthropology and biology: "Because most societies have valued warfare and women cannot hold their own on the battlefield, where men have traditionally won both power and glory. By contrast, the experience that most women know best—the pain of childbirth—has been underrated in all societies." Armed with such facts about world history, Zhang Shenfu proposes a quixotic solution to the predicament of women: test-tube babies. "The noted British biologist J. B. Haldane has already experimented with this, and it will surely be the hope of the future" (222).

But to wait for this technological solution to the pain of childbirth is to put off the revolution in human nature too long. In the meantime, Zhang insists, women must start to wean themselves from the "habits of dependency" that have become second nature: "One must look at the tragic phenomenon of educated women to understand how deep-seated is the desire to be taken care of, to be so safe in one's inferior status. Whereas before marriage educated women think of themselves as quite emancipated, their pursuit of romantic love lands them in the same predicament as that of less enlightened women. It is the ideal of romantic love that, again and again, draws women toward the marriage grave" (223).

Zhang Shenfu's hard-hitting words of 1930 appear to echo Liu Qingyang's 1924 essay about the hell of virtuous wives. By 1930, however, Liu was in such a grave herself. No one who read Zhang's article and who knew of his common-law marriage with her could have mistaken the implication behind all the talk of educated women.

Was Zhang trying to rescue Liu Qingyang? Or was he venting his irritation that she had become so dependent, so burdensome, like his previously uneducated wives?

The self-serving meaning of Zhang's words did not become fully apparent until the mid-1930s, when he strayed from Liu Qingyang into another love affair. But there was more than selfishness in Zhang's critique of women's dependency. He was also trying to understand why love was such a peculiar curse in the lives of women. He was determined to show how romantic attachments bind and weaken women by fostering debilitating fantasies: "When women try to fall in love," Zhang wrote in 1930, "when they seek to become lovable in the eyes of a man, they end up making themselves hopelessly incomplete" (224).

WINTER 1930–31. Zhang is now drafting the conclusion for his book *Thought as Such*. The last article, entitled "The Mutual Understanding Between Men and Women,"[36] is a modest treatise, quite unlike his 1922 Paris essay on "An Unproblematic Solution to the Man-Woman Problem." The later version is more subdued. It is, at first glance, simply a review of Russell's recently published *Marriage and Morals* (1929). In this work Russell pressed his critique beyond the sexual freedom he had advocated over tea with Zhang Shenfu in 1920. Russell no longer believes that mutually satisfying sex is as easily attained as food. Nor does he content himself with an attack on the social institution of marriage. Instead, Russell begins to probe the values that have upheld the marriage institution for centuries.

Zhang's essay is meant to introduce this last stage of Russell's thinking to China. But it serves also to probe his own concern with the psychological barriers to intimacy between men and women. As in earlier essays, Zhang begins with a negative assessment of what has been accomplished in China over the past decade: "Although there is more open social contact between men and women today than ever before, the two sexes are as far from really understanding each other as they have always been" (225).

The reason for this lack of understanding, according to Zhang, is mutual mistrust and an ingrained habit to act out the roles of dominator and dominated. Unlike the true friendship that can exist between two men or two women, the most common emotion between the sexes is resentment.

In Zhang's view men must bear the primary responsibility for this sorry state of affairs. It is they who have made women into the dependent creatures that they are today. It is men who continue to benefit from women's well-practiced inferiority. To support this argument, Zhang Shenfu appeals to the latest Western scientific work on the subject, *The Dominant Sex: The Sociology of Sex Differentiation*, written by a German couple named Vaerting.

On the basis of this theoretical book, Zhang Shenfu asks a more practical question: How are men and women to overcome their long-standing antipathy to each other? His answer: by first recognizing the deep-seated origins of misogyny in men and of men-hating in women. To acknowledge that each side has been misshaped by unequal dependence is the first step toward the revolution of human nature. Self-awareness and self-control, according to Zhang

Shenfu, provide the only way out of the endless cycle of domination and subjugation (227).

Contrary to assertions in earlier essays, Zhang Shenfu suggests here that
there can be a genuine *interdependence* between men and women. He assumes
that they need and will continue to need each other. Thus, love—both the
emotion and the word—is now endowed with more positive connotations. (To
underscore this transition Zhang uses a new word for love: *aiqing* [natural and
spontaneous affection, as between parent and child] rather than *lianai*, the use
of which he had contested for so long.) To be sure, it has to be a love devoid of
possessiveness, especially in sexual matters. But it is love nonetheless that
Zhang Shenfu writes about as he concludes his 1931 book of philosophical
ruminations.

In the decades after 1931 Zhang Shenfu experimented with love more than
he wrote about it. The challenge and the difficulty of mutual understanding
with women, however, remained an important issue in his life. Like his mentor
Bertrand Russell, Zhang Shenfu took delight in his sexual exploits. At the
same time, he refused to reconcile himself to the unfair conditions that made
him freer to explore free love than the women who shared his affairs.

The Feminist Womanizer

The same attraction to strong, independent women that in 1920 had led Zhang
Shenfu to his affair with Liu Qingyang drew him away from her a decade and a
half later. In the early 1930s, as his philosophical prestige was reaching its
zenith and his family life was growing more mundane, Zhang thirsted for new
adventures. In 1932, after publication of his book *Thought as Such*, Zhang
accepted the editorship of "World Thought," a special column published in the
North China newspaper *Dagong bao*. Here was a unique opportunity to reach
the kind of mass audience Zhang had only dreamed of before. His previously
private ruminations now continued on a monthly basis in this column.

AUGUST 27, 1933. Zhang Shenfu is answering one of the letters to the editor in his newspaper column. The top page is, as usual, filled with philosophical articles on Marxist theory. Most weeks, Zhang Shenfu adds a few paragraphs
of his own, entitled "Thought as Such Continued," which usually deal with
two of his main concerns: the Japanese aggression in North China and the
convolutions of analytical philosophy developed by "Ludwig Wittgenstein and
earlier pioneers such as Moritz Schlick, born in 1881."[37]

Today, however, Zhang takes time to answer a query by Hebi, an anonymous
intellectual who chose a pen name meaning, literally, must it be necessarily so?
In this letter, Hebi interrogates Zhang about his views on women. Following
the logic of Zhang's own ideas about the problem of understanding between the

Sun Junquan,
president of
Beijing's Number
One School for
Girls, in 1933.
(Courtesy of
Zhang Shenfu)

sexes, Hebi asks: "What would you do if you were a woman? Would you condescend to marry someone who was not a match for your intelligence and wits? What is your opinion of such 'wild' and 'weird' women as Rosa Luxemburg?"[38]

Zhang's answer is straightforward enough: "I really cannot answer your question since I am not a woman. I cannot and do not claim to understand a woman's feelings. What I can say, however, is that I am a great admirer of brave and intelligent women like Rosa Luxemburg."[39]

A few months after this exchange, Zhang Shenfu met Hebi. The writer of the letter turned out to be Sun Junquan, the female president of the Number One School for Girls in Beijing.

JUNE 13, 1981. Zhang Shenfu spends the afternoon talking about the women in his life. As always, he starts out with Liu Qingyang. He relives the pleasures of the initial conquest, along with the pain of their separations: "Throughout the 1930s, I made Liu Qingyang angry. She felt humiliated by my affair with Sun Junquan. In February 1936, when I was arrested, my children went to Sun's house for aid and advice. Liu Qingyang was also arrested but was released before me. We were accused of being ringleaders for the North China Communist Party underground. Ha! How untrue.

"When I was released from jail, things did not get better. I remember a meeting in Wuhan in 1937. Liu Qingyang got up and flew into a rage against me, against Sun Junquan. We separated shortly after that. I did not live with Liu Qingyang again until the end of the war with Japan, sometime in 1944. The only woman I lived with for a while was a former student of mine from China

University, Dong Guisheng. But it was nothing sexual. Just a platonic relationship. We slept on the same bed and never touched each other."

I have heard about Sun Junquan and Dong Guisheng before. But today Zhang appears more relaxed, more willing to talk. So I ask about them all over again.

"Sun, oh, she was a fiercely independent woman. We became close around the time of the December Ninth student movement [1935]. She was very active politically, very temperamental, too. She ended our relationship in 1937 because she was jealous of Dong Guisheng. No reason, of course. But she was angry. Jealous, like Liu Qingyang. Sun's life ended so sadly. She committed suicide by hanging herself in the early 1950s. They found her naked, with a note that read, 'I go out of the world as I came.' Awful.

"Dong? Oh, she was young, very innocent. Very devoted to me. She helped me with the magazine *Wartime Culture*, which I was editing in Chunqing. There was nothing more than that between us. I helped find her a husband among my former students. I think I still have some of her letters to me. Some from Sun Junquan, too. Let me show them to you."

NOVEMBER 7, 1937. In her last letter to Zhang Shenfu, Sun Junquan pours out her anger. She is unforgiving about his interest in Dong Guisheng and outraged at his expectations of fidelity on her part: "I have received all your letters since I got home [to Wuhan]. They are so insulting! How dare you, at a time when our relationship is ending, still be jealous of me, and with no reason at all? I hope you take pains in the future to learn how to behave like a true man and do so accordingly. Furthermore, you must understand that I am an independent woman. Therefore, there is no need whatsoever for you to send money to me."[40]

Sun Junquan's accusations help me understand the disparity between Zhang's conduct and convictions. The man who had advocated the importance of nonjealous love was now acting possessively in the midst of a dying affair. Full of anger at his betrayal, Sun could not imagine Zhang's offer of money to be anything but a desire to patronize her. By then there was no time or trust left to change the love affair into a friendship. Sun Junquan had seen the old-fashioned man inside the public feminist and decided to withdraw from his affectionate concern. This, however, was not the case with Dong Guisheng, the young woman who had caught Zhang's fancy in 1937 and for whose sake he risked, and eventually gave up, the relationship with Sun Junquan.

JUNE 10, 1938. Zhang Shenfu has been living with Dong Guisheng for almost a year in Chunqing, China's wartime capital. Friends like Liang Shuming had visited and taken note of Zhang's new companion. Introduced as his secretary, Dong is clearly something more to Zhang. On days that they must be apart, she writes lengthy letters, addressing him as father, teacher, or darling.

Today's letter calls him darling and reports on a visit to the dentist: "He wants to take out four of my teeth and replace them with new ones. It will cost eighty yuan. Do you think I should go ahead, darling? Oh it's such a nasty thing to go through. Every tooth of mine has been touched by you and become pure and precious. I hate to get rid of them."[41]

MARCH 6, 1939. Zhang Shenfu is trying to disengage from the intimacy of the relationship with the ardent young girl who was his student at China University in 1930. He clearly values her help with his journalism projects but is unable to shield her from the gossip of living with a married man. (Liu Qingyang lived not far from them in Chunqing.) As before in his life, Zhang is beginning to feel the burden of responsibility. The most acceptable solution appears to be a separation, following which Zhang is to arrange an engagement for Dong Guisheng to one of his worthy students.

But the separation is not easy for Zhang to carry out. Today's letter seeks to broach the subject and to console all at once: "I am going away now and will not be able to see you for a while. I am not sure whether I have treated you as I should. For the past year, you have concerned yourself about me both personally and in terms of my work. I am now involved in so much else. Still, I cannot bear to think that we have ended like this. I am feeling all the difficulty of life. Gui, Gui, please do not be too tough on me. As I think of our future, I'm trembling."[42]

MAY 23, 1939. Dong Guisheng's delayed response makes it clear that she is hurt but not angry. In Zhang, she found, even if temporarily, an empathetic friend. This is more than she imagined possible in a world that frowned on all friendship between men and women: "For the past three years who have I talked to but you? Who knows my hurts but you? Now that it's to end like this, my life will be nothing but remorse. . . . Still, I would like to talk with you one more time before we leave each other forever. After three years of closeness, what harm can there be in meeting one more time. I just want to cry my heart out to you, then start going my own way."[43]

In the affair with Dong Guisheng, Zhang's foibles were overlooked—or more likely, unrecognized—by a young woman in love and eager for understanding by an older mentor. Zhang, in turn, was free to play the role of teacher-lover. In this role, he did not face the burden of a long-term commitment. Yet even when Zhang relied on "Cutie" (as Dong liked to call herself for his pleasure) for help in his publishing projects, he was not unaware of how he might burden her. By the end of the war with Japan he was once again looking toward his relationship with Liu Qingyang. Here was a concrete way to work out what Zhang had identified in 1930 as the "problem of mutual understanding between men and women."

MARCH 11, 1944. The war with Japan is drawing to a close. Zhang Shenfu and Liu Qingyang are living together again. Both are active members of the Democratic League, a loose congregation of intellectuals seeking alternatives between the Communist Party and the Guomindang.[44] The need to lay the foundation for constitutional democracy is foremost in Zhang's mind as he prepares a new collection of essays entitled *Independence and Democracy.*

On this day, Zhang finishes the draft of a new essay, "Women and the Constitution." In this work, the first on the subject of women since the mid-1930s, Zhang makes it clear that he is forsaking his previous interests in sexual freedom. Instead, he dwells on legal guarantees necessary for the equality between the sexes. His conclusion calls for safeguarding "relationships between men and women that depend on prolonged loyalty and devotion of the two people involved."[45]

Prolonged loyalty is what Zhang Shenfu hoped for and was beginning to explore again with Liu Qingyang in 1944. But civil war and the ideological demands of the Communist Party cut short his time for such explorations. By December 1948 Liu Qingyang published a public renunciation of her relationship with "the enemy of the people, Zhang Shenfu."[46]

JUNE 6, 1981. Zhang is recalling his separation from Liu Qingyang in 1948. Today, as often before, Zhang retells the end of their story with bitter regret: "Our separation was forced upon her, you know. She became controlled by the Party. She had cut off all contact with me when I became a target of public attack. She had no choice but to protect herself and the children. . . . After liberation, we did not speak to each other. But she continued to ask about me through intermediary friends."

To the very end, Zhang insists on placing himself at the center of Liu Qingyang's life. His self-importance fills in the gaps of what he did not know or did not understand about Liu Qingyang. I am left with the dilemma of the man who wrote so much about women yet understood them so little.

In the late afternoon sun, I slowly close the gate of Zhang's house behind me. Too much of what was said between us is troubling to me. On the way to the bus that takes me back to Beijing University I am reminded of Bertrand Russell's split with Dora Black, of the bitterness of their daughter, Katherine Tait, who tried to come to terms with her father's so-called feminism and his selfishness in relationships with women.

AUGUST 20, 1981. Back home in Connecticut I reread Katherine Tait's essay "Russell and Feminism."[47] In it she struggles with the discrepancy between her father's convictions and his actions. Russell, like Zhang Shenfu, professed a belief in equality between men and women. Yet, he was unable to act accordingly.

At the end of the essay, Tait faults her father for never troubling himself to understand how women really felt. Without denying the impact of Russell's public feminism, she argues: "A feminist can perfectly well be general and public and social and entirely concerned with changing the laws and customs for the benefit of women; lots of feminists are and they are genuine feminists. You need not understand a women's heart to fight for justice for her. A feminist need not even understand women" (9).

Tait makes me realize how far I am from solving the puzzle that is Zhang Shenfu. Maybe a solution will always evade me. Maybe solutions simplify too much. I try not to fall into the trap of Communist Party historians. They too tried to iron out the contradictions in the life of Zhang Shenfu and Liu Qingyang. I hold on to loose ends. These are my threads through the labyrinth of twentieth-century Chinese politics.

3

AN ECCENTRIC AND

ALMOST FORGOTTEN

COMMUNIST

Critical history
begins with a
dissatisfaction with
memory and a
desire to remedy its
deficiencies.
—Bernard Lewis,
History

NEW YEAR'S DAY, 1921. Zhang Shenfu arrives in Paris from Marseilles. He has every reason to consider himself the most senior Chinese Bolshevik in Europe. He has been a trusted intimate of Chen Duxiu and Li Dazhao for more than four years. Throughout 1920 Chen and Li invited the young philosophy instructor to share in their discussions about the founding of a Communist Party in China. Before leaving in November, Zhang had visited Chen Duxiu at his home in Shanghai. Again, as often before, Zhang received the older man's confidence and political counsel. The Europe-bound philosopher was also entrusted with a new mission: to recruit Chinese students living in Europe into the nascent Communist organization.

And this Zhang did with notable success. In three short years he brought into the radicals' fold some of the men and women who would shape the fate of revolution in China. Among them were Liu Qingyang, Zhou Enlai, the future premier of the People's Republic, and Zhu De, the general who brought Mao to victory in 1949. Furthermore, in spring 1921, Zhang Shenfu started the first Chinese Communist cell in Europe. One year later, in 1922, he became the official link between the enlarged network of Chinese Communists in Europe and the Party organization at home.

And yet, following a brief but pivotal career as Party founder, Zhang Shenfu vanished from the public record of the Communist revolution. For decades it was as if he had never existed. Mao Zedong, the self-educated leader of the peasant masses, increasingly dominated the limelight. Chinese Communism appeared to have sprung from Mao's forehead, like Athena from Zeus. Even when Party histories broadened the narrative terrain after Mao's death in 1976, there was little room for eclectic, highly educated intellectuals like Zhang Shenfu. At most, he was used as a source for information about the early career of Zhou Enlai.

A Berlin outing at Lake Wannsee, 1922. *Left to right*: Zhao Guanchen, Zhou Enlai, Liu Qingyang, and Zhang Shenfu, then official correspondent of the Chinese Communists in Europe. (Courtesy of Zhang Shenfu)

AUTUMN 1922, BERLIN. One photograph provides two versions, two visions of Chinese Communism in Europe. I encounter the first version in books about Chinese students in Europe, published in the People's Republic in the 1950s. These works recount how Chinese students became radicalized and drawn into the Communist movement during their sojourn in Europe. To illustrate the narrative better, these works point out that Chinese premier Zhou Enlai was among those students.

Thus, an image is created—"Premier Zhou in Europe." The photograph (reprinted with the more modest title "Zhou in Berlin" in *The Coming of Grace* by Ed Hammond)[1] shows Zhou with his hands on the oars of a boat. A serious young man dressed in a Western suit and tie looks out at the camera. He is the epitome of the determined Communist revolutionary. Here is a version of what history must have been in order to explain the "inevitable" victory of Communism in China. This vision reads history backward from 1949.

Another, very different image confronts me in a photograph that Zhang Shenfu pulls out of his files in November 1979. Zhou Enlai still holds the oars of the boat, but he is not alone. Now in full view, the rowboat holds four young Chinese intellectuals on an outing at Berlin's Lake Wannsee.

At the stern of the boat sits the long-haired, bespeckled Zhang Shenfu—the man who became corresponding secretary for the European branch of the Chinese Communist Party in Europe. Liu Qingyang, the first female member of the Communist Party in Europe, wears a fox fur draped on her shoulders. She is seated between Zhang, her lover, and Zhou Enlai, her longtime friend and associate from Tianjin. Behind Zhou sits another friend from Tianjin, Zhao Guangchen.

I realize that the image of Zhou Enlai promoted in the 1950s was cut out of the original picture and reproduced separately. The reconstituted whole tells a story quite different from its dismembered parts. "Premier Zhou in Europe" had placed Zhou Enlai at the source of a narrative with a predictable conclusion: the victory of Chinese Communism in 1949. The solitary Zhou Enlai symbolized the power of the forward-looking Party. It was a vision cut off from the details that surrounded, and complicated, the lives of Chinese Communists in Europe.

With Zhang Shenfu at the stern, however, with Liu Qingyang in a fox collar, the photograph reveals nuances. It suggests that Zhou was just one of many young Chinese trying to find themselves and seeking their mission in Europe. Along with their Western clothes, these young people tried on a series of identities and ideologies. Whatever they called Communism was clearly something more tentative than what became codified as Marxism-Leninism under Mao Zedong. Uncropped, the 1923 photograph opens a window onto a whole world of personal and intellectual exploration—and amusement—that had been consigned to oblivion during the long period of Maoist historiography.

MARCH 2, 1962, GUANGZHOU (CANTON). Zhou Enlai himself tries to break through the amnesia surrounding his early years as a Communist. In a speech to the National Conference of Spoken Arts, he acknowledges that he was one of the "formerly bourgeois intellectuals" who are still needed by the Chinese Communist Party. If China is to recover its economy and mend its broken spirit after the hardships of the Great Leap Forward, intellectuals must once again be appreciated.[2]

To facilitate this Zhou reaches back into his past to a man condemned as a counterrevolutionary rightist in 1957: "I would like to thank Liu Qingyang and Zhang Shenfu, for it was these two who introduced me when I entered the Party. Zhang Shenfu's thought is very broad. He studied Russell most intensely. His aim was to fuse the ideas of Russell, Marx, Freud, and Einstein. . . . In sum, one thing must be positively acknowledged: all of us came from the old society. No matter where we are now, in the past we all belonged to the bourgeois intelligentsia."[3]

Zhou Enlai's forgiving, appreciative attitude toward intellectuals like Zhang Shenfu was not allowed to flourish for long. After a brief moment, during which once-frowned-upon thinkers such as Russell and Freud could be discussed alongside Mao and Marx, the Cultural Revolution broke out in 1966. From 1962 to 1966, a few more intellectuals were drawn into the Party (though Zhang himself was not "rehabilitated" until 1979). During the early 1960s, too, more pragmatic economic policies were tried, and new questions about Party history were aired in public.

But the outbreak of the Cultural Revolution in 1966 snuffed out the possibilities for reform. Heroic narratives of Mao Zedong leading the peasant masses replaced previous attempts at a more truthful version of Party history. Bourgeois intellectuals were cast into "cow pens" and out of the Party annals. The story line narrowed, growing ever more apocalyptic. It was as if nothing important had happened in Party history before Mao Zedong entered the Communist stage at the First Chinese Communist Party Congress in Shanghai in July 1921.

Cells before the Party, the World before Mao

SEPTEMBER 17, 1979. Zhang Shenfu is interviewed by Party historians about his version of the origins of Chinese Communism. The interview appears in print a year later in a limited-circulation volume entitled *Before and After the First-Party Congress*, a collection of documents and recollections put together by a new generation of scholars who are trying to free Party history from the burdensome legacy of Mao Zedong.[4] They are now giving Zhang Shenfu an opportunity to record—under his own name—a Mao-less version of the birth of the Chinese Communist Party:

"The Chinese Communist Party began to be established in August 1920 in Shanghai and Beijing. In Shanghai, there was Chen Duxiu. In Beijing, Li Dazhao and myself. When the Comintern's representative, Grigori Voitinsky, arrived in China, he first came to Beijing to talk to us about founding a party.[5] Later, with Li Dazhao's introduction, Voitinsky went to Shanghai to talk to Chen Duxiu about starting a party. Chen sought out Hu Hanmin, Dai Jitao, Zhang Dongsun, and others to talk with. But they could not agree. Chen Duxiu could not decide by himself whether to call the party the Socialist Party or the Communist Party.

"So he wrote me a letter, telling me to share it with Li Shouchang [Dazhao]. It was a long letter, mostly dealing with the Party-founding issue. In it he said: 'As far as this matter is concerned, you and Shouchang are the only ones I can talk to at Beida'" (220–21).

Two months after this interview, Zhang tells me the same story when we meet for the first time at the Beijing National Library. He also adds, "That letter has long been lost." Lost, I now realize, not just from Zhang's own library but also from the public record. Before 1979 official histories were not interested in any details of Party-founding discussions before Mao's emergence on the Communist scene in 1921. Most Party historians before 1979 started with the July 1921 Communist Party Congress in Shanghai. There, at a French girl's school, Mao Zedong was one of thirteen delegates. This was assumed to be the beginning of "real" Party history.

OCTOBER 6, 1980. The *People's Daily* is giving public credence to Zhang's version of Party history. In an article entitled "The Beijing Cell of the Chinese Communist Party," the author, Zhou Zhixin, writes: "According to the recollection of Zhang Shenfu, the *earliest founder* of the Communist organization in Beijing, the date of the establishment of the Beijing Party cell is October 1920."[6]

Here, a recently rehabilitated intellectual is being quoted as a source of Party history. In one short year, from 1979 to 1980, Zhang Shenfu was transformed from a persona non grata into an acceptable authority on the history of Chinese Communism. His recollections were now accepted as fact in the public domain. From our conversations on Wang Fu Cang Lane, I know that this evolution puzzled and delighted Zhang Shenfu. He had outlived Mao and now had the chance to have his say about how Communism began in China.

A whole new year has been added to Party history before Mao's debut at the First Party Congress in Shanghai. It is filled with the emergence of *xiaozu* (small groups that became known as Party cells). This new term allows Zhang to talk about the evolution of Chinese Communism at a time when the lives of intellectuals were not yet bound by the dogma of Marxism-Leninism.

The brief 1980 *People's Daily* article alludes to and uses Zhang's recollections but does not dwell on the details of the Beijing cell that Zhang already provided in the 1979 interview. It overlooks the story of how, in the late summer of 1920, Li Dazhao and Zhang Shenfu gave their assent to Voitinsky's suggestion. It is silent about their advice to Chen Duxiu that the new organization be called the Chinese Communist Party.

Zhang Shenfu's 1979 interview, on the other hand, details the problem of recruitment faced by the new Communist organization: "Discussions had to be carried out in secret, because Chen Duxiu still had his position as dean of humanities. He was known by a lot of people, many of whom disagreed with his involvement in politics."

The idea of informally gathered cells was thus born out of practical consideration. "In Shanghai, Chen Duxiu reached out to a few young men recently returned from studies in Japan. In Beijing, there were only two Party members, Li Dazhao and myself. We agreed that the Party needed expansion, but first we had to reflect on the process with care. Then we reached out to Liu Qingyang. She was a very able young woman, prominent in the Tianjin student movement and good at raising funds in Southeast Asia. When she got back to Beijing we called her into the library office for a conversation, in preparation for her joining the Party.

"She refused, and the matter did not develop further. Zhang Guotao [another Beida student who had been with Liu Qingyang on the fund-raising mission to Southeast Asia] was approached next. Thus, the third Party member became Zhang Guotao. In October, I went back to Shanghai to prepare for study abroad.

Later I heard that the Beijing party grew to include Liu Renjing, Deng Zhongxia, and others—all were Beida students."[7]

The Party cell, in Zhang's version of history, was a natural, conversational outgrowth of student activism in the May Fourth movement. A small band of like-minded intellectuals who knew each other well gathered together in yet another association. The rules and obligations of this new group were still thoroughly fluid. Cells like Zhang's in Beijing and Chen's in Shanghai also sprouted up in other places—most notably in Hunan, where Mao Zedong and others had already started an organization called the New People's Society.

During the cell-building period, old associations and ideas were not relinquished. Joining the Communist Party was something one did in addition to, not instead of, the commitments already undertaken in the heat of the May Fourth movement. It was this loose network of friends and comrades that attracted and maintained the interest of Zhang Shenfu. In 1920 the new association asked no more of him than that he be "for revolution." Zhang had been for this since 1911.

SEPTEMBER 20, 1920. Zhang Shenfu writes an open letter to the Young China Association, the national group that had been most congenial to him in the months after the May Fourth incident. A year later, however, the association is having growing pains. Founded before the event of 1919, it used to attract young people in rebellion against politics—against the corrupt, selfish world of the warlords. Now many new members were swept up by the student movement and were actively involved in a wide variety of organizational activities. Some had already gravitated toward the Communist cells in Shanghai and Beijing.

Zhang's 1920 letter is meant to tip the debate within the Young China Association in favor of an explicit political commitment, especially toward communism. At this moment, though, communism means little more than an ardent, encompassing opposition to the social and political order of the day. Fittingly, the letter opens with Zhang's cri de coeur—"My basic opinion is simply this: destroy the state, burn down class barriers and marriage.

"Having realized the evil that is capitalism, I bitterly hate the prospect of its endless days. So, very naturally, I have an absolute faith in socialism. Communism is the essence of socialism, so naturally I have an absolute faith in communism. Whoever looks at society and reflects deeply on things cannot but understand that socialism is opposed to capitalism. I absolutely believe that politics can cure the evils of today, and that we must carry through with socialism. I believe that if we want to change the circumstances of the present, there is no other way but to change toward socialism."[8]

The Young China Association went on debating for two more years the issue that Zhang hoped to settle in 1920. A 1921 conference on whether the association should embrace Communist politics ended inconclusively. By 1922 a loose definition of youth no longer sufficed for political unity. Members of Young China drifted off in different ways—some toward socialism, some toward communism, some toward the Nationalist Party and others toward purely cultural pursuits.

But Zhang Shenfu's 1920 letter remained as a signpost: it marked the birth of the Chinese Communist Party and showed how one of its founders could—and did—move easily between anarchism, socialism, and communism. Boundaries drawn with ideological fervor later on were nonexistent in 1920.[9] What mattered was impassioned commitment toward the end of the old order. In Zhang's case, this commitment was fueled by avid reading of Russell and by the exhilarating prospect of his departure for Europe.

FEBRUARY 12, 1980. We are looking at Zhang Shenfu's photographs from Germany again. He identifies his old friends with care. I try to figure out what it was like to be a Chinese Communist in Europe. "What did it mean for you to *introduce* Liu Qingyang and Zhou Enlai into the Party?" I ask, trying to hear a much-used phrased anew.

"Nothing more than a letter from me to Chen Duxiu in Shanghai," Zhang answers simply, as if Party introductions were no more, no less than extensions of an old conversation. "I had come to Europe with the full confidence of Chen. He knew me and trusted me. If I thought someone was all right for us, I wrote to him. That was enough. So, a letter from me to Chen—that is how Liu Qingyang and Zhou Enlai joined the Party. That is how our small cell began in Paris in 1921."

Informal communism: no more than a network of personal friendships that ran through this whole first year of Party building. Europe, for young Chinese Communists, was a fluid world without Leninist rules to weed out heterodox beliefs or individualist behavior. When such rules became the norm, Zhang Shenfu was one of the first of the May Fourth intellectuals to refuse to buckle under.

AUGUST 22, 1980. The *People's Daily* publishes a short article entitled "The European Branch of the Chinese Communist Party." For the first time since Mao's death (in 1976) readers are introduced to the historiographical distinction between cell (*xiaozu*) and Party (*dang*). The Maoist version of Party building is being replaced here by a view of history closer to Zhang Shenfu's recollections.

The tone of the article, however, remains cautious. It stays well within the canons of Maoist historiography. Most attention is still given to Cai Hesen, Mao's coprovincial leader from Hunan who was martyred in 1931. Although

Cai left France in 1921—a year before the "European branch of the Chinese Communist Party" is conceived by Zhang Shenfu, Zhou Enlai, and others —Cai Hesen's activities take the most space.

Toward the end of the third paragraph, the *People's Daily* mentions Zhang Shenfu, "who has been a member of the Communist Party since 1920 and was the chief organizer of the Paris cell in 1921."[10]

MAY 1981. A Tianjin-based journal publishes an interview with Zhang Shenfu. The subject is timely and safe: Zhou Enlai's early years as a Communist in Europe. As Mao's shadow recedes from the historical scene, Zhou is assuming center stage. And through Zhou Enlai, Zhang Shenfu is getting a public hearing as well.

The interviewers seek out Zhang Shenfu to talk about the organizational life of Chinese Communists in Europe. Zhang gives them his personal story, dwelling on the network of homegrown friendships. Throughout the interview, Zhang's voice is cautionary and corrective. He insists that Zhou's entrance into the Communist Party was both more and less than an ideological conversion. It was, in Zhang's narrative, a gesture of friendship, of trust in Zhou's May Fourth friends from home—especially in Liu Qingyang and himself.

To complicate his questioners' understanding of Chinese Communist activities in Europe, Zhang dwells on the informal nature of both the Paris and the Berlin cells. In each of these, Zhang first guided and then collaborated with the man who would become China's premier. Personal friendship, Zhang tells his guests, was the bedrock of the trust that grew between them. "Our mutual respect also led me to suggest Zhou's name for an appointment at the Whampoa Military Academy in the winter of 1923–24."[11]

One source of tension between Zhang Shenfu and his Tianjin interviewers lies in their questions about the nature of the Party organization in Europe. The guests want to confirm a Leninist structure; the old man remembers matters quite differently. He tells them repeatedly that the early CCP was an informal gathering of like-minded intellectuals.

From the questions that are printed alongside the answers here, it is clear that the interviewers want a more focused version of history than Zhang is willing or able to give them. When, for example, they say, "Tell us something about the circumstances surrounding the Chinese Communist Youth Party in Europe in 1922," Zhang replies, "The Chinese Communist Youth Party is a misnomer used by quite a number of people. As I recall, there never was such a thing. Rather there was a Youth League started by our Paris cell group" (90).

Here, self-aggrandizement and critical history merge in the mind of an octogenarian who is being asked to set straight the record of Chinese Communist activities in Europe. For Zhang Shenfu, it does not matter that the name Youth

Party was in fact used briefly from summer 1922 to winter 1923. He only wants to correct the record in a way that increases his own prominence and that of the Communist cells he worked with in Paris and Berlin.[12]

Like his interviewers, Zhang uses the past to justify the present. The more he can inscribe himself into the official record of the Communist past, the more secure is his place in contemporary society.

JULY 10, 1985. Zhang Shenfu's public rehabilitation reaches a climax. Hu Yaobang, chairman of the CCP, has sent greetings and a gift of fruits in recognition of Zhang's "contributions to the revolution and the mother land." In a story written by Zhang Shenfu's daughter, the old man is described as "surprised and grateful for the Party's solicitude toward him personally and toward the people in general."[13] One year later, after Zhang Shenfu's death in June 1986, the *People's Daily* calls him an "old friend of the Party."[14]

Rehabilitation in the public realm, however, cost Zhang Shenfu a great deal. His life story became condensed, edited down in keeping with Party directives, drained of flesh and blood. No wonder Zhang sought to breathe life into the public image by taking me—and himself—on recollected circumambulations of his years in Europe.

A Small Band of Fellow Travelers

MAY 27, 1985, PARIS. Zhang's memory leads me, again, straight to his home in this city: 50, rue des Ecoles, the site of his Communist cell meetings. Sixty years later, no signs of the young Chinese from the 1920s remain. How am I to re-create Zhang's Paris world? His early Communist days in a foreign land seem so different from the communism I grew up with in Romania after the war. By then, Russia had imposed harsh Leninist and even harsher Stalinist rules on its European satellites. My father flirted with communism briefly, in the late 1940s. He left the Party in 1952, sickened by anti-Semitism. (He was asked to change his name to make it sound less Jewish.) He also had a distaste for the crude methods used by Communist cadres, who routinely persecuted small shopkeepers and peasants for being capitalists.

My father used to dwell on one story, in which a Party official had hidden a gun inside the hut of a man he wanted charged with a trumped-up crime. My father saw the official hide the gun. He confronted the man with the evidence and was expelled from the Party.

Zhang Shenfu's world in Paris, by contrast, seems so fluid, so gracious. I imagine Zhang opening the fine white drapes that covered the tall windows on rue des Ecoles. I imagine his stepping out onto a small, iron-railed balcony, holding a cup of tea, or maybe even coffee, in his hands. Looking over the roofs of the Sorbonne, I imagine Zhang wondering what the day held for him.

Zhang Shenfu's residence during 1921–22: 50, rue des Ecoles, across the street from the Sorbonne. (V. Schwarcz)

A psychology class taught by the renowned Pierre Janet? A visit from some Chinese cultural dignitary—perhaps the president of Beijing University, Cai Yuanpei? Or maybe something more intimate, such as a few hours with Liu Qingyang or Zhou Enlai? These were indeed daily occurrences in the life of this Chinese Communist in Paris. His Party circle was no bigger than his circle of friends. Their activism was mostly conversation.

I look again at the solid, imposing house on rue des Ecoles. It looks like a good place to learn, to make love, to talk politics for a while. This is a forgotten place in Chinese Communist history. The apartment near the Sorbonne exists solely in Zhang's memory, and in the French police archives that I have been exploring for the past few days. After six hours of delving, I find two items in a folder marked "492—Agitation révolutionnaire des Chinois en Paris." Here is Zhang's address, obtained from the notebook of a Chinese student who got in trouble with French authorities in autumn 1921. This file also documents Liu Qingyang's having lived at the Paris YMCA for four months. No dates, just a snippet of confiscated information.

MAY 19, 1980. After seven months of conversation, Zhang Shenfu is filling out the picture of his years in Europe. Today we spend more time on the Paris scene than in any of our previous meetings:

"I arrived in Paris on New Year's Day 1921. I did not have any difficulty upon arrival. You see, I had traveled first-class on the French ship *Cordillère*. My papers stated that I was personal secretary to Mr. Cai Yuanpei, president of Beijing University. Though not exactly true, it was a useful and necessary formality. In fact, I had been recruited by Cai to be a faculty member of the Franco-Chinese Institute in Lyon, which was to open soon.[15] I had been given an income of eight hundred francs per month. Not bad at all compared to the Chinese work-study students who had to make do on less than half of that. So I could afford the apartment at 50 rue des Ecoles. I also had free time to study, to attend classes, to write.

"At the same time, I was organizing the Communist cell. The first person I recruited was Liu Qingyang, in January 1921. We were lovers by then. In February Zhou Enlai joined the group—I wrote to Chen Duxiu about that. Soon we were joined by two others, Chen Gongpei and Zhao Shiyan. Zhao was a dynamic man who came on the work-study program from Siquan. Chen and Zhao arrived with recommendations from Chen Duxiu—the Party chief in Shanghai. They were Party members before joining our Paris cell.

"My goal from the beginning was to set up a publication, an organ for the dissemination of socialist views among Chinese students and workers in France. There were so many Chinese in France after the war. I needed funds and finally got them after I made contact with Zhang Shizhao, who was in Europe at the time. He was a well-known intellectual and former official and had come to take a firsthand look at political changes in Europe after the war. In England, Zhang had met with such famous celebrities as H. G. Wells and George Bernard Shaw.

"I knew Zhang Shizhao when I was in China. He was an eminent scholar-politician from Hunan and a friend of Li Dazhao. I had also been good friends with Zhang Shizhao's wife, Wu Ruonan, while I was still a student at Beida. When Zhang came through Paris, I spoke to him about the publication project. He became interested and provided the funds that were used to start *Shaonian*, our journal in Europe. I started it in 1921, with the financial help of Zhang Shizhao."

FEBRUARY 1981. Zhang Shenfu's recollections have inspired a new generation of Chinese historians. Among them are Liu Ye, Zhu Yuhe, and Zhao Yuanbi, coauthors of an article entitled "The Organizational Origins of Chinese Communism in Europe," appearing in the Party's official history journal, *Dangshi yanjiu*.[16] This essay uses Zhang's version of the early 1920s to construct a narrative of the birth of Chinese Communism that highlights Zhou Enlai and Zhao Shiyan—a big shift from earlier Mao-centered Party histories.

The new story line accommodates Zhang's view that he founded the Paris cell but rejects the possibility that *Shaonian* was started by Zhang Shenfu as well. There seems to be a deep-seated resistance here to the notion that the foremost Communist journal of Chinese students in Europe was published with support from such a political establishment figure as Zhang Shizhao (who became a controversial minister of education in 1925). Criticism of Zhang Shizhao as reactionary forecloses the possibility that he might have helped the Communist cause in 1921.

Zhang Shenfu is, by contrast, an acceptable character in this narrative. For the first time in published sources his story is used extensively to distinguish between the small Paris cell and the larger group of Chinese worker-students congregating around Cai Hesen in Montargis, south of Paris. The Montargis group had been recruited from China through the Society for Frugal Study by Means of Labor (*Qingong jianxue hui*). The aim of this society (founded in June 1915) was to encourage and enable poor students to work in France by providing part-time employment. Unfortunately, the end of World War I in 1919 and the unemployment that followed in France greatly diminished work opportunities for Chinese students. Little wonder that they were surprised—and outraged—by the material comforts of the government- or family-sponsored Paris group.[17]

Unlike the Paris Communist cell, the Montargis group had been documented in Chinese Party histories throughout the 1950s. This group, especially its leader, Cai Hesen, has long been praised for the progressive role of a demonstration it organized in front of the Chinese Embassy in Paris in February 1921. Unlike Zhang Shenfu (who was materially secure on his professorial salary), Liu Qingyang (who was supported financially by her brother), and Zhou Enlai (who had income from his family's commercial enterprises), the students in Montargis were poor, jobless, and in danger of losing the small subsidy they received from Chinese government funds. On February 28, 1921, they gathered in front of the Chinese Embassy to criticize Ambassador Chen Lu. The demonstrators plastered the embassy walls with slogans that dramatized their rage. Their words—"Donne-moi du pain!" (Give me some bread) and "O! j'ai faim, j'ai faim" (Oh, I'm hungry, so hungry)—expressed the frustrations of young men and women who had come to France to study and were now forced to seek rapidly diminishing factory jobs. Or, as they put it, "to work for starvation wages."[18]

Zhang Shenfu and his fellow members of the Paris Communist cell took a negative view of the embassy demonstration. Although some of their friends and coprovincials turned up at Chen Lu's gate, members of the Paris cell held on to the conviction that laboring with one's hands was the still best way to broaden study in France. For Zhang Shenfu adherence to this point of view was a matter of abstract principle. His generous salary and comfortable living arrangement spared him from all factory work. On the other hand, Zhao Shiyan, the Siquanese Communist, lived out the credo of the Paris group. He continued to work in various factories for the rest of his stay in France. Zhao never wavered from the belief that manual labor brought him closer to real proletarians, whom he considered his most important political teachers.[19]

Whether engaged in manual labor or not, all five members of the Paris cell supported the *Qingong jianxue tongmeng* (Thrift-diligence study association) founded by Zhao Shiyan in March 1921.[20] The purpose of this new group was to uphold the work-study principle articulated in 1915, which appeared under attack during the demonstration of February 28.

JULY 12, 1921. Zhang Shenfu writes an open letter to Chen Duxiu in China. It is published in *New Youth* magazine, the new cultural journal that is now the official voice of the Chinese Communist Party. Zhang's letter is titled "The British and French Communist Parties and China's Reform."[21] The subject confirms Zhang's position as the Party's chief correspondent in Europe.

Zhang Shenfu, however, does not fit easily into the role. His essay reports on the activities and publications of English and French Communists. But Zhang also criticizes Chinese radicals in Europe—especially the Montagris-based demonstrators later canonized in Party historiography: "In France, there are quite a few Chinese workers—students who claim to believe in Marxism. But in fact, they don't understand it at all. Still, they feel they cannot live without revolution, and throw away their lives for it" (1–2).

Here is the voice of arrogance and concern combined. In the aftermath of the February 28 demonstration, Zhang witnessed the increasing pace of radicalization among Chinese worker-students in France. An increasing number of them were quoting—and perhaps reading—Marx. These young radicals made scathing denunciations of bourgeois life in France, including the life-style of the Chinese educational authorities in Paris and Lyon who lived off fat government grants. These activists were also full of suggestions for the course of revolution at home. They did not look kindly on Zhang Shenfu's efforts to define the meanings of Marxism for them.

MAY 26, 1983. Sixty-two years after Zhang's letter to *New Youth*, one of the Chinese students in France still recalls with bitterness the arrogance of Zhang Shenfu. Now an aged and prominent politician, Xu Deheng—who was Zhang's schoolmate at Beida and later joined many of the patriotic and democratic associations that Zhang was part of in the 1930s and 1940s—tells me in an interview today what kept him from joining the Chinese Communist Party in Europe in 1921: "I heard that Zhang Shenfu was in charge, and I could not bear the thought of working under him."

MAY 28, 1983. Zhang Shenfu retells the story of his own radicalization in Europe: "In February 1921 our Paris cell was not much involved in the students' demonstrations. By September, however, things had gotten much worse. The Franco-Chinese Institute in Lyon was occupied by hundreds of outraged worker-students, who were protesting the news that their long-awaited study center was to be opened by a new group of wealthier students recruited from China.

"In October I heard that the demonstrators had barricaded themselves in the dormitories and tried to open negotiations with school authorities. The French police, with full support from the Chinese educational authorities in Lyon, deported many Chinese students from Marseilles. Among those forced to leave were Cai Hesen and a member of our Paris cell, Chen Gongpei.

"The Lyon incident brought home to me the terrible situation of the worker-students. Zhao Shiyan, from our Paris cell, was deeply involved in the Lyon protest as the chief negotiator for the students. He got out of Lyon just before the others were kicked out of France. I heard the news in Paris and was outraged. I went to talk to the Chinese authorities myself. Wu Zhihui, a May Fourth luminary I knew from home, was president of the Franco-Chinese Institute then. I demanded that he hear the demands of the worker-students. They had, after all, been living in poor conditions in France for over a year—all for the promise of a chance to study in Lyon.

"Wu did not change his mind. So, as always when my principles are at stake, I had nothing more to do with Wu or his institution. I handed in my resignation and gave up the position and the salary. I made my stand on the side of the worker-students. This made things more difficult for me personally. Without an income, and with prices soaring in France, I had no choice but to move.

"We had heard from other Chinese students that rents and food were much cheaper in Germany. In February 1922 Zhou Enlai, Liu Qingyang, and I embarked on the night train to Berlin. I will never forget that ride. I talked to them about the significant contributions of the three Jews who shaped Western thought: Marx, Freud, and Einstein."

I try to imagine this train ride—another momentous journey, like the one that brought Zhang Shenfu and Liu Qingyang to France at the end of 1920. On the *Cordillère*, Zhang had lectured Liu on the virtues of communism. Two years later they are lovers and friends; his conversation on this journey is focused on broader intellectual interests and unencumbered by obligatory praise of communism.

A delighted smile crosses Zhang Shenfu's face today, as he recalls his captive audience on the night train in 1922. He had Liu Qingyang and Zhou Enlai all to himself for an entire night. He shared with them the story of three Jews who had fired his own imagination since May Fourth.

Is Zhang Shenfu reminiscing about Jews for my sake? I have no way of telling. What Zhang Shenfu wants me to understand is the enduring solidarity of his small circle of Communists. Zhao Shiyan had stayed behind to work in a factory in France, "though letters went back and forth frequently between us." In Berlin, the Chinese Communists' circle expanded and reconsolidated again. This time, too, around Zhang Shenfu.

MAY 1981. In the interview with the Tianjin historians, Zhang Shenfu is asked: "When you were in Germany, was the Chinese Communist Party organization called 'cell' or 'branch'? How many party members were there? Was it subordinate to or independent from the French cells?"

Zhang answers: "They were simply called cells [xiaozu]. I was the only person in charge. There was no explicit organization. I just oversaw things, that's all. Party members in our Berlin group included Zhang Bojun, who had already entered the Party before leaving China. In the second half of 1922, we expanded to include others. Party members became more numerous. Zhu De was also brought in at this time. When he arrived [in Berlin], Zhu was already a military man of considerable stature and reputation in China. So he did not feel quite at ease asking to join the Party directly. Instead, he broached the subject indirectly, modestly: 'I am seeking to become more progressive.' We understood the meaning of these words—he really wanted to join the Party. So we decided to let him in. This was also the time when Sun Bingwen entered the Party."[22]

Informal associations endured and flourished in Berlin, as they had earlier in Paris. Zhang still saw himself at the center of an expanding circle of friends. He helped attract to the Communist cause men who later became famous —especially Zhu De, Mao's chief military ally in the 1930s and 1940s. But this urge to imagine himself as the fulcrum of the German group did not diminish Zhang's determination to bear witness to the loose, many-sided affiliations that prevailed among the Chinese Communists in Europe.

Retrospective criteria of correct Marxism-Leninism have little room in Zhang's recollections. Friendship is shown to have been the glue that held the Berlin cell together, just as it had been in Paris. Both Sun Bingwen and Zhang Bojun became Zhang Shenfu's intimates in Germany. A tall, lively young man with intellectual (indeed philosophical) pretensions, Zhang Bojun challenged and stimulated the logician from Beida. The two men became lifelong associates in a variety of political causes that included the Third Party (in the late 1920s) and the Democratic League (in the 1940s). Sun Bingwen, a Beida graduate, was a more established, more prominent figure in domestic politics. Having befriended Zhu De (then an opium addict) in 1916, Sun had become a fierce critic of warlordism at home and an equally ardent proponent of revolutionary literature in Berlin.

Zhang Shenfu's recollections of Sun Bingwen were tinged with melancholy.

This Beida schoolmate was Zhang's friend and a publicly venerated martyr who was sacrificed to the Communist cause by Chiang Kaishek's coup of 1927. Zhang Bojun, on the other hand, was no hero. He was still frowned upon as a rightist from the Communists' own anti-intellectual campaign of 1957. To recall Zhang Bojun was to keep faith with history. It was also a political risk, because Zhang Bojun had remained a prominent public enemy in China. To take chances, however, was nothing new for Zhang Shenfu. In 1957 he had already risked—and lost—what was left of his political capital to defend Zhang Bojun at the height of the antirightist campaign.

Berlin, where the two friends met, was a testing ground for new loyalties. The Chinese Communists' cell grew as their friendship grew. Throughout this period Zhang Shenfu served as informal leader. This vision of Zhang is not limited to his own memory. It is confirmed in an article by Wu Qi, one of the Chinese students who had gravitated to Zhang's orbit in Germany.

Wu, too, is an old man now. Unlike the publicly prominent Xu Deheng, Wu Qi does not have to adjust his recollections as carefully to the changing demands of official historiography. In a Tianjin publication he remembers Zhang Shenfu as a catalyst in the political and intellectual maturation of Chinese students in Europe. Wu describes the Berlin cell as a study group that met on Saturday nights in Zhang Shenfu's apartment: "On these nights, Zhang Shenfu would frequently lecture to other comrades on the philosophial background of Marx and Hegel."[23]

Intellectual Life inside the Band

LATE AUTUMN 1922, GÖTTINGEN. Eight Chinese gather for a formal photograph in one of the drawing rooms at the university. Seated at the far left—his looks as manicured as ever—is the twenty-nine-year-old Zhang Shenfu. To the far right, seated in a more awkward position is Zhu De, sporting cropped hair and ill-fitting Western clothes. Facing him is a sensuous-looking young woman, Chen Yuzhen, his wife at the time. Standing next to Zhu De is his longtime friend Sun Bingwen. In center back, arms crossed, a self-satisfied smile on his face, stands twenty-seven-year-old Zhang Bojun.

The clothes, like the poses of the eight Chinese, provide visual testimony of the loose coherence of the group: each person seems engaged in a quest; each has taken on the trappings of the host culture; each is envisioning a different future for China and for themselves. Beneath the Western dress and formal gazes, beneath the Communist determination attributed to them retrospectively, lies a more tenuous commonality: a thirst for fresh ideas and experiences.

Zhang Shenfu's lectures on Marx and Hegel were welcome in Berlin, because they nourished the quest for a new *rensheng guan*—a new worldview.

Chinese Communists in Göttingen, Germany. Seated: *far left*, Zhang Shenfu; *far right*, Zhu De, facing his wife, Chen Yuzhen. Standing: *far right*, Sun Bingwen; *second from right*, a smiling Zhang Bojun. (Courtesy of Zhang Shenfu)

This quest had begun during the May Fourth movement but had been deflected in the course of the students' political activism. In Germany, however, students could try on new worldviews just as they did new clothes. Zhang Bojun began auditing philosophy classes at Berlin University; Zhu De sat in on social science lectures at Göttingen; Zhang Shenfu, the most highly trained among them, followed the latest developments in mathematics and physics.

At cell meetings in Berlin, Zhang spoke about Marx and Hegel. In Göttingen, however, he was drawn by a more intimate passion: modern science. Through the introduction of Chinese friends, he was able to meet David Hilbert, the senior scholar in charge of Göttingen's Mathematical Institute. Born in 1862, Hilbert had early on distinguished himself in mathematics and physics. Three Nobel Prize winners in physics—Max von Laue, James Frank, and Werner Heisenberg—spent considerable time at the Göttingen Institute during Hilbert's tenure.

JUNE 14, 1981. "Hilbert was already famous when I met him in 1922. He was the founder of modern formalism—an effort to place mathematics on a firm foundation through logic. His work was closely related to Russell's theories in *Principia Mathematica*. I went to Göttingen to talk with Hilbert as often as I could. He opened up for me new ways of looking at the relationship between physics and mathematics. This was of great interest to me at the time.

Chinese students in Berlin, 1922: Seated: *second from right*, Zhang Shenfu; *third from right*, Jiang Menglin, former chancellor of Beijing University. Standing behind Jiang is Fu Sinian, founder of the New Tide society at Beijing University in 1919. (Courtesy of Zhang Shenfu)

"Liu Qingyang and Zhou Enlai did not go to Göttingen as often as I did. For me this university town was a refuge from the crowded world of Berlin. It was a more gracious world, full of lofty minds. Not like my apartment in a working-class part of Berlin.

"It was in Göttingen that I decided to translate into Chinese Einstein's treatise on relativity. At home, in March 1920, I was already interested in Einstein. In an article called "A Revolution in Science," I was the first to draw attention to the broader significance of Einstein, to the historic breakthrough of his ideas on relativity. These ideas made the universe more finite, more comprehensible. Einstein's theory also had great beauty. It summarized and altered all the concepts of physics. It made physics more philosophical."

The book on Einstein that Zhang Shenfu began in Göttingen was never finished. It became yet another casualty of Zhang's all-too-catholic curiousity. The unfinished project testifies to his ability to devour everything new, to take on his mentors' interests. Einstein's work, however, continued to inform Zhang's later writing on the philosophy of dialectical materialism. It led him to take a far more eccentric path toward dialectics than did other Chinese who had become Communists in Europe.

NOVEMBER 11, 1920. Another tribute to Zhang Shenfu's catholic mind is a letter by Bertrand Russell to a French student, the brilliant young mathematician Jean Nicod: "Dear Nicod, This is to introduce to you a Chinese colleague, Mr. Zhang Shenfu. He is being sent to France by the University on an educational commission and wants to know about French university matters. He knows my writings, all of them, far better than I do, and has constructed an inconceivably complete bibliography of them. He will want to know about your one law of thought."[24]

JUNE 9, 1980. Zhang still has this letter sixty years later. Regretfully he tells me that he never did ask Jean Nicod about his law of thought:

"Everything, anything new in science, yes, that is what I was always after. Jean Nicod represented that to me. He was a rebellious mathematician who died young. In 1920 I got interested in his ideas about the single axiom in calculus and asked Russell for an introduction to him in Paris. Once there, I was too shy to look him up, because my conversational French was still weak. Later, after he died in 1924, I still continued to be interested in his work. I especially liked his book *The Logical Problem of Induction*. Others picked up on the clues I left behind. The poet-historian Guo Moruo, for instance—an opportunist windbag who followed Mao's every whim later on—developed an early fascination for Jean Nicod's life from my writings. He even wrote a play, I think, about the tragic end of a young mathematical genius modeled on Nicod. But Guo Mouro set the action in the Qing dynasty."

Again Zhang Shenfu imagines himself as sowing seeds—not just of communism and not just among his circle of friends in Paris and Berlin but among others, too, who profited even more than Zhang himself from his fertile, far-reaching curiosity.

Today Zhang laughs at himself when he describes how far he has strayed from Nicod and even Wittgenstein, another one of Russell's students: "I did come back to Wittgenstein, though. In China, after the failure of political revolution in 1927, I was the first to translate the *Tractatus* into Chinese.

"But in Paris and Berlin, I just read whatever I could on whatever subject interested me. Freud and psychoanalysis was foremost in my mind then. I was always interested in sex and truth telling. Freud helped me understand the mechanisms of self-deceit. So I decided to audit some psychology classes at the Sorbonne. I especially enjoyed the courses taught by Pierre Janet, Freud's forerunner in clinical psychology. Janet too began with work on hysteria. By 1921, he was a noted lecturer at the Sorbonne and the author of several books on psychology."

JULY 1921. Zhang Shenfu is finishing his open letter to *New Youth*, edited by Chen Duxiu. After criticizing the naïve, self-destructive passion for Marxism among Chinese worker-students, Zhang warms up to his real subject: the intellectual life of English and French Communists in Europe.

In keeping with the style and theme that marked his debut in the pages of *New Youth* in 1918 (in the impassioned "Plea for Reading Magazines"), this letter is also a survey of periodicals. In it, Zhang Shenfu enumerates each of the major Socialist and Communist journals, including Henri Barbusse's *Clarté* and the London-based *Communist Review*.

In the middle of this overview, Zhang allows himself a digression on a new subject: "the pathbreaking work in psychology currently done in France by Pierre Janet, who is pioneering a new research effort in mental illness [*jingsheng bing*, literally, sickness of the spirit] quite similar but not identical to that of Freud." And then, sensing that this departure from the subject of Communist periodicals needs explanation, Zhang adds: "I think that research in psychology is extremely important: on one hand, it is a necessary link to philosophy, while on the other hand, it is a key to the resolution of social problems. Today, fully 99 percent of the people may be said to be suffering from some kind of psychological illness. Without a change in the human mind there is no hope for social change."[25]

Changing the human mind was not a new goal for Zhang Shenfu or for his generation of May Fourth intellectuals. But Zhang's enduring attachment to it in Paris, in new political circumstances, reveals an agenda quite apart from Party building. In Paris, as in Berlin, Zhang continued to seek enlightenment, *qimeng*—an all-encompassing transformation of self and world that he first articulated among the circle of cultural rebels at Beijing University.

Commitment to communism did not affect Zhang's interest in qimeng. During the five years that he remained a member of the Party, he never once held back his words, or his questions, no matter how idiosyncratic his point of view. He remained, from start to finish, a maverick intellectual guided by his own vision of truth. He read voraciously, wrote on any topic that crossed his mind, and never tired of reminding his comrades of the spiritual revolution that must accompany the social one.

OCTOBER 1922. The new pen name "R" appears on all of Zhang's articles for the European-based *Shaonian*. Sixty years later he explains to me: "I used this pen name to signal all my passions at that time: Russell, Red, and Revolution."

Zhang's longest essay in the October 1922 *Shaonian* is dedicated to "An Unproblematic Solution to the Man-Woman Problem."[26] He had already written about the subject at home in the *New Youth*. But in Berlin—with Janet's classes still fresh in mind and Freud's work increasingly accessible in the original—sex is addressed more explicitly, more psychologically than was possible back home. In China, the social institutions of arranged marriage had consumed Zhang's anger and intellectual energy. In Europe, settled into the affair with Liu Qingyang, he could, and did, raise other questions.

Following Freud's recent publications on psychoanalysis, Zhang Shenfu takes it upon himself to educate Communist cadres about the meanings of *instinct*, *desire*, and *libido*. He transliterates and explains each term in Chinese. Zhang then proceeds to warn his fellow Communists: "These powerful forces cannot be overlooked or repressed—either in social theory or social action. Instead, they must be acknowledged and satisfied whenever possible through freely engaged intercourse. Eventually, they can be channeled toward an encompassing project, like political revolution."

Here, as in Zhang Shenfu's letter to Chen Duxiu one year earlier, the idea of social revolution is likened to a change in human nature. To prevent revolution from becoming narrowed to politics alone, Zhang continues to stoke the fires of intellectual curiosity in himself and his fellow comrades. Other Chinese Communists in Europe were no less curious about sex than Zhang. But by the end of 1922 they were preoccupied with other concerns, such as the organizational life of French and German workers, and with aspects of Marxist theory that might be applicable to the Chinese class struggle.

While Zhou Enlai, Zhao Shiyan, Deng Xiaoping, and others filled the pages of *Shaonian* with articles on the practical problems of organizing a Chinese Communist Youth Party, Zhang Shenfu remained in a world of his own making. Even when writing about such partisan matters as "the Communist youth movement in Europe or the future policies of the Chinese Communist Party," Zhang is marching to a drummer all his own.[27]

While other Communists in China were coming around to the idea of a united front with the more established Nationalist Party, for example, Zhang Shenfu used his distance in Berlin to counsel something else. He believed—in spite of all the evidence of organizational weakness within the nascent Chinese Communist Party—that it was possible for the Party to make revolution alone.

Just as the Comintern was drawing up a plan for Communists to join the Guomindang in a united front, Zhang wrote in *Shaonian*: "The Chinese Communist Party has already become a major force in Chinese politics. Our task now is to rouse our members to fight for our lofty ideals. . . . While pursuing a policy of united front with the Guomindang, we should not forget that for a Communist, the ultimate goal is not the united front but the dictatorship of the proletariat. Our final goals continue to be public ownership and a society without classes, state, or government. We must retain the organizational independence of the Party and proclaim its goals at every opportunity."[28]

Away from the complexities of the Chinese scene, Zhang Shenfu ended up as a purist defender of Communist theory and practice. The philosopher who had let comrades like Zhao Shiyan and Zhou Enlai take care of all the messy details of organizing worker-students in France now called for fidelity to the "dictatorship of the proletariat."

The situation had a certain built-in irony. Zhang had long been better off materially than most Chinese youths who had to work in European factories. He also had time to read books and magazines in French, German, and English. The same circumstances that in 1921 had set him apart from worker-students in the Montargis group now led him to drift away from Chinese Communists at home and abroad. They continued to be pragmatists and compromisers, while he chose to defend an idiosyncratic vision of Communist strength. In 1925, three years after the essay that questioned the united front, Zhang Shenfu withdrew from the Chinese Communist Party. To the end of his Party membership, Zhang remained convinced that the Communist Party was stronger than its so-called ally, the Nationalist Party.

The Beginning of the End

FEBRUARY 20, 1923, BILLANCOURT, FRANCE. The Chinese Communist Youth Party votes to expel Zhang Shenfu. Founded in autumn 1922, this group was, in principle, under the aegis of the European branch of the CCP. Instead of accepting guidance, however, the youth group rejected the Party's foremost representative in Europe.

The news of the expulsion did not reach Zhang Shenfu until a few weeks later, when Zhou Enlai returned from Billancourt to Berlin. The man who for over two years had considered himself the most senior Chinese Bolshevik in Europe flew into a rage. According to the recollections of Zheng Chaolin, one of Zhang's Communist comrades at the time, "The kingmaker of Chinese Communists in Berlin railed against the upstarts in the Communist Youth Party, using the following words: 'Would you dare to, would you presume to, oust Chen Duxiu from the Communist Party if he were here in my place?'"[29]

Zhang Shenfu saw himself as having the same importance among Chinese Communists in Europe as Chen Duxiu, the Party secretary, had in China. Zhang had founded the Paris cell and continued to guide the Berlin-based one. He had helped get funding for the Communist journal *Shaonian*. He thought he knew more Marxism than other students and wanted them to respect and obey him.

Instead, they had rebelled against Zhang Shenfu. The February 1923 rebellion did not catch Zhang by surprise. He had been aware that a mass youth organization was coalescing during the summer of 1922. In June of that year, Zhao Shiyan had written Zhang Shenfu and Zhou Enlai in Germany to seek advice about how to build an umbrella group that might embrace all Chinese Communists and their sympathizers in Europe. The idea of a Communist Youth

Party was thus born, just as Zhang Shenfu was beginning to consolidate his control of the small cell in Berlin. In Zhang's mind, the Youth Party was a mass organization, quite distinct from the European branch of the CCP.

Zhang had no objection to the larger group as long as he remained the nerve center of the Communist Party branch. This position was acknowledged in autumn 1922, when Zhang Shenfu became official corresponding secretary while Chen Duxiu acted as chairman of the Chinese Communist Party in Shanghai.

While writing to Chen—whether as a friend, as Party chairman, or as editor of *New Youth*—Zhang Shenfu always insisted that youth movements and the Communist Party were two different entities. Zhang left no doubt in anyone's mind that he considered the first subordinate to the latter. To buttress his point of view, Zhang Shenfu wrote an article for *Shaonian* that dealt with the second Congress of the International Youth League. It gave Zhang the opportunity to quote—with evident approval—the careful words of Lazar Schatzkin, a member of the Central Committee of the Soviet Youth League: "We are not Communists. We are only a political organization of the masses. We will gather together the laboring youth and educate them. We are not a Party, but we have a close relationship to it."

In his editorial comments on Schatzkin's words, Zhang Shenfu makes it clear that the essence of communism was "Party discipline." And for Chinese Communists in Europe, Party discipline meant subservience to Zhang Shenfu. Not that Zhang really wanted to be bogged down in all the details of Party organizing. These he left to the more active and more able Zhao Shiyan. The role that Zhang Shenfu preferred to play was that of unchallenged mentor. And this is what most irked some young people.

Zheng Chaolin, an early member of the Communist Youth Party and of the European branch of the CCP, recalls the attack on Zhang Shenfu at the February 1923 Billancourt meeting as follows: "Some students felt that Zhang had schemed to become the 'power behind the throne.' With one hand he guided Zhou Enlai, with the other, Zhao Shiyan. In this way, Zhang Shenfu tried to control the entire organization.

"Zhao Shiyan and Zhou Enlai, who were present at the Billancourt meeting, were in a tough spot. They were Zhang Shenfu's closest friends and political associates from the Paris cell. They knew his intellectual gifts, but they also knew his arrogance."[30]

To make matters worse, Zhao Shiyan was chairing the meeting at which the discussion of Zhang Shenfu occurred. All that Zhao could do as chair was to remain silent. The only person to defend Zhang Shenfu was Zhou Enlai, the Communists' representative from Germany. "Among those accusing Zhang Shenfu most explicitly were Chen Yannian [Chen Duxiu's son] and Yin Kuan.

At the Billancourt meeting, Yin said that Zhang Shenfu interfered with the work of the Communist Youth Party by using his position as corresponding secretary for the European branch of the CCP. Yin went on to say: 'R keeps his authority and position in his pocket. When he needs it, he takes it out. If he doesn't need it, he keeps it there in reserve.' Others said that Zhang Shenfu had threatened to withdraw from the Party several times whenever anyone disagreed with his instructions or his point of view.

"Zhou Enlai tried to respond to all this, with caution. But having decided that Zhang Shenfu had violated Communist discipline, those at the meeting expelled him. When Zhou Enlai returned to Berlin to inform Zhang Shenfu, Zhang stamped his feet in fury. Because it was Zhou Enlai who had delivered the news, Zhang became convinced that Zhou was involved in the plot to oust him. Zhou tried to reason with him, saying: 'You're too arrogant. The masses are too dissatisfied. They had to attack you a little.' "[31]

Zheng Chaolin's memory of this dialogue is striking. He repeats almost the exact words when he speaks about this sore subject with Zhang Shenfu's daughter Zhang Yanni. He has granted the interview out of gratitude to the father's role in his own intellectual radicalization: "I became a Marxist in large part because of some articles written by Zhang Shenfu for *New Youth* magazine. He was an intellectual of integrity, a theorist, but not a revolutionary. That is why he eventually withdrew from the Communist Party in 1925."[32] In Zheng Chaolin's recollection, Zhang Shenfu is a lively, arrogant figure. He is at once inspiring and vindictive, even toward Zhou Enlai.

MARCH 22, 1980. Today is the first and the only time that Zhang Shenfu shows some emotion when we talk about his expulsion from the Chinese Community Youth Party in 1923. He does not dwell on the event, nor on any rift between Zhou Enlai and himself. All blame is put on a radical student named Ren Zhuoxuan, the most notorious of the French-returned Communists to break with the Party:[33] "He was a man who later called himself Ye Qing and became a shameless enemy of communism in China. It was Ye Qing who instigated the whole silly vote against me. He was the most hot-headed among the many naïve students in Europe at the time."

The finger points toward a man who became an enemy of the Party. It moves swiftly away from the son of Party elder Chen Duxiu and from Zhou Enlai, whom Zhang wants to remember as a true friend.

"And anyway, history justified me, you know. Soon after the vote, the Comintern ordered the Communist Youth Party to change its name to the European branch of the Chinese Communist Party and to reinstate my position as corresponding secretary. And so, in July 1923, when all this nonsense blew over, I returned to Paris. Liu Qingyang and I came back to get our son before going home via Moscow. While in Paris, I made a speech to the Communist Youth group there. I still remember the title of my talk: "The Role of Peasants in the Chinese Revolution." You can see how forward-looking I was even then. Others still talked about collaborating with the Guomindang, of subordinating the Communist Party to the bourgeois revolution. But I knew where the future lay. Even though I had not researched the peasant question in any depth, I could talk about it well.

"In Moscow, I was greeted by Zhao Shiyan, who had led a delegation of Chinese students there before my arrival. I also met Soviet officials, including [Nikolai Ivanovich] Bukharin. It was in Moscow, too, that I first met Jiang Jieshi [Kaishek], who impressed me with his sharp insight on military matters. Back in China, I met him again at the Whampoa Military Academy in 1924. I was lecturing there while working for the Communist Party in Canton. When the political commissar of the Whampoa Academy asked me to recommend some people to him, I put Zhou Enlai's name at the top of the list. And so, I helped launch this part of Zhou's revolutionary career as well."

These details of Zhang's recollections are confirmed four years later in a public collection of memoirs about the Whampoa Military Academy.[34] Again, as with Party building in Europe, Zhang Shenfu's role is acknowledged only very briefly. This volume of essays, I learn from Zhang's daughter, was prepared before anyone had solicited or accepted an essay by Zhang Shenfu. No one on the editorial board, it seemed, had thought it necessary or worthwhile to include in this book a recollection by a relatively unknown, almost forgotten, intellectual. Then Zhang himself reminded the editors that it was he who brought Zhou Enlai to the academy. Again, as with the European branch of the CCP, Zhang Shenfu manages to have his say only if and when his story crosses that of Premier Zhou Enlai.

What is lost in the public memoir, however, is the rich texture of Zhang's relationship to the Communist movement—its ambiguities, its quirks of fate. These details are suppressed in the political rehabilitation of memory. Yet such details proliferate in other domains, in less-monitored spaces, such as Zheng Chaolin's conversation with Zhang Shenfu's daughter in Shanghai, in the stories that Zhang tells me on Beijing's Wang Fu Cang Lane. Here, in off-the-record narratives, the temperamental arrogance of Zhang Shenfu and the fluidity of the Communist Party organization in Europe are finally given their due.

Party Politics, Operatic Exit

AUGUST 12, 1986. My first visit to Wang Fu Cang Lane after Zhang Shenfu's death two months earlier. I have come for a short visit, to wrap up loose ends, to pay my personal respects to his family, to see the urn of his ashes deposited at the heroes' cemetery in Babao Shan.

I read the official summary of Zhang's life—the Party's verdict on his significance—printed in the *People's Daily* several weeks earlier. Today Zhang Shenfu's daughter Zhang Yanni speaks to me about the struggles involved in working out the final wording. She shows me several drafts of the death announcement, the *bugao*. One phrase had been at the center of the debate between the family and the committee in charge of finalizing Zhang's place in Communist history.

The family won its victory behind the scenes. The first version of the committee draft had described Zhang's relationship to the Party as follows: "In 1921 Zhang Shenfu established a Communist Party cell in Paris. He was one of the main representatives sent by the Central Committee to France and Germany. In 1925 he attended the fourth Chinese Communist Party Congress in Shanghai, and quit [*tuo dang*] the Party shortly thereafter."

Tuo dang is the phrase that the family wanted changed. They suggested *tui dang* (withdrew from the party), a milder term that leaves the possibility of an enduring, sympathetic relationship to the Party that still rules Chinese politics and historiography today. To quit the Party, to tuo dang, connotes a hasty departure. It implies an ignominious exit, an escape, a running away from, as suggested by the term *tuo tiao* (running way from responsibility) something akin to fear or cowardice.

Tui dang, by contrast, connotes a gracious, more civilized departure, a temporary renunciation of involvement. It can be used when turning down excessive honors or simply retiring from office, as in *tui xiu*.

Zhang Shenfu's family held out for a change in wording for several weeks before they won. They did not want Zhang's exit from the Party to be remembered—and inscribed in marble over his ashes—as a hasty, clumsy gesture rooted in self-righteousness. The family's reputation would then suffer as well. When finally published, the *People's Daily* obituary for Zhang Shenfu uses tui dang and calls him "an old friend of the Party."[35] His posthumous rehabilitation is thus complete. And with this rehabilitation, the family's position in public life is more secure as well.

But what of Zhang Shenfu himself? Would he care about the change in wording? Would he worry or lose sleep over this public interpretation of a turning point in his political career? Most likely, I imagine, he would lean back and laugh.

APRIL 28, 1980. Zhang's laughter today comes from deep within. This is the day he hits upon the phrase *ning zhe bu bian* (rather break than bend). As a summary of his own temperament, the four-character expression brings a ripple of delight. Even when talking about Zhou Enlai and their meeting at the January 1925 Communist Party Congress in Shanghai, Zhang uses the phrase, with two characters reversed, *ning bian bu zhe* (rather bend than break). "Zhou, you see, went along with the policy to compromise with the Nationalists. He voted for the united front. Not me. Zhou Enlai was an endlessly bending compromiser. . . . His merchant-family background was so unlike mine. I came from a rigid, more scholarly family."[36]

As the thin light from the spring afternoon cuts through the curtain, Zhang Shenfu dwells on details of the January 1925 meeting in Shanghai: "It was the end of a cold winter month when the fourth Party Congress took place in Shanghai. As usual I stayed at Chen Duxiu's house. He was an old friend from my days at Beijing University and still secretary of the Central Committee. Others in attendance at this meeting were Zhang Tailei, Zhou Enlai, Qu Qiubai, the Comintern representative Voitinsky, whom I had known since 1920. The most heated policy discussion took place around the issue of the united front. The main proposal called for altering the Communist Party's commitment to proletarian revolution for the sake of the alliance with the Nationalist Party. I spoke out against the compromise. I believed—and still do—that the working class was strong enough to carry out its own agenda.

"But Cai Hesen [Mao's coprovincial who had been expelled from France after the Lyon incident of 1921] called me laughably naïve. I can still hear those words in my ears. I was furious and walked out. In the hallway, Zhou Enlai told me he agreed with my views but pleaded with me not to break with the Party. During the following months in Beijing, Zhao Shiyan tried to change my mind too. But, I was not to be moved. That is my temperament: I would rather break than bend. . . . Maybe this is a shortcoming of mine."

A trace of regret breaks through the self-satisfied laughter. The breach, however, is so slight that it does not affect the old man's pride in his own backbone. So slight, in fact, that it blocks out the memory of how he himself once labeled Cai Hesen and other worker-students "naive Marxists" in the pages of *New Youth*. Maybe the name calling at the fourth Party Congress was Cai's retaliation for European squabbles.

There is an echo here, too, of the 1923 meeting in Billancourt. Two years before the fourth Party Congress in Shanghai, Zhang Shenfu's arrogance and opposition to the united front were already well known. Zhang's outlook had not changed, but circumstances had. He could no longer count on the Comintern's deus ex machina. In 1925 there was no Comintern order to reverse the negative tide against Zhang Shenfu. By 1925 the Communist International (under Soviet orders) was actively pressing for a united front in China, pressuring Communists toward compromise with the more powerful Nationalist Party (the GMD). Thus, after January 1925 Zhang began another stage in his long, though not unaccustomed, journey toward a politics of his own making.

MARCH 1980. Zhang Shenfu is finishing revisions on an essay entitled "Recollections of the Circumstances Before and After the Founding of the Chinese Communist Party."[37] The essay is to appear in *Before and After the First Party Congress*, a collection of Party-commissioned essays that are controversial enough to be considered *neibu* (for internal publication only).

This collection is so sensitive that I do not tell Zhang Shenfu that I have obtained it until two years after its publication. The essay, contemporaneous with our conversations on Wang Fu Cang Lane, reveals Zhang's public persona. There is little in this published history that contradicts the stories I heard about the Party cells in Paris and Berlin. What is missing in this narrowly political narrative are the details about Zhang Shenfu's intellectual life: his interest in Janet, Freud, Hilbert, and Einstein.

At the end of the essay, Zhang includes a brief paragraph to explain his departure from the Chinese Communist Party—the very organization that this book is meant to celebrate and commemorate: "In 1925 the working people of Canton elected Premier Zhou to represent them at the fourth Party Congress. Premier Zhou was one of the chairmen of the congress. Others included Chen Duxiu, Zhang Tailei, and Qu Qiubai. All together, some seventy or eighty people attended the Congress. I attended this meeting too, as did Voitinsky. During the meeting, a great debate arose around one of the Party's policy documents. There were some young Party members there who called me laughably naïve. I flew into a rage and let them know I would withdraw from the Party [tui dang]. Later, back in Beijing, Li Dazhao, Zhao Shiyan, and others tried to convince me not to quit the Party [*tuo dang*]. But I am a bad-tempered man. When the majority approves of me, then I do anything. When the majority disapproves of me, I just get out (*gundan*). It was in this way that I quit the Party (tuo dang)" (548).

In the end, Zhang settled on tuo dang over tui dang. Perhaps he was required to use the harsher term to placate the political sensitivities of 1980. He describes himself as quitting the Party in a fit of anger. He calls himself a bad-tempered man. Temperamental attachment to his own point of view is reduced to a shortcoming. There is no hint here of the pleasure of ning zhe bu bian. No hint either of the laughter that accompanied our conversation. There is no mention of Cai Hesen, the man who called Zhang laughably naïve. Cai, Mao's coprovincial from Hunan, remains a hero in Party historiography. The public record concludes with Zhang's self-incrimination as a "Party quitter."

JULY 1921. Zhang Shenfu is writing from Paris for *New Youth*. An essay entitled "Truth Speaking," in which he describes his fondest political hopes, is published in Shanghai on the eve of the First Congress of the Chinese Communist Party: "If we want to change the present world, which has hypocrisy as its main feature, I believe we must organize some sort of Honesty Party [*shihua dang*]. Only such a party is capable of challenging the psychological tendency of people to deal untruthfully with one another."[38]

The Party that was officially founded in Shanghai in 1921 was not called the Honesty Party. Truth telling was not a main feature either during the five years that Zhang took part in its activities, nor has it been in the decades since. When the Party became a Leninist organization with a penchant toward forcible adherence to its ever-changing line, Zhang Shenfu quit. Whether tuo dang or tui dang, Zhang moved on to work out his own compromises, his own combinations —mostly on the philosophical plane.

AUGUST 18, 1986. Today, a cup of tea with an old friend. I have known this gray-haired, vigorous cadre for over seven years. He is retired now but once held a high position in the Ministry of Education. My friend has often complained about his frustration at the slow pace of economic and political reform. Over the past seven years, he has also become a thoughtful listener to my stories about Zhang Shenfu. Unlike other prominent intellectuals, he has not discouraged my work on this "marginal" man. Rather, this gentleman is amused by each new detail I come up with. He often probes his own memory for bits about Zhang Shenfu. Two years ago he was the first to tell me about Zhou Enlai's speech in 1962—the one in which he publicly acknowledged Zhang Shenfu as the man who introduced him into the Communist Party.

Today I muse aloud about Zhang's withdrawal from the Communist Party in 1925. I know this is a sensitive subject for my friend who has been a Party member for forty years. But I want to hear his version of how one leaves the circle of the true believers. I have read published memoirs by and public accusations of intellectuals who left the Party. These do not help me understand Zhang's self-description: "I'd rather break than bend." I also know there is more to the public confession: "I am a bad-tempered man. When the majority disapproves of me, I just get out."

My friend laughs while listening to Zhang's story. Then he goes on, in the lilting accent of southern Chinese: "Ah, this reminds me of all the operas I grew up with. . . . You know, the exit of the virtuosos, those pretty young boys called *xiucai* [candidates for the first degree of the examination system]. These boys are like maidens, with their soft green, richly embroidered robes. So full of high-minded ideals of bookish virtue. When they come upon some worldly mess, some situation that demands compromise, they retreat from the stage with a dramatic sweep of their long, flowery sleeves."

At this point, my friend jumps up and acts out the scene for me. Although he is over seventy, he manages to make me see the maidenly sleeve of the scholar. In its billowing folds, I recognize the righteousness of Zhang Shenfu, the thirty-two-year-old xiucai. Beneath all the controversy about tuo dang and tui dang, I glimpse a moment of stylized drama. Zhang Shenfu, after all, loved old-style opera. He also hated to be reminded that the world was full of muck, weakness, and half-truths.

4

BETWEEN RUSSELL

AND CONFUCIUS

The longing to resemble is an incipient resemblance. The word which we shall make our own is the word whose echo we have already heard within ourselves.
—Maurice Friedman,
To Deny Our Nothingness

DECEMBER 17, 1979. My third visit to Wang Fu Cang Lane. Zhang Shenfu is drawing me deeper and deeper into the crevices of his philosophical system. I feel lost, unprepared, over my head. In just one month we have strayed far from the political events of his life. Nothing in my training as a historian of modern China has prepared me for this. We have left the May Fourth movement of 1919 behind. We have been over his role in the founding of the Chinese Communist Party. We have already explored his political associations with Zhou Enlai and Liu Qingyang.

Today Zhang Shenfu wants to talk about the virtues of traditional Chinese philosophy. He is using our conversation to work out his ideas. He wants to find a place for himself in native Chinese thought. Zhang is looking for a worldview that he can claim as his own.

Zhang fills the page in front of me with synonyms for his favorite idea in Chinese philosophy—*zhong* (the golden mean). He is struggling to explain to me the connection between this ideal and a psychological state of mind that he calls *rong* (forbearance). Forbearance, Zhang believes, must accompany the quest for a genuinely balanced worldview. Digressing at one point, he offers a long, tangential criticism of Chinese Marxism. He likens the Chinese effort to emulate Soviet models of thought and economic development to a man who enters a river without knowing how to swim: "He can do nothing but drown."

As in every conversation since we met in the National Library, Zhang Shenfu comes back to Bertrand Russell, his private raft, as it were. This is what seems to have kept Zhang afloat over the years—even when China became submerged in wave after wave of revolutionary fervor. But today he adds something new: "I believe I understand Russell. Maybe I am the only one in China who really does. . . . Russell himself did not understand Confucius. But his thought is in fact very close to Confucius. I see this similarity even if nobody else does. Even if Russell were to deny it. My philosophy brings them together. I am like a bridge [*qiaoliang*], you might say."

I try to make sense of these water metaphors—a bridge, drowning. I try to hear what lies beneath Zhang's unabashed arrogance, beneath his claim that he alone understands Russell in modern China. Zhang sees himself as linking unlinkables. But, as we both know, China is still struggling with the dilemma of modernization, with the challenge of crossing over from Confucian politics and values into a world shaped by Western technology and revolutionary ideas. What problems, then, did Zhang Shenfu solve?

I look up from my notes to see Zhang's ironical smile. He knows his claim about Russell and Confucius sounds extravagant. He wants to see how far I will travel along his thought paths. In the end, what seems to matter is not whether I accept or reject his version of himself as the most important philosopher in twentieth-century China. Rather, what he looks for in my face is a sign that I sympathize with the problem of bridging East and West.

Russell and Confucius—the more we go on, the more I understand them as the objects of Zhang's love: "Among all philosophers I have read, and there have been so many, those two are the ones I respect and admire the most." Before they became objects of thought, before Zhang embarked on the difficult task of distilling the best from each, Russell and Confucius captured Zhang Shenfu's imagination. They echoed and expanded his own concerns. They were life-saving devices when all else appeared unmoored, in flux around him. To this day, they remain a source of endless interest for him because they matter in a deep, personal way.

WINTER 1930. Zhang has finished the introduction to his first book of philosophy, *Suosi (Thought as Such)*.[1] He has previously completed translations of two other philosophers' works: C. E. M. Joad's *Introduction to Modern Philosophy* in 1926 and Ludwig Wittgenstein's *Tractatus Logico-Philosophicus* in 1927. This time, Zhang Shenfu has collected his own intermittent essays, written between 1919 to 1930, which he is about to publish as his philosophical statement. At thirty-seven, he appears ready to cast a glance backward, to sum up the main themes of his work. The introduction to *Thought as Such* identifies two principal concerns: humanism and the scientific method. These, Zhang writes, "are what I believe to be the two most precious things in the world" (2).

The introduction leaves little doubt about the sources of Zhang Shenfu's values. Humanism is "what Confucius wrote about." Scientific method is "rooted in Bertrand Russell's philosophy of logical analysis." With these roots acknowledged, the author moves off in his own direction, which he describes by using the English concept of polarity and the Chinese phrase *chun keguan* (pure objectivism). These odd twists of tongue (and thought) enable Zhang

Shenfu to look at issues—such as dialectical materialism—that Russell never considered. He can also write about sexual intimacy and the problem of episte-mology, subjects Confucius ignored or considered immoral.

By 1930 Zhang Shenfu is swimming in alien waters. He has strayed far from Chinese contemporaries, as well as from Western and ancient Chinese mentors who guided his philosophical maturation. By the end of the brief introduction to *Thought as Such*, Zhang pleads with the reader as follows: "Whenever you do not understand my words, I hope you will look around, especially at the facts of your own existence. I hope you will expend a bit of energy to integrate them concretely. The facts of one life, however, are just a fragment and cannot be substituted for the totality of facts that exist in the world" (3).

Fragments and totalities, these constitute Zhang Shenfu's subject. Bits and pieces are what *Thought as Such* is all about. This style of episodic essay, Zhang acknowledges, has as its precedent the works of Blaise Pascal and the German philosopher Novalis. The content, however, is unmistakably his. If a reader wants to make sense of these fragments, there is no other way but to retrace the idiosyncratic itinerary of Zhang Shenfu's philosophical loves and hates.

The Making of a Russell Admirer

NOVEMBER 9, 1920. Zhang Shenfu is writing his most impassioned letter to Bertrand Russell, whose work he has been reading for more than five years. During the past few weeks, Zhang has met Russell in Shanghai and heard his lectures in Beijing.

But today, Zhang is after something more personal. He confesses a deep admiration for Russell, tinged with the impending loss of a still-unconsum-mated friendship. With awkwardness, Zhang writes in English: "Probably I will leave Peking for France on the 17th, or later. I am very sorry we would separate so soon. But even I go to France, I will continually study your philoso-phy and as I always attempt to read anything you write, henceforeward when you publish books or articles (even reviews), please kindly make me knowing at once. Thank you in anticipation for the trouble you will take.

"May you favor me with a copy of your photograph with your autograph? I only wish this because I worship you."[2]

Sixty-three years later, in 1983, I read this letter in the Russell Archives of McMaster University in Canada. Zhang's fervent admiration for Russell leaps off the yellowed page undiminished by the passage of time. It foreshadows Zhang's enduring attachment to Russell over the course of his long life.

The letter also puzzles me. What did Zhang Shenfu really mean by "wor-ship you"? I first read these words in a 1982 article by Suzanne Ogden entitled "The Sage in the Inkpot: Bertrand Russell and China's Social Reconstruction in the 1920's."[3] Ogden never met Zhang Shenfu but used his letter to show the zealousness of some of Russell's Chinese admirers on the eve of his visit to China. In a footnote on Zhang Shenfu, Ogden suggests that he was "China's Russell specialist" at the time of May Fourth and that he was "instrumental" in bringing Russell to China. She then quotes the sentence containing "I worship you," leaving the impression of Zhang's blind reverence.

With the original letter now in my hand, with Zhang's face and words fresh in mind, I am convinced that this was not uncritical veneration.

MAY 11, 1983. A few days ago, I gave Zhang Shenfu a copy of Suzanne Ogden's article. Today Zhang tells me that Ogden—like Russell's biographer Ronald Clark—overestimates his role in inviting Russell to China.[4] Zhang gives credit to Liang Qichao, a more senior scholar-official who provided the money and organized Russell's itinerary. His view mirrors a photograph in the Clark biography of Russell—the one in which Russell and Dora Black take center stage in front of the entrance to Beijing University, while Zhang stands on the side, almost out of the photograph. Zhang's own narrative, like the photograph, shows him to be marginal in organizing Russell's China journey:

"I did not invite Russell to China—Liang Qichao did. I did not translate his public lectures. Zhao Yuanren, an American-educated young man, did. I did not even translate Russell's lecture notes. A member of the *New Tide* Society, Sun Fuyuan did that job. I was not even involved in the founding of the Chinese Russell Society in 1921. I had already gone to France. Your friend does not tell my story but that of others who stayed on in China after I left.

"I did something else, something maybe more important. I translated Russell's philosophy. I introduced him to Chinese readers as an important modern thinker. I think I set the stage for informed appreciation of Russell's thought."

Zhang's self-presentation contradicts Ogden's use of "I worship you." If Zhang did worship Russell, it was not as an idol or an infallible god. By 1920 Zhang Shenfu was deeply involved in the iconoclastic New Culture Movement. He had already allied himself with those who challenged idolatry, both Chinese and Western.

When he writes "I worship you," Zhang Shenfu is trying to say something new about Russell. And about himself. Something concerning the possibilities that informed admiration can reveal within the worshipper. How it can augment, multiply really, the mirrors of self-knowledge. Zhang wanted a signed photograph from Russell to help him along his path toward becoming an iconoclastic philosopher. In worshipping Russell, Zhang sought to explore possibilities that were imminent within him.

Why, then, did he use the English word *worship*? A short essay by Zhang Shenfu written in 1928 answers this question. Entitled "A Free Man's Worship," the essay is a distillation and defense of Russell's 1903 work by the same title. Although Zhang did not translate this key text until he had returned from France, until after he had left the Chinese Communist Party, until after he had witnessed the collapse of the social revolution in the summer of 1927—this essay makes it clear that Zhang had read and loved Russell's "A Free Man's Worship" many years earlier.

JANUARY 15, 1928. The Shanghai-based magazine *World* (*Shijie*) publishes Zhang Shenfu's commentary on "A Free Man's Worship," a title that the British philosopher had used twenty-five years earlier to describe a personal spiritual crisis.

Russell's essay was the work of a lonely, troubled man. Orphaned by the age of four, Bertrand Russell had been raised by an austere grandmother. Presbyterian and Unitarian by turns, she was a guardian who never doubted the voice of God in moral matters. Russell's first wife, the fervantly Quaker Alys Smith, had no doubts about religion either. Yet the budding mathematician did. He arrived in Cambridge in 1890 with some belief in the Deist's God. But then the modern world, with its Henrik Ibsen, Friedrich Nietzsche, and Oscar Wilde, poured in on him.

In 1903, while vacationing in Italy with Alys (with whom he was becoming increasingly unhappy), Russell wrote "A Free Man's Worship" in great haste and with great stylistic verve. It was to be his most impassioned feature about the kernels of belief possible in a world ruled by the laws of physics and mathematics. True freedom, Russell concluded, is to be found "in the determination to worship only the God created by our own love of the good, to respect only the heaven which inspires the insight of our best moments."[5]

In 1920, in China, Zhang Shenfu faced a spiritual crisis that was at once personal and social. Russell's words were particularly timely, Zhang argued, "because they remind us that a free person, must think freely. A free person's worship transcends all religions, all idols. It transcends all desire to rely on supernatural forces. It is nothing more than the worship of the creativity inherent in one's own thoughts, especially in what is most noble and spirited in one's thinking."[6]

Zhang Shenfu's spiritual crisis, unlike Russell's, was not about Christianity. It revolved not around notions of God but, rather, around Confucianism, women, personal freedom, and the right to define truth in keeping with one's inner lights.

In 1920, as Russell prepared to leave China and the charmed intimacy of their conversations came to an end, Zhang Shenfu begged him for a signed photograph as a reminder of what "free worship" was all about. By 1928 Zhang Shenfu had grown impatient with a range of dogmatic faiths, most recently that of Marxism-Leninism. Since having tea with Russell, Zhang's need to worship *freely* had grown stronger.

FEBRUARY 1983. Zhang Shenfu is dictating an essay entitled "My Admiration for and Understanding of Bertrand Russell" to his daughter Zhang Yanni.[7] He hopes it might serve as an introduction to a collection of his essays about Russell. I read the draft of this essay in 1986, two months after Zhang died, at which time the work was languishing in a publishing house plagued by new pressures to show quick profits. For the moment, such a work is not deemed profitable enough.

Nonetheless, the 1983 essay brings *me* some profit. It helps me understand what Zhang Shenfu—as distinct from Russell—meant by "a free man's worship." The concept of free worship is dealt with indirectly in a text meant for circulation only in the People's Republic of China. There is no room here for the passionate defense of *ziyou chongbai* (free worship)—the explicitly religious and iconoclastic phrase that Zhang Shenfu had used in 1928. Instead, Zhang gives this essay a more cautious title. He writes of his *zanpei* (admiration or esteem) for Russell. And yet, in spite of this shift in connotation, Zhang's approach is the same. His 1983 essay, like that of 1928, leaves no doubt that in discovering Russell, in cultivating admiration for him as a man and as a thinker, Zhang Shenfu had cultivated his own commitment to critical thought.

The story of Zhang's free worship begins in 1913, when he was a student in the preparatory program of Beijing University. It describes the spiritual awakening of a young man in love with books:

"At that time, the library was nothing but a space for storing books located in the innermost courtyard of the university campus. The books could be borrowed, but there were few readers. In the following year [1914], when I entered Beida's undergraduate school, the library finally opened a reading room. Books in Western languages were placed on bookshelves along the walls. But the shelves were locked up most of the time. Still, I came often. Because of my frequent appearances, I became very familiar and friendly with the librarian. So I was allowed to read whatever I wanted from the locked shelves. There were very few books in the reading room at the time. Other than a few texts on engineering, there was almost nothing that I did not read.

"One day I found a very interesting book published in the United States in 1914. The title was *Our Knowledge of the External World* by Russell. From the first time I read it, I sensed that it was full of new meaning for me. Then I read it two more times, each time becoming more interested in its author, Bertrand Russell" (3–4).

What started out as an accidental encounter among the engineering books developed into a passion. Zhang was not satisfied with one book by Russell. He wanted more—anything he could get his hands on. The quest for Russell's texts opened the door to a new world of periodicals published by Chicago's Open Court bookstore: "This bookstore published two periodicals, the *Monist* and *Open Court*, in which there were always some articles by Russell. I sub-scribed and read them all" (5).

Excerpts from the *Monist* and *Open Court*, however, did not satisfy Zhang's deepening interest in the man who wrote the philosophical texts. Following the thread from abstract ideas to concrete embodiment, Zhang Shenfu found his way to Russell's *The Problems of Philosophy*. Published in 1912, this slim volume had been commissioned by a popular press with the express purpose of widening the readership for modern philosophy. It was meant as a "handbook for shop assistants"—a simplified and more intelligible version of the philo-sophical issues that Russell had been struggling with over a decade.[8]

Zhang Shenfu was no shop assistant. By this time, he was a sophomore majoring in mathematics at the National Beijing University. With the aid of Russell's *Problems of Philosophy*, Zhang developed an even stronger interest in logic. Russell's simple, lucid text opened up for Zhang a new way of looking at philosophy. Whereas it had been the province of musty classicists in the Chi-nese context, philosophy now became the subject of scientific study. After all, Russell had combined mathematics and philosophy: his scientific magnum opus, *Principia Mathematica* (written with A. N. Whitehead), began to appear in print two years before *Problems of Philosophy* and was completed (with vol-ume 3) one year after, in 1913. Seventy years after these momentous publica-tions, Zhang Shenfu recalls how *Problems of Philosophy* led to his commitment to walk in Russell's footsteps, how he decided to become a philosopher himself:

"In this book, Mr. Russell uses the example of the painter to talk about how an artist becomes interested in the appearance of things. By contrast, the prac-tical person wants to know what things are really like. The philosopher, in turn, is moved by an even more profound desire to know the inner quality [*benti*] of things. According to Russell, philosophy is not the process through which one finds concrete, definite answers to this or that question. Unlike the physicist, the philosopher studies the questions themselves. Philosophical questions broaden our conception of reality. They enrich our inner feelings and imagina-tion and diminish arbitrary self-righteousness.

" 'Arbitrary self-righteousness,' Russell wrote, 'is difficult to undo.' More difficult even than acquiring reason. Still, undoing 'self-righteousness' is the most important object of philosophy. According to Russell, philosophy's con-cerns are not limited to man but extend to the universe as a whole. The subject is so great that it must, by necessity, stretch our minds as well. To put it simply, it is possible for us to strive to obtain truth—a truth that is part of the great objective truth of the universe."[9]

In the wake of this realization, Zhang Shenfu changed his major from math-ematics to philosophy and plunged more deeply into reading and translating Russell. The tide of Zhang's interest in Russell crested in 1919–20, when he translated, annotated, and wrote ten articles on Bertrand Russell in less than fourteen months.[10] This outpouring represents Zhang Shenfu's contribution to the positive reception that Russell received in China in 1920. Though Zhang could not take credit for inviting the eminent British philosopher to Beijing, he did create a climate of interest and appreciation for Russell as a technical philosopher and social activist.

On October 8, 1920, when Bertrand Russell and Dora Black arrived in Shanghai, Zhang Shenfu was there to welcome them. He had, by that time, already made plans to go to France on the same boat as Liu Qingyang and Beijing University president Cai Yuanpei. The month and a half that remained before his departure tested and confirmed Zhang Shenfu's fervent admiration for Russell. After their public meeting in Shanghai, Zhang Shenfu and Russell continued conversation over tea the following month in Beijing. They developed a mutual respect that lasted even after 1948, although Zhang never met Russell face-to-face again.[11]

For Zhang Shenfu, Russell's voice was as exciting as his mind. In 1920 Zhang had the opportunity to hear Russell explain his philosophy in his own words, an experience that left an enduring impression on the young Chinese philosopher. In 1983 Zhang recalled: "Russell's speeches were easy to understand, fluent, humorous, and inspiring. When analyzing a problem, Russell explained the problem in simple terms. His reasoning powers were penetrating, but not without irony. But it was not a hurting sort of irony. To me, his voice sounded like spring water from a sacred mountain. It cools and calms. It also leaves one with a chilly, alert, pleasant sensation."[12]

JANUARY 1988. One of Zhang Shenfu's students, Sun Dunheng (who took Zhang Shenfu's logic courses at Qinghua University in the mid-1930s), is recollecting his teacher's lecture style. Sun's impressions of Zhang echo Zhang Shenfu's recollections of Bertrand Russell—and through no accident. In the decade after he met Russell, Zhang Shenfu went on to fashion himself into a philosopher of the Russell mold. In his own teaching, Zhang mirrored the approach of the man who first revealed to him the everyday significance of philosophy:

"In his logic classes, Mr. Zhang Shenfu sat in the center of the dais. With his glasses on, he never stopped looking at us while he lectured. With a piece of chalk in his right hand, he would cover the blackboard with abstract signs like a circle, or a plus or a minus sign, or with formulas such as AEIOPQ. Often he dwelt at length on the thought of the great English philosopher Russell.

"In general, the study of logic dealt with abstract concepts. But Professor Zhang Shenfu's knowledge was broad, many-sided, mind-expanding. He would always enrich his subject with examples from everyday life, from commonplace existence. This made things easier to understand. For example, he would say: 'Logic is the study of propositions, the study of form, the science of all sciences. To see how its reasoning works, let me give you an everyday example. If it rains the ground gets wet. So rain seems to imply a wet ground. If it rains, the ground is definitely wet. But if the ground is wet, it is not necessarily because it rains. It could be wet because the street cleaner has just sprayed water over the ground.'

"Each of Mr. Zhang's sentences was like a piece of crystal sugar. It could be pondered with increasing pleasure for a long time. Each class was full of 'asides.' These consisted of leisurely digressions from the dry subject of logic. They were anything but useless diversions. They were the harvest of his own truth seeking. He used them to make his lectures more lively."[13]

Here a student pays unwitting tribute to the teacher's teacher. Zhang Shenfu, the dispenser of crystal sugar in the 1930s, had received his first taste of lucid, earthbound philosophizing while drinking from Russell's mountain spring in 1920.

MAY 21, 1942. Zhang Shenfu continues to savor the pleasures of Russell's thought. He continues to relish the cool and calming effect of the British logician's philosophy, even in war-torn China. Though the Japanese invasion forced him to leave Beijing and resettle in Chunqing, Zhang continues to read as much as possible by and about Russell.

On this day, writing for a Communist-supported newspaper, *Xinhua ribao* (New China Daily), Zhang takes the opportunity to mark his mentor's seventieth birthday. He takes space out of a special column dedicated to science and dialectical materialism to comment on the enduring significance of Russell for philosophers and for the world in general: "Bertrand Russell is the greatest philosopher of mathematical logic. He is a veteran soldier of the new enlightenment trend that has brought science to the study of human nature. Every new philosophy has its own methodology. Russell's pathbreaking method is that of logical analysis. If you want to truly understand Russell's philosophy, you have to understand the tradition of British empiricism out of which Russell emerges. His goal was to set mathematics on a firm foundation of logical proof. In this he succeeded admirably."[14]

APRIL 12, 1946. The anti-Japanese war has been over for about a year. Zhang Shenfu is deeply involved in negotiations about the future form of China's national government. Nonetheless, he manages to take time out to write about Bertrand Russell again. Unrestrained by the kind of Party censorship that silenced him after 1949, he titles his essay "Russell: The Greatest Philosopher Alive Today." Published in *New Criticism* (*Xinwen pinglun*) this article allows Zhang to speak even more effusively than he had in 1942:

"Russell is the most well known modern thinker in the world of Western philosophy. Russell's works have been translated into more foreign languages than that of any philosopher alive today. Russell's philosophy is complex and cannot be explained in a few simple terms. The source of his original contribution must be traced to his masterwork, *Principia Mathematica*, which opened up a new page in both mathematical logic and philosophy. Russell has often said, and I always agreed with him: 'No problem in philosophy can be truly solved unless there is a breakthrough in mathematical logic.'

"Currently Russell is working on an autobiography that is eagerly awaited by readers all over the world. His thought, like his personal demeanor, is thoroughly revolutionary. He is capable of evoking intense admiration. This can be seen in the powerful loyalties he has generated among the women who have shared his life. Because Russell is a powerful and attractive personality, he has naturally been envied, and even hated, by some people. His commitment to science and democracy has not always received a supportive response. Some people hate him just because others love him too much, especially women."[15]

After this tribute to his mentor, Zhang goes on to praise himself as the conduit through which Russell has reached Chinese readers:

"In China, some of the most important new theories and new personalities [from the West] have been introduced first by me. Quite a few new names and works were first translated and explained in my writings, and then became popular later on. This is especially the case with Romain Rolland, Auguste Rodin, [Henri] Barbusse, and many others. This was even more apparent in the circumstances surrounding Russell's reception in China. Here was one of my main contributions to the nation. This is what I myself consider most glorious. Now these seeds have been scattered across the broad public. But, naturally, I have no way of knowing what kind of significance, if any, they will have in the world at large" (22).

FEBRUARY 1983. Thirty-seven years after the publication of "Russell: The Greatest Philosopher Alive Today," Zhang Shenfu is less doubt-ridden about the impact of his glorious contribution to the nation. Now Zhang is less worried about Russell's impact on China ("already proven") and more interested in Russell's significance for himself. As he dictates to his daughter, Zhang's tone is unequivocally admiring. At the same time, the octogenarian's words continue the search for self-justification:

"To be a great philosopher, a person must be creative. He must have something original to say about the human condition and have a noble purpose in philosophizing. Russell did not fail to meet all of these criteria. To sum up Russell's life: he was not only a great philosopher but also a theorist of education. He also fought for justice and peace. He was tireless in his appeal to critical reason and in the fight against fascism. His great achievements in mathematical logic have transformed the entire philosophical world. Thus I write this article to show my admiration and respect for Russell."[16]

Zhang Shenfu was, from beginning to end, a fervent admirer of Russell. In 1920 he worshipped Russell as a model of critical thought. By 1983 he acknowledged that Russell was a creative philosopher beyond himself. Zhang Shenfu rested on his laurels as China's Russell expert.

The Making of a Russell Expert

NOVEMBER 10, 1920. The day before Russell is to have tea with Zhang Shenfu at the Continental Hotel, a gulf develops between the two men. Russell's letter inviting Zhang identifies it. In response to Zhang Shenfu's earlier questions about the importance of biology to philosophy, Russell writes: "Yes, philosophy depends, as you say, especially upon biology, but, at the moment even more on physics."[17]

This, at first glance, is a brief, mild reference to Russell's current interest in physics and in the work of Albert Einstein. Zhang adopted these interests in the following decade. And yet there is a premonition here of a more significant difference: for Zhang, biology and philosophy will remain related concerns. They will, in time, open the door to a further divergence from Bertrand Russell as Zhang moves closer to dialectical materialism.

Dialectical materialism is not yet on Zhang's intellectual agenda in 1920. Russell nonetheless senses its shadow. He closes his letter of November 10 to Zhang with the following words: "I am very sorry you are going away so soon. I would have made more attempts to see you, but was persuaded you hated me on account of my criticism of Bolshevism."

Zhang Shenfu answers on the same day. He accepts the invitation to tea but takes issue with Russell's letter. With effort, in English, he writes: "Many thanks for your reply. I will see you tomorrow at the time requested. I am delighted very much by your so estimable reply.

"Its last sentence surprises me also very much. Not only I never hated you at all, but I hope eagerly that there would be no hatred at all. Even Mr. Anatole France's saying 'to hate the hatred,' for me, is not quite right. Your criticism of Bolshevism are all right, and valuable, I believe.

"Even if not so, there would be no reason for me to hate only on account of this. You said, 'If I be a Russian, I would defend the socialist gov't' (cited from memory). This attitude, I quite admire. Though I consider Russia as the most advanced country in the world at the present, and though I believe in communism, I am not a Bolshevik. This is of course also your opinion. I believe I agree with you at nearly every point and believe myself I can *almost* always understand you quite correctly."[18]

Before sending the letter, Zhang Shenfu inserted the word "almost" before the phrase "always understand." This was the only sign that there might be a breach in understanding between Russell and himself. It was, however, a momentary concession. Overall, Zhang believed that he understood Russell fully. More important, he was convinced he had found in Russell's thought a key to a new Chinese philosophy. In 1920 Zhang Shenfu was convinced that the British logician's lectures and writings were true and sufficient unto themselves. That conviction would erode in the years that followed their meeting at the Continental Hotel.

JUNE 11, 1981. Today we have our most extensive conversation about mathematical logic. Zhang Shenfu is explaining, line by line, a narrative poem he wrote in 1960. As a diversion from illness and political repression, Zhang had composed a ten-page overview of the history of mathematical logic.

As always, our conversation—and the poem—starts and ends with Bertrand Russell. Even as Zhang reviews his appreciation for the contributions of Gottfried Leibniz, George Boole, G. W. Pierce, William Jevons, and other pioneers in mathematical logic, he reserves highest praise for Russell: "It is Russell who sets the whole field of mathematical logic on a firm theoretical foundation. His contribution is the greatest. He has expended great effort to rebuild philosophy through the theory of types, through the theory of description and through the logic of relations."

I have a hard time following Zhang's list of technical developments in logic. It is hard enough to thread my way through the thickets of Zhang Shenfu's political career. This material on mathematical logic is tougher still. How am I to make sense of Chinese words summarizing Russell's *Principia Mathematica* when I do not even understand them in English? Russell's breakthrough—the translation of mathematical problems into symbols of logic and the elucidation of logical puzzles by distinguishing proper names (such as table, chair, square) and denoting phrases (for nonexistent objects such as a round-square)—leaves me as confused as the lay list of Western logicians' names in front of me now—in Chinese! An almost hopeless puzzle.

I am not sure what all these names mean to Zhang Shenfu in his old age. Leibniz, Boole, Pierce, and Gödel appear as so many denoting-phrases—as so many round squares in Zhang's overly condensed history of mathematical logic. Sometimes I have the feeling that these names are like mantras, incantations that Zhang Shenfu uses to maintain some philosophical lucidity in old age.

But this is not the case with the name and work of Bertrand Russell. Russell's opus and life remain real, detailed, and richly nuanced in Zhang Shenfu's mind. And today he wants to underscore his own contribution to clarifying Russell's thought in China:

"I was the first to translate most of Russell's key texts into Chinese. Others followed with longer books, more technical works. But I introduced all the key phrases, all the key themes. I was the first to notice and to emphasize what was new in Russell's thought. For example, I was the first to emphasize the concept of philosophy as 'the science of the possible'—though I am not sure where this concept appears in Russell's work. I was also the first to translate and interpret in the Chinese context the logical concept of 'falsification' that is fundamental to all of operations in logical analysis.

"I also translated the concept of 'analysis' very differently from all others. I used the Chinese term *jiexi* instead of the more commonly used *fenxi*. Why, you wonder? Because I believe jiexi is more logical. It also sounds newer somehow. Fenxi suggests something being cut up, scattered, severed—as if by one blow. Jiexi, by contrast, is not so simple.

"How is it more complex, you ask? I feel that there are many more steps involved in jiexi. When something is subjected to logical analysis, it is a slow, systematic unraveling of a problem, like peeling an onion. Fenxi was widely accepted as a synonym for philosophical analysis when I began my work on Russell. But I did not think it conveyed the full implications of Russell's thought. It was too simple. So I made an innovation through translation. Maybe this is my most important contribution to clarifying Russell's work in twentieth-century China."

Fenxi versus jiexi—this strikes me, at first, as a petty claim on the part of a man who wants to convince me of his grasp of the complexities of Russell's thought. But the more I listen to Zhang Shenfu, the more I understand how Zhang's philosophical commitment is rooted in the meaning of words, in the attention lavished upon specific turns of phrase. Zhang Shenfu is a philosopher of the word. In Bertrand Russell he has found a new vocabulary for his thought. Or, as Maurice Friedman put it, "The word which we shall make our own is the word whose echo we have already heard within ourselves."[19]

So I go back to 1920, to the year when Zhang's longing to resemble Russell was most explicit, when the longing signaled an incipient resemblance: this is the year in which Zhang Shenfu made the most concentrated effort to introduce Russell's vocabulary to Chinese readers. This is the year in which he chose to translate logical analysis as jiexi instead of fenxi. This is the year that he became convinced that Russell's logic opened up a new path in scientific philosophy. This is the year in which Zhang became convinced that philosophy is the science of the possible. This is also the year in which he began to develop a more independent philosophical outlook. From 1920 on, much like his mentor Bertrand Russell, Zhang Shenfu expressed his thoughts by clarifying words. He believed that truth lay in words.

The significance of Russell for China lay in words, too.

MARCH 16, 1920. Russell has not yet landed in Shanghai, but already Zhang Shenfu is defending him in Beijing. Seven months before his mentor began to lecture in China on philosophy, logic, and social issues, Zhang was already on the alert against any possible misreadings. John Dewey, the American exponent of pragmatism, was also lecturing in China in 1920, and Zhang was concerned that Dewey might distort or eclipse Russell's philosophy in this Chinese intellectual context.

In a letter to the editor of *Chenbao*, the most influential newspaper in North China, Zhang Shenfu takes issue with Dewey's characterization of Russell: "The night before last, Mr. Dewey talked about Russell as a despairing pessimist. In fact, Russell stands for ethical neutrality [*lunli zhongli*]. Russell stands beyond judgment in all categories of thought. . . . Furthermore, Dewey is thoroughly mistaken when he describes Russell's philosophy as elitist. This leads us to think of him as somehow antidemocratic. In fact, Russell is a thorough realist who upholds logical atomism [*duoli yuanzi lun*] and the principle of absolute pluralism [*duoyuan lun*]. Russell's philosophical method is to dissect all categories of thought, be they political, scientific, or philosophical. To make this clear I have translated his 'Dreams and Facts' which appeared first in the January issue of *Atheneum* and was reprinted in the February 1920 issue of *Dial*."[20]

Less than two months after Russell published an essay in the West, Zhang Shenfu was ready to defend and explain its meanings in Beijing. Zhang's vigilant alertness testifies to his admiration for Russell. Informed admiration, in turn, enabled Zhang to quarrel with the ignorance of his contemporaries.

OCTOBER 30, 1920. Zhang Shenfu enters the fray of public debate again. He is defending Russell's philosophical position once more. Now that the British guru has set foot on Chinese soil—a true sage in the eyes of youthful admirers who only a few weeks earlier had sat at the feet of John Dewey and who a few months later would flock around the Indian philosopher of mysticism Rabindranath Tagore—interest in his ideas is spreading like wildfire. Zhang Shenfu is ever on guard against distortions of Russell's point of view. On this day, Zhang is picking a bone with a young Chinese philosopher, Zhang Dongsun.

Though not much older than Zhang Shenfu, Zhang Dongsun has an established reputation as political activist. He is an associate of senior statesman Liang Qichao and editor of the Shanghai-based *Shishi xin bao*. By October 192? Zhang Dongsun had produced a Chinese translation of Henri Bergson's 1907 work *Creative Evolution*. He was also looking for a spiritual ally in the battle against Bolshevism. Having heard about Russell's negative reactions to his visit to the Soviet Union and about his reservations concerning the applicability of Marxist analysis to the Chinese situation, Zhang Dongsun is beginning to take an interest in Russell's philosophy.

Zhang Shenfu loses no time in taking Zhang Dongsun to task for misreading Russell. Convinced that Russell is far more complex than Zhang Dongsun's picture of him as an anti-Bolshevik, Zhang Shenfu sends off another letter to the editor of *Chenbao*. As always, his argument revolves around words: "Mr. Zhang Donsun's is thoroughly misreading Russell when he describes his philosophical realism with the Chinese words *shiyong zhuyi*. The English equivalent for this is 'pragmatism,' not 'realism.' This is a fundamental mistake. Anyone who knows anything about contemporary philosophy and about Russell's work knows that Russell is a firm opponent of pragmatism. His views are very different from those of Henri Bergson and John Dewey, in the same way that his mathematics is fundamentally different from that of Galileo Galilei.

"Since last year, when he began to study modern psychology, Russell has developed a new theory which suggests that there is no difference between mind and matter. They are both part of a continuum of varied perception. In this respect, Russell's theories are quite close to those of William James. Russell's idea that 'truth propositions correspond to actual facts' is nonetheless different from James's notion that 'truth is an assumption we need in order to proceed with the work of philosophy.' It is also very different from Dewey's notion that 'truth is an assumption about what works in a given situation.' The difference in their positions is amply evident in *Principia Mathematica* and in other of Russell's works. So how can one of our so-called illustrious commentators make such a fundamental mistake?"[21]

Setting words straight—this was Zhang Shenfu's philosophical ambition in 1920. And it has remained so ever since. Defending Russell's realism in public gave Zhang an opportunity to defend his own philosophical position. Each time he translated a work by or wrote an essay about the British logician, Zhang was, in effect, stretching the limits of his own language and thought.

In the same month that he took on Zhang Dongsun, Zhang Shenfu also edited a special issue of *New Youth* magazine dedicated to Bertrand Russell. This was a rare opportunity to make an enduring impact on the most inquisitive minds of China. *New Youth*—the most cosmopolitan publication of the day —had published only three special issues in its history: one dedicated to Henrik Ibsen in June 1918, one to Marx and Marxism in May 1919, and one to Bertrand Russell in October 1920. As special editor of the October issue, Zhang Shenfu had an opportunity to set the tone for subsequent Chinese discussions of Russell.

OCTOBER 1920. Zhang's introduction to the Russell bibliography in *New Youth* focuses on linguistic and philosophical issues. The emphasis is a bit odd in light of the fact that Zhang Shenfu, like other young Chinese, was amply aware of Russell as a social theorist and activist for peace. Russell's views on freedom of marriage, women's rights, and socialism were of immediate interest to young radicals of the May Fourth era. Nonetheless, Zhang Shenfu's introduction to *New Youth* emphasizes Russell's contribution to scientific philosophy. This essay dwells on the significance of "new realism" in British philosophy and traces its evolution from G. E. Moore to Russell. New realism, as Zhang Shenfu grasped promptly, challenged idealism by linking philosophy to science in two complementary ways: by reducing most complex propositions to their simplest parts (like atoms in the laboratory) and by rebuilding a verifiable system of scrupulously logical notations. In this introduction to Russell's thought, Zhang takes great care to explain the mathematician's key dictum: "Whenever possible, logical constructions are to be substituted for inferred realities." Zhang Shenfu is clearly at great pains to find the right Chinese word for Russell's method of "logical atomism."

He finally hits upon the rather cumbersome but evocative Chinese expression *mingli yuanzi lun* (or the atoms of logic). With this in mind, he argues that philosophy can be placed on a "realistic," that is to say, scientific, foundation. Unlike other philosophers of the past—and even some contemporaries—Russell does not use logical analysis to examine only philosophical statements. For him, logical atomism is a powerful method of investigation and justification beyond philosophy. It takes philosophy out into the world. Logical analysis (*mingli jiexifa*) is a most important invention. It makes philosophy truly "scientific."[22]

With this essay on Russell, Zhang Shenfu established himself as a Russell expert, not just a Russell admirer. His mission, however, would not remain unchallenged. Many others became more expert in the intricacies of mathematical logic—most notably, the Western-trained logician Jin Yuelin, who became Zhang Shenfu's colleague in the Qinghua University philosophy department in the 1930s. Other Chinese philosophers, Liang Shuming foremost among them, called into question Zhang's admiration for Russell.

MARCH 1921, SHANGHAI. Zhang Shenfu is in Paris organizing a small cell for the Chinese Communist Party. Russell is lying ill in Beijing, given up for dead, according to one Japanese newspaper. Liang Shuming goes public with his reservations about Russell as a philosopher and moralist. Liang's essay is published in a major Shanghai daily under the title "My Reservations about Russell."[23]

Liang begins this critique of Zhang Shenfu's philosophical mentor with the following acknowledgment: "To my friend Zhang Shenfu who already loves Russell's theories: over the past seven, eight years, he has not stopped talking about and praising Russell's theories. Following Mr. Zhang's urgings, I have also tried to read Russell's works and to like them. And in fact found that some aspects of his theories accord well with my own thought—such as his social psychology. Also his theory of impulsion [here Liang uses the English word *impulsion*] is quite coherent.

"I also found Russell's theories of cognition and of the essential continuity of all matters very suggestive. Last year, when Russell passed through Nanjing, he gave a very convincing lecture on the subject using the example of the concept of 'hat' to prove that hats seen by people in the present are nothing more than extensions of hats that they have seen before—though they might not actually be the hats bought originally. So I accept some of Russell's theories. But my dissatisfaction with Russell's thought is more serious. I am full of doubt about its foundation.

"What gives me great unease about Russell is the way he criticizes—quite unfairly and ignorantly—the theories of Bergson [Liang's favorite Western thinker]. Although I do not know much about mathematical logic, I still have deep reservations about Russell's unscholarly attitude in intellectual debate. It is well known that Russell opposes Bergson. But he has never bothered to understand the other's point of view. In Beijing, he attacked Bergson for 'mythical idealism' without any basis at all."

In conclusion, Liang again pays tribute to Zhang Shenfu's overview of Western thought, while continuing his critique of Russell: "Finally, I also want to warn my readers about the quest for an all-encompassing, comprehensive philosophy. Truths attained through such comprehensive philosophies might sound good. Indeed, they appear to be perfect in their claim to certainty. But the real truth is always more complex. It is neither as pleasant nor as fine sounding as Russell likes to claim.

"A scholar is an expert only in his own field. Outside of it, he is just a commoner. Zhang Shenfu is right in saying that 'today, philosophy belongs either to Russell's school or to that of Bergson.' One is a leader in rationalism; the other is a leader in nonrational thought. Russell and Bergson are the two greatest contemporary philosophers. Although they are different, each has a claim to truth" (103).

"But from Russell's shortsighted words it is evident he is not open to learning. He seeks truth but cannot attain it. In this Russell has forsaken the outlook of a true scholar. I write this not only to criticize Russell. There are many people who discuss philosophical issues the same way as Russell does. I have been feeling pity for them for a long time now. The reason such persons cannot be true scholars is that they are not prudent in their outlook. They do not know that only one who is calm, careful, and insightful can be a truly great philosopher" (105).

Was Liang Shuming referring to Zhang Shenfu here? Did he sense as early as 1921 that Zhang did not have the inner qualities of a "great philosopher"? Liang Shuming said as much to me during our first meeting on April 29, 1983.

In 1921, however, Liang did not yet have the evidence of Zhang's life, a longevity spent in the teaching of logic and the pursuit of political activism. Nonetheless, Liang was already emphasizing the need for calm and prudence. Zhang never treasured these qualities of mind as much as Liang Shuming did. Neither did he produce a coherent work of original philosophy as Liang had managed to do by the late 1940s. Even in 1921 Zhang Shenfu was attracted to what Liang criticized as all-encompassing philosophies. He had already embarked on the search for one comprehensive answer to China's many problems. For awhile, mathematical logic seemed to promise such an answer through its formulas and step-by-step processes of deductive reasoning. Mathematical logic eventually gave way to dialectical materialism in Zhang's worldview and, finally, to an idiosyncratic combination of Russell and Confucius.

To the end of his life in 1986, Zhang Shenfu was aware of his failure to convert Liang Shuming to Russell's point of view. He nonetheless took endless pride in having exposed Liang to the works of Bertrand Russell. Zhang remained a critically minded Russell expert while Liang went on to become a philosopher in his own right.

During his long career as philosopher-activist, Zhang Shenfu was far from blind to Russell's shortcomings. Although Zhang never wrote a detailed critique of the British mathematician, his philosophical journeys took him far from Russell's arrogant certainties. In all the far-flung journeys through Confucianism and dialectical materialism, however, Zhang maintained his interest in Russell's thought. Over and over again Zhang translated or abstracted the latest book by the prolific Englishman; he expressed his admiration for the political courage manifested in Russell's stand against war and fascism; and he showed his enjoyment of "Bertie," the irreverent private man inside Russell the public philosopher.

MAY 1, 1931. Zhang Shenfu is writing his most personal essay about Russell, a confession of his enduring interest in the man who invited him to tea in Beijing in November 1920. The essay is a meditation on "What Russell Loves and What Russell Hates," but it is also an oblique recognition that Zhang's interest in the man behind logical atomism might not be strong enough to nurture prolonged philosophical work in the Chinese context.

By 1931 Zhang had made his imprint as a Russell expert on Chinese intellectual life. He had produced translations and interpretations of Russell's works during two distinct periods: the first in 1919–20 during the May Fourth movement, the second in 1927–28 in the wake of the failure of revolution. Whereas the first period was marked by the careful introduction of key terms in Russell's analytical logic, the second was marked by an attempt to delve into the scientific and social foundations of Russell's work. The second phase of appropriation began with a translation of Russell's 1927 essay "Is Science Superstitious?" and went on to include essays on "The Meaning of Meaning," on "A Free Man's Worship," on "The ABC of Relativity," and on "Russell's New Views of the Atom."

Translation was a particular kind of appropriation, but writing a book about Russell's philosophy was quite another task, one that Zhang Shenfu kept putting off. In May 1931, having recently been appointed as professor of logic to the prestigious philosophy department of Qinghua University, Zhang imagined that he would still write such a book. He never did.

Instead, Zhang Shenfu wrote yet another translation-essay published in the *Qinghua University Weekly*. This article centered around a recent interview in *The Little Review* in which Bertrand Russell spoke about his loves and hates. Zhang's preface to the Russell interview contains a confession of his own frustrated desires:

"I have been wanting to write something about Russell for a long time. He will be sixty years old next May. I very much wanted to write a big, thick book about his thought by way of congratulation. What I have here, instead, is sort of a foreword to that project. It is only an expression of my personal interest in Russell.

"But actually, if you stop to think about it, what other criteria is there for truth but that of interest, or rather beauty. What is life for, if not for the expression, the fulfillment of interest? Whether my interests will find an echo among readers is beyond my ability to predict."[24]

Zhang's self-doubt here is colored by the conflict between the desire to write a big, thick book about his British guru and the proclivity to follow a wide array of interests. Zhang Shenfu never did write his book about Russell or any other subject. This set him apart from Liang Shuming, whose many books assured him a place in the annals of twentieth-century Chinese philosophy.

Nonetheless, *The Little Review* essay allowed Zhang Shenfu to look behind the solemn aura of Russell as a public philosopher. Zhang excerpted the interview for Chinese readers because he was convinced that "among the fifty famous people interviewed by *The Little Review*, Russell's answers were the most interesting, the most profound, and the most humorous."

To make his point more concrete, Zhang goes on: "When asked what do you like best and would you have liked to be? Russell answered, 'I would have liked to know physics best and to be a physicist.'

"What are you most afraid of? 'I fear most becoming a boring companion to my friends.' When was the happiest and the most unhappy time in your life? 'The unhappiest was the time of my birth. The happiest will probably be when I die.'

"What do you like most and least about yourself? 'What I like the most about myself is that many people like me. What I dislike is that I hate myself'" (10).

Even with Zhang Shenfu's appreciative introduction, Chinese readers could not but raise eyebrows at the kind of man revealed in the answers published in *The Little Review*. Zhang concludes on a critical note. On the face of it, he is troubled by Russell's repeated praise of physics—the source of their old disagreement from 1920, when Zhang was already quite taken by psychology and biology: "Russell says that physics is the most important realm of theoretical research and that it helps us to understand everything, including social phenomena. But ten years ago, I already discussed with Russell the importance of psychology for philosophy. Even then he told me that philosophy must rely more on physics. It is a pity, though, that he never developed the specific reasons for his preference of physics."

The question of Russell's infatuation with physics is but the tip of the iceberg. Beneath it lies a host of buried doubts about the social usefulness of the kind of cool rationalism that informed Russell's answers to *The Little Review*.

How useful could such rationalism be for a thinker like Zhang Shenfu—or for a country like China—who needed a more compassionate analysis of society and a more comprehensive view of the dynamics of social change?

SPRING 1897. Using the pen name Orlando, the twenty-five-year-old Bertrand Russell writes a brief essay entitled "Self-Appreciation." A recently elected fellow of Trinity College, the iconoclast who joined G. E. Moore in the rebellion against Immanuel Kant and Friedrich Hegel now lays bare his likes and dislikes even more sharply than in his subsequent answers to *The Little Review*: "I am quite indifferent to the mass of human creatures, though I wish, as a purely intellectual person, to discover some way in which they might all be happy. I wouldn't sacrifice myself to them, though their unhappiness, at moments, about once every three months, gives me a feeling of discomfort. . . . I care for very few people and have several enemies—two or three at least whose pain is delightful to me."[25]

Zhang Shenfu did not read this extreme version of Russell's antihumanism. But he sensed it in the answers to *The Little Review*. Zhang had had a glimpse of Russell's antihumanism even earlier, in 1920, when he tried to convince Russell of the importance of biology—the science of living, changing organisms. Russell, on his side, remained firmly committed to the razor-sharp approach of analytical logic. It helped to cut away, not through, the muddy problems of social life.

In the course of his long life, Zhang Shenfu never lost interest in Russell the man or even in Russell the philosopher. But the chilly, formalistic core of his mentor's worldview forced Zhang to look beyond Russell. Though he did not say as much in 1931, Zhang Shenfu could not deny the truth in Liang Shuming's 1921 accusation: Russell *was* arrogant and one-sided. For a corrective, Zhang Shenfu, like Liang Shuming, turned to the humanistic traditions of native Chinese thought.

Chinese Roots

JUNE 16, 1981. We are talking about the connection between materialism and realism. I cannot follow the thread very well, because I am untrained in technical philosophy and because Zhang Shenfu tends to drift off into a low mumble whenever we circle back to ideas that decades ago became code words for him. Once in a while, however, his voice clears. Then he surprises himself, and me, with something new about the evolution of his philosophical worldview.

Today Zhang stops in the middle of a sentence about the utility of Western logic in fostering a scientific, realistic view of the world. He adds: "But Russell, you see, ended up so one-sided in his philosophical outlook. His philosophy is useful in seeing only discrete parts of a problem. I wanted to think about the whole. In many ways Russell was biased. He opposed materialism. But materialism and idealism are just two sides of the same coin. Materialism does not see the heart and mind (the *xin*), whereas idealism fails to appreciate outward realities.

"My own philosophy seeks a more comprehensive view of experience, a more thorough realism, an expansive objectivity. So I went back to certain ideas in Chinese philosophy—especially to the Confucian notions of *ren* [tolerance, humanism] and *zhong* [the unprejudiced golden mean]."

"But didn't Russell himself hold Confucianism in contempt?" I ask. I remind Zhang Shenfu of what Russell wrote in *The Problem of China*: he was "unable to appreciate the merits of Confucianism" because "Confucius' writings are occupied with trivial points of etiquette," and he felt that "the master's main concern was simply to have people behave correctly on various occasions."[26]

Zhang loses no time in answering me: "Yes, it is true Russell did not understand or respect Confucius much. But that is just another example of his one-sided view of things. He reduced Confucius to empty rituals. But my philosophy took the best in each. Never blindly. And to this day, the two philosophers I admire most deeply are Russell and Confucius."

Here, Confucius does not evoke the itinerant teacher from the State of Lu who lived in the fifth century B.C. Confucius never becomes human in Zhang Shenfu's thought. The ancient native philosopher does not provide a full-bodied polarity to Zhang's many-sided fascination with Russell, a contemporary Westerner. And yet, truncated as Confucius might be, reduced to a few key ideas, a few euphemisms, he draws Zhang back to the recesses of Chinese humanism. After two decades of fierce attachment to Western science and mathematical logic, the native sage provides a starting point for what Zhang calls his "more dialectical approach" to the problems of Chinese society.

NOVEMBER 12, 1934. Fourteen years after tea with Russell in Beijing, thirteen years after the British logician confessed disinterest in Confucius, Zhang Shenfu is writing a critical defense of the Chinese sage. This essay, like the 1931 article on Russell, appears in the weekly journal of Qinghua University. Its title is "Can Worship of Confucius Save China?"[27]

As in most of Zhang's essays written in the 1930s, this one too is provoked by specific political circumstances: in February 1934 Jiang Kaishek had launched a New Life Movement, the purpose of which was to revive the so-called Confucian virtues of honesty, modesty, obedience to superiors, simple living, and cleanliness. Jiang's campaign for good manners resembled what Russell might have imagined as a natural outgrowth of Confucian moralism. One month later, on March 1, 1934, the Manchu scion Puyi ascended the throne as the Confucian emperor of the Japanese puppet state of Manchukuo.

Zhang Shenfu's essay is a direct response to these events. The author faces a tough task: how to discredit the abuses of Confucianism in contemporary political life while salvaging some core of appreciation for the sources of native Chinese philosophy? Furthermore, how is he—a man publicly identified with the iconoclastic May Fourth movement of 1919—now to argue for the rehabilitation of Confucius?

Zhang's answer is to drive an ideological wedge between Confucianism (as a social philosophy that supports the governing class) and Confucius (a thinker of merit concerned with the moral ideals of benevolence, tolerance, and impartiality). This essay marks the beginning of an effort by Zhang Shenfu to modify the extremist May Fourth slogan: "Down with Confucius and Sons!" Zhang Shenfu's new credo—repeated with increasing fervor throughout the early years of the anti-Japanese war—becomes "Down with Confucianism! Save Confucius!" (7).

In this 1934 essay Zhang Shenfu is already concerned with the problem of national survival. His title, "Can Worship of Confucius Save China?" is a deeply felt response to a cultural and political emergency. By 1934 the Nationalists in Nanjing and the Japanese in Manchukuo were grasping at Confucianism as a raft full of holes. Zhang's own view is that worship of Confucius will definitely not keep China afloat in this period of menancing imperialism. Rather, what is needed is a critical, informed, selective appreciation of the master's teachings:

"Most of the reasons behind the current movement to worship Confucius are regressive. They are marked by politically motivated nostalgia. The moving force of history, however, is progressive. If national confidence is to be restored today in the face of the peril of national extinction, it must be done on a firm foundation. Otherwise it will unleash an even more counterproductive revolution against Confucius. If Confucius is worshipped today in the same way that he has been worshipped for two thousand years, then there will be dire results."

To make his warnings more precise, Zhang adds: "In our times, common understanding of Confucius has deteriorated and so the master is open to manipulation by whoever needs his words. In fact the historical Confucius was not at all that 'great.' To dwell on his 'greatness' is to make him more open to manipulation, to make him omnipotent, absolute, infallible. Confucius was simply a great Chinese thinker, educator, and political activist. To view him as an absolute norm and to worship him is really to do him harm" (8).

The problem of the worship of Confucianism neither began nor ended in 1934 with Jiang Kaishek's New Life campaign or with Puyi mounting the throne of Manchukuo. It did not subside until the war against Japan was over. Zhang never ceased to worry about what it would take to build national confidence in a protracted war of resistance to Japan. He continued to write essays about the need to learn from Confucius—but always with a critical eye. The problem was political mobilization against Japan. The solution lay in something personal: Zhang Shenfu's own quest for a philosophical worldview that modified the cold, harsh edge of Bertrand Russell's dissective genius.

SEPTEMBER 27, 1932. Zhang Shenfu has just edited the fourth installment of a special column for the North China daily *Dagong bao*. Entitled "Trends in World Thought," the new project brings Zhang a national readership and new social contacts (Sun Junquan among them). For the moment, Zhang Shenfu is concentrating on introducing readers to the latest and the best of Western and Marxist philosophy. In this column he also takes the opportunity to continue his episodic essays that began in the 1931 book *Thought as Such*. The new essay series is entitled "Thought as Such, Continued." In this series the Pascalian project begun in the 1931 introduction is continued in an even more condensed fashion. In a few sentences his *pensées* brush over subjects as wide-ranging as logic, sex, imperialism, and Chinese philosophy.

In today's installment Zhang recalls a passage by the ancient Taoist philosopher Zhuangzi. He then proceeds to muse about Russell's extreme scepticism, which, Zhang believes, prevents Russell from penetrating the emotional component of reality. Finally, Zhang concludes that Eastern and Western philosophy have their own disparate genius: "Oneness and universality are the strong points of Eastern philosophy. Multiplicity and distinction are what is prized in Western philosophy. Russell is certainly the most inspired among those who talk of the many and who distinguishes himself by analyzing differences between them. He believes that oneness and universality are nothing but superstitions.

"Someone who seeks to understand multiplicity and distinctions cannot but emphasize logic, cannot but seek absolute certainty.

"My own goal is to glimpse the One among the many. I seek, through distinctions, to arrive at what is truly universal. When thinking of One I try not to forget the many. I moderate what exists with an understanding of what is universal."

Then, as if the implicit refutation of Russell's dissective genius were not enough, Zhang concludes rhetorically: "Is absolute knowledge anything but superstition?"[28]

The man who was once so taken by Russell's claims for absolute certainty in the 1910s now uses Russell's own criticism of superstition to indict as vain the quest for absolute certainty.

APRIL 8, 1980. My first meeting with Zhang Shenfu's younger brother, Zhang Dainian, a tall, grey-haired man and a well-known expert on traditional Chinese thought in the Beijing University philosophy department. He is a more traditional, more academic scholar than Zhang Shenfu. Nonetheless, Zhang Dainian has shared the political fate of his revolutionary older brother. Both men were condemned as rightists in 1957.

Like the firstborn son, Zhang Dainian makes a professional career of philosophy. He began his studies at Qinghua University during Zhang Shenfu's tenure there. For a while he also embraced his elder brother's fascination with Western scientific philosophizing. Today Zhang Dainian recalls his first articles about philosophy, which, with Zhang Shenfu's guidance, he published in 1933–34 in the special column "Trends in World Thought." Like Zhang Shenfu, Zhang Dainian wrote a great deal about Russell: "In fact I translated some of the most technical parts of Russell's work into Chinese. Then I decided to turn all my attention to the history of China's own traditions of thought. My brother also became interested in Chinese philosophy—later than I did, and never wholeheartedly."

Our conversation drifts back and forth over Zhang Shenfu's philosophical maturation. His younger brother is an urbane, highly trained, careful historian of philosophy. His help is valuable in untangling the various, often contradictory threads in Zhang Shenfu's work. Zhang Dainian emphasizes how important Russell had been in deepening Zhang Shenfu's interest in mathematical logic. Then Zhang Dainian adds, "Zhang Shenfu also gained a great deal by not cutting himself off from traditional Chinese ideas. . . . This was not a comfortable stance in the ideologically torn world of Chinese philosophy in the 1930s. Among dogmatic adherents to Western materialist and narrow-minded defenders of Confucius, Zhang Shenfu stood out like a light. He was conversant with the latest ideas from the West. And yet he found it possible —indeed necessary—to affirm the value of certain key ideas from Confucian thought, especially of ren, the ideal of active benevolence. The best place to start to understand my brother's attachment to ren is in the introduction to *Thought as Such*. There the mathematical logician already credits Confucius with a truly balanced view of the world. There you can see how Zhang Shenfu passed beyond his early infatuation with narrowly scientific rationality."

FEBRUARY 4, 1934. Zhang Shenfu is continuing his meditations on Chinese philosophy. In this month's "Trends in World Thought" he develops one of his main concerns: Confucian humanism. As often before, Zhang states his point of view through a play on words:

"What Confucius means by ren [benevolence or humanness] is quite the opposite of what is often understood as ren [passive forbearance]. Benevolence requires an active pursuit of the ideal society. It demands acknowledgment of true freedom between two people. To be ren in the true sense is to be nothing more than human [also ren in Chinese]. To be fully human is not only to look out for what is beneficial to oneself but to think of how not to bring harm to others. Therefore it can be said that to be ren [humane or benevolent] is to be objective. Not an easy proposition."[29]

This condensed play on words echoes much of what Zhang had written in other essays during the late 1920s. It repeats his arguments against the use of Confucian ideas to enforce a passive acceptance of fate by those deemed inferior in the Confucian hierarchy—as in the relation of women to men, of young to old, of commoners to political authorities.

In 1934, however, Zhang Shenfu goes one step further: he insists that ren —genuine benevolence—is a necessary precondition for the realization of one's humanity. Humanity, in turn, requires commitment to an "ideal society." The activist in Zhang Shenfu thus finds a way to stretch tradition to accommodate the urgent challenge of national salvation.

Zhang's play on words is also grounded in classical texts—especially in the *Zhongyong* (the doctrine of the mean), an ancient text supposedly written by Confucius's grandson. Full of quotations from the *Analects*, this book became one of Zhang Shenfu's favorite sources of quotation. Chapter 20 of the *Zhongyong* contains the very words Zhang Shenfu uses to weave together his 1934 meditation: "*Renzhe ren ye*"—"benevolence is the characteristic element of humanity."[30] *Benevolence* (ren) as used here is nearly synonymous with *humanity* (ren). This ancient verbal echo confirms Zhang's own sense that humaneness is an ideal accessible to all. This interpretation also enables Zhang to challenge his contemporaries to develop the richest potential in themselves: the will to social action.

The doctrine of the mean is also the source of Zhang Shenfu's other Confucian ideal—that of zhong. The first chapter of the ancient text describes the state of mind that Zhang came to view as a prerequisite to genuine objectivity: "When there are not stirrings of pleasure, anger, sorrow or joy, the mind may be said to be in a state of equilibrium [zhong]. Equilibrium is the great root from which originates all the human actions in the world" (255).

But as with ren, Zhang Shenfu's interpretation of zhong was consciously activist. He insisted that a true understanding of the Confucian golden mean necessarily demanded struggle against injustice in contemporary society. By the mid-1930s, Zhang Shenfu's quarrel with socially conformist Confucianism had escalated into a full-fledged war. He was more convinced than ever that true equanimity required an active commitment to the world as it really was. His concern with Confucian benevolence was giving way to an urgent recommitment to the value of objectivity, but from a new, more expansive perspective than had been made possible by Russell's logical atomism.

Expansive Objectivity

JUNE 2, 1980. After eight months of conversation, Zhang is most concerned that I understand—and acknowledge—his contributions as a philosopher: "I am one of the greatest thinkers in twentieth-century China, you know. [A slight ironic twinkle crosses his eyes.] I have tried to bridge the impossible: the best in ancient Chinese philosophy with the latest ideas from the West. I have tried to build a common ground between Confucian humanism and Russell's mathematical logic. Maybe they are impossible to bridge. But I tried. And I am still convinced that my concept of expansive objectivity [da keguan] was what was needed to bring these two different worlds together."

The arrogance in Zhang's tone is nothing new. Still, each time he uses unequivocal superlatives about himself, I am taken aback. His own story calls into question the steadfastness of his commitment as a philosopher. Zhang Shenfu has documented the many political causes that took him away from systematic philosophy. Almost all of our sessions end with regret about his not having written "one thick book."

And yet, here is an old man bent on wresting a philosopher's pride out of an inconsistently lived life. He is urging me to consider what it took to bridge unbridgeable worldviews in his time. Zhang Shenfu is determined to show me how a selective return to the roots of Chinese philosophy enabled him to look at the world more objectively—"even more objectively than Russell's one-sided, partial realism" allowed him to do.

Zhang Shenfu's claim that he developed a new kind of objectivity forces me to rethink key concepts in Chinese thought: *keguan*, the term used to denote "objective" in modern thought, means, literally, "guest perspective," as opposed to *zhuguan*, or "host perspective." This is a very human, socially embedded definition of objectivity and, as such, offers a great contrast to Western notions. In China's naturalistic cosmology, there is no radically transcendent Principle, First Cause, or Primal Mover. In classical Chinese philosophy, to be objective is to be quanmian (well-rounded), as opposed to pianmian (partial or prejudiced).

Zhang Shenfu calls Russell pianmian: "If Russell had one major shortcoming, it was his inability to see something from different sides. His forceful analysis cut through to the core of discrete phenomena. But it left out too much. It made him prejudiced [pianmian]—as evidenced in his opposition to dialectical materialism. I tried to be more comprehensive [quanmian]."

In Zhang's Chinese universe objectivity—keguan, the quest perspective —has an intimate relation to well-roundedness, to quanmian. The quest in this sense is not transcendent but simply less prejudiced in his well-rounded appreciation of a given problem.

JANUARY 1927. Zhang Shenfu has just finished "The Method of Pure Objectivity" ("Chun keguan fa"), one of his longest philosophical essays.[31] Most of his previous meditations were published in Beijing newspapers. Earlier jottings ran three or four paragraphs; a few went on for ten. This time, though, Zhang has worked out one key idea in some detail and has even coined a philosophical phrase for it, which he uses as a descriptive title. This essay stands in contrast to the elusive play on words that marks other essays in his book *Thought as Such*.

This work on objectivity is also kinder to the reader. From the beginning, Zhang acknowledges that he is about to lay out an argument that is at once simple and complex. He even goes so far as to draw a diagram that will help the reader follow his vision of pure objectivity. The drawing consists of three circles joined by vectors that form a triangle. The purpose of the diagram is "to illustrate that pure objectivity can transcend the subjective, can look at subjectivity objectively. One who has attained pure objectivity can look at objectivity subjectively. This perspective incorporates and transcends them both" (195).

At the base of the triangle are two points of view: objectivity and subjectivity, labeled A and B, respectively. The apex represents the possibility of a point of view that is informed by the two below and reflects their interaction. This is what Zhang considers his innovation. This is the pure objectivity that he describes and pleads for in the rest of the essay: "According to commonly held philosophical views, subjective is the opposite of objective. In fact, however, they cannot exist independently. They are informed by each other. Their opposition is false unless their interaction is grasped from the point of view of pure objectivity. Only this vantage point allows the inside to be seen from without. Only in this way can the subjective world become truly objective."

To guide the reader toward the apex of the diagram, Zhang goes on to say: "In order to achieve the perspective of pure objectivity, the subject must step out of his or her own narrow position and move toward a more comprehensive point of view. In this process one becomes transformed as well. What was previously subjective has now been objectified. . . . To look at A and B—at subjectivity and objectivity—from the position of pure objectivity is to see that what we commonly call subjective and objective are both part of a shared world and can be investigated through a dynamic philosophy. From the point of view of the philosophy of pure objectivity, everything is seen as a series of self-evolving events" (196–97).

Zhang Shenfu's determination to overcome duality is more pronounced in this essay than in all of his previous writings. To be sure, he had used the phrase *pure objectivity* before—especially in 1925 during his political withdrawal from the Chinese Communist Party—when he argued that both objectivity and materialism are artificial, narrow, prejudiced dichotomies adopted by "those who are not aware of what else exists beside themselves, or not conscious of what they are. Such people cannot envisage others and are unfit for coping with others."[32] But by 1927 previous renunciations about the partiality of materialism and idealism had blossomed into a philosophical statement about Zhang Shenfu's own epistemology.

The fuller definition of pure objectivity is, to be sure, indebted to Russell's work on the problems of perception and philosophical truth. Nonetheless, Zhang moves the argument forward on thoroughly Chinese grounds, seeking to strip and to cleanse Russell's notions of objectivity of their one-sided opposition to the inner world of the subject. Subjectivity, according to Zhang, is the private experience of the self seen from within. Objectivity—when identified with what is public and common—is "the world of the subject viewed from without." Pure objectivity, in turn, is not concerned with the omniscient perspective of objects. Rather, it is a world full of ever-changing events.

In the conclusion of his January 1927 essay, Zhang Shenfu acknowledges that pure objectivity introduces both a tongue twister and a mind twister: "If I were to look for a more simple expression maybe I would settle for one word —*realism*. But the English word *realism* has too many meanings. . . . All I can say is, Know what motivates the subject, and then you will know the subjective objectively. Know what makes a falsehood false, and you will know the truth at the heart of falsehood."[33]

OCTOBER 1932. Zhang Shenfu has finished yet another column in his series "Thought as Such, Continued." Though longer than the previous essays, this one reflects the same spirit in its scattered meditations on assorted subjects.

One idea, however, can be followed through all the essays in spite of a meandering approach—that of da keguan. The idea is not exactly new, but the term is novel, because Zhang had previously written about pure objectivity.

The tone of the 1932 essay is calmer and more playful than the formulaic effort of 1927. In January 1927 China's social revolution was just gaining momentum. Zhang Shenfu was responding both to the exhiliration and the mounting danger of the Nationalist Party's crushing the Communist initiatives in urban and rural mobilization. During the first half of 1927, everything was up in the air: Zhang Shenfu's salary, his teaching position, his editorial work. No wonder, then, that he worked to refine the idea of a pure objectivity.

By 1932, however, Zhang Shenfu was an established professor at Qinghua University. He was living on a gracious suburban campus and benefited from the extra income of his column for the *Dagong bao*. Life then was more slow-paced, more expansive than it had been in 1927–28. It provided Zhang with an opportunity to develop his concern with objectivity.

The opening to the 1932 essay confirms Zhang's sense of expansive contemplation: "The universe is so varied and complex. The scientist has his universe, the philosopher has his universe, the logician has his universe. Even among the philosophers there are divergent notions of what the universe is. The perspective that is most open to change is closest to reality. Only such a point of view can accept the vanishing nature of all material existence."[34]

From this broadly philosophical opening, Zhang moves to his real point, a more nuanced restatement of his 1927 position: there is no firm boundary between subjectivity and objectivity, between idealism and materialism, between realism and pragmatism.

The Western epistemology that distinguished between these concepts had excited Zhang Shenfu in the late 1910s. Twenty years later, however, he is challenging its presuppositions in the name of expansive or greater objectivity: "Whoever holds to the point of view of expansive objectivity will not fall either into the fallacy of misplaced concreteness—the shortcoming of materialists—or into the prejudice that all reality is comprised of mind and spirit—as is the case with the idealist. Rather, expansive objectivity enables one to act in keeping with reality, to have genuine equanimity, to see things from many different points of view, to be able to make distinctions without making them absolute. . . . From this, it can be seen that the enmity between materialism and idealism is truly empty and should be abandoned."

To make his point about the emptiness of all absolute distinctions even more dramatic Zhang Shenfu concludes the essay with five poetical epigrams:

The wisest is stupid.
The bravest is like a virgin.
The most tragic is he who overcomes personal feelings.
The mind of a great man is like that of an unformed child.
Must one who holds to expansive objectivity dwell in the
  abode of objectivity all alone?[35]

In 1932 Zhang Shenfu styled himself as the lonely resident of the lofty abode of expansive objectivity and believed that he had achieved a worldview of his own making. But da keguan—the phrase as well as the expansive state of mind that nurtured it—was short-lived. Zhang Shenfu was swept up in a new wave of political activism. As Japanese aggression mounted in North China, it became less feasible to maintain the unsullied standpoint of either pure or expansive objectivity. By 1935 Zhang Shenfu rushed into the fray of yet another patriotic movement—this time for national salvation. Political activism, in turn, opened up new philosophical questions for him. During the war with Japan, Zhang became increasingly drawn to dialectical materialism. The graceful bridge he had wanted to build between Russell and Confucius, between Chinese humanism and analytical logic, collapsed under the pressure of political events.

5

IN THE REALM

OF RED DUST

Myth is the part of reality we create and choose to remember. History corrects for the heroics that we would project upon the past. Only myth tells us who we would become; only history tells us how hard it will really be.
—Robert Cover, *Folktales of Justice*

AUGUST 8, 1989. The events in Tiananmen Square are still vivid in my mind after a spring journey to Beijing—my first trip back to China since the death of Zhang Shenfu three years ago. This spring, China went from hyberbolic elation about the prospect of democracy to deep despair in the wake of the June 4 massacre. Politics—the never-ending siren song of Chinese public life—engulfed young intellectuals, much as it had the long life of Zhang Shenfu, who was enveloped and defeated all at once.

This year China celebrated the seventieth anniversary of the May Fourth movement. For a brief moment, the event of 1919 and its participants were discussed in terms that reflected the intellectuals' own dilemmas. For a week or so in early May, the heirs of China's first enlightenment movement looked back over the past seventy years of history and asked themselves what intellectuals could do and be in the China after Mao. I participated in commemorative conferences, mindful of Zhang Shenfu's ambivalent relationship to Mao Zedong in particular and to revolutionary politics in general.

But time for discussing intellectuals' ambivalence toward politics ran out too soon. As so often before in twentieth-century China, intellectuals were overwhelmed by events beyond their control. Another campaign to chastise intellectuals is now in force on the mainland.

My return to this book is shadowed by the events in China. Back home, fresh from the exhiliration and despondency I witnessed in Tiananmen Square, I search the record of my dialogues with Zhang Shenfu for survival techniques in the midst of revolution and autocracy. Here is a concrete opportunity to explore the ambiguities of political engagement in modern China —ambiguities that plagued Zhang's work and life much as they did the student movement of 1989. Zhang, like the students this spring, wanted to be close to and beyond politics all at once. Zhang, like the young students in

Tiananmen Square, found it impossible to sustain prolonged disengagement from revolutionary events.

JUNE 11, 1981. Today a break in our conversation about Zhang's philosophy and mathematical logic. In this interval Zhang Shenfu speaks to me about politics: "Philosophy must never, never be affected by politics. But politics—ah well, politics is really boring [*zheng zhi, hai, zhengzhi hen wuliaode*]. If philosophy ever becomes influenced by politics it becomes tedious, partial. It loses its objectivity. My philosophy seeks to be objective. I am incapable of prejudice."

I press on, knowing that Zhang's life has been lived, both by choice and by forcible necessity, in close proximity to politics: "But didn't you take part in countless political movements? Didn't you make a career out of revolution? How, then, can your philosophy avoid being involved in politics? Have you really been able to remain impartial?"

"Sure, sure, I did politics in my time. Still, philosophy and politics ought to be considered separately. Take Marxism, for example. When making revolution, it has a clear purpose. But I never let it affect my logic. Politics should not invade scholarship. Politics are inherently one-sided. Scholarship cannot, must not be partial. What is true is true, what is false is false. This must be kept clear, separate. But politicians don't care about such distinctions."

A nervous, confessional laughter accompanies Zhang Shenfu's words, letting me know that we are near a difficult subject. Politics have, after all, dominated every aspect of Zhang's life and thought. Revolution has been his obsession, whereas philosophy was always an avocation.

Today he tells me that "politics is boring." His voice is weary from decades of Party-imposed political study. An old man tired of the dogmatism of the Chinese Communist Party now looks back over his life and wishes that politics and philosophy had been separable after all. He longs to see himself as impartial and wishes for an Olympian stance above the fray of political action, above the enforced partialities that always accompany a revolution.

For the moment Zhang Shenfu imagines himself beyond the realm of the red dust (*hongchen*). This Buddhist metaphor comes to mind as I hear him longing for a philosophical position beyond the realm of mortals enchained by passion and desire. In traditional China, men who were steeped in the sensual pleasures of everyday life, men who pursued the dream of a career in politics, were chided by Buddha's followers for their attachment to earthly rewards. Red dust, although glittering, disintegrates when pressed hard, bringing the pain of loss and disillusionment. But Zhang does not appear troubled by the lure of sexual passion and desire. He seems to think, though he never says so, that illusion is limited to politics alone.

But then again, Zhang Shenfu is no Buddhist. He is heir to a long tradition of Confucian activists. The Confucian gentleman made his mark among mortals. He always tested and proved himself in the realm of red dust. Like Confucian literati before him, Zhang Shenfu repeatedly brought his ideas to bear on the crises of the day, attempting to solve them through a combination of logic and Marxism, philosophy and revolution. It is amid red dust that Zhang wrote and published essays about Sun Yatsen as a master logician in the late 1920s and about the contribution of dialectical materialism to constitutional democracy in the 1940s.[1] Today all this is momentarily forgotten by an old man who needs to imagine a retrospective boundary between politics and scholarship.

But neither communism nor Confucianism sanctions such a divide. In fact, it was Mencius, Confucius's main disciple, who first codified the Chinese intellectuals' sense of social responsibility by declaring that "those who know are the first to awaken; those who are enlightened must awaken the others."[2] Zhang Shenfu has lived out this Mencian dictum with passion. A "knower" by profession, he never tired of trying to awaken his compatriots, to make himself, and them, more responsive to history. Political engagement was an expression of Zhang's own responsiveness to twentieth-century history.

The activist passions of red dust were never far from Zhang Shenfu's door. Though he left the Chinese Communist Party in 1925, his wife remained active in the Party's Women's Bureau. Many of his closest friends were Communists as well. These intimate associations as well the Japanese aggression in North China kept drawing Zhang Shenfu back into revolutionary action. Although he continued to read Russell and to write philosophy, Zhang always circled back to politics.

MAY 20, 1983. Today I met with one of Zhang Shenfu's oldest, most trusted political comrades—the newspaperman Xu Yin. A short, slight man in his seventies meets me at the door of Zhang's house; Xu Yin feels very much at ease here. Zhang and Xu have known each other for fifty years—ever since Zhang Shenfu began the special column on world philosophy for *Dagong bao*. In the early 1930s, Zhang Shenfu was a prominent professor at Qinghua, while Xu Yin was getting a start in the publishing world. A bond of mutual respect has endured, at the heart of which lies what Zhang wants to overlook in late age: politics.

"My most enduring impression of Mr. Zhang," Xu Yin tells me, after casting a warm glance toward the subject of our conversation, "is that of an impassioned political activist. He was a fiery speaker with a quick pen throughout the 1930s. Whenever there was a national political crisis, you could count on a strong statement from him. He spent all his time building various organizations to work for national salvation."

"But what about philosophy?" I ask, looking at Zhang Shenfu. "Wasn't

Mr. Zhang a professor of philosophy first and foremost? Mr. Zhang always tells me that he wants to be remembered as a philosopher, that scholarship must stand apart from politics." I catch an ironic smile on Zhang's face. I have disagreed with him on this subject often before, and I know he expects me to continue to challenge him today in the presence of a trusted friend. Zhang Shenfu helped set up this meeting. He has told me how he introduced Xu Yin to his future wife in the 1930s, how they both suffered as rightists in 1957. Zhang Shenfu is also grateful for how much Xu Yin has done recently to promote Zhang's reemergence in public life.

"No, I must beg to differ." Xu goes on: "I never got the impression that Mr. Zhang was a philosopher. His main activity was always politics. I never attended his classes at Qinghua, of course, so I can only tell you what I perceived in the newspaper world. But from that I can assure you he was no philosopher. He lived, from beginning to end, for politics."

Xu Yin stops short of calling Zhang Shenfu a *zhengzhijia* (politician). All three of us around the table know the disparaging connotation of this Chinese term. Politicians are self-serving opportunists—officials who follow the winds of power. Most intellectuals in China use the pejorative phrase zhengzhijia to describe Guo Moro.

"If not a politician, what was Zhang Shenfu's role in the 1930 and 1940s?" I ask, unwilling to let the subject drop. "You did not attend his classes, but you know about his activities in political organizations such as the National Salvation Association and the Democratic League. What compelled a philosopher to get involved this way?"

Xu Yin hesitates for a moment as his eyes search Zhang Shenfu's face once more. He is not sure why I continue to refer to his friend as a philosopher, when he is convinced Zhang was never that removed from the world, never that impartial. Finally, his eyes back on me, Xu Yin retells the history of *Dagong bao*, the newspaper that brought them together in the 1930s: "After 1927, you see, the revolutionary movement suffered a terrible setback. All parties appeared corrupt or impotent, or both. The *Dagong bao* newspaper was reorganized in 1927, around two slogans: 'Intellectuals must talk about politics' [*wenren tan zhengzhi*] and 'Essays can save the nation' [*wenzhang jiuguo*].

"And so, people like me and Mr. Zhang had a source of support, even of income. The newspaper gave us a chance to get involved in politics, to stay involved with politics. It made writing not just a private project but a matter of national significance. It prepared us, especially Mr. Zhang, for a prominent role in the political organizations of the anti-Japanese war period. *Dagong bao* was our school, our laboratory for promoting independent thinking among the masses."

Xu Yin's words bring to life for me a world beyond Russell and Confucius.

This is the murky world of political action that has claimed Zhang Shenfu's sympathy for longer than he cares to acknowledge. Impartiality might have been a goal for a young newspaperman like Xu Yin, as well as for a seasoned logician like Zhang Shenfu. But the 1930s brought them up against politics far more complex than the slogans of 1927.

Was there ever a time when literati did not "talk politics" in Chinese history? Never, I sense from Xu Yin and Zhang Shenfu. The pressing question was how to talk politics, especially after disillusionment with the concept of revolution in the late 1920s. How did Zhang Shenfu and Xu Yin manage to keep on talking about political mobilization after the outbreak of the White Terror in April 1927? That month the Nationalist Party severed its united front with the Communists and launched a wholesale attack on Party members and sympathizers. Zhang Shenfu had been both. He was also deeply attached to the vocabulary of revolutionary politics now used by the GMD to hunt down its former allies.

JUNE 1928. Zhang Shenfu is making yet another disclaimer about politics under the pen name "TSS." His essay "My Attitude Toward the Chinese Revolution" is published in *Revolutionary Critique*, a semiofficial journal of the left-wing remnant of the GMD.[3] In this article Zhang writes about his profound disillusionment with revolution one year after the outbreak of the White Terror, one year after Jiang Kaishek usurped all talk of revolution for his own Nationalist Party politics.

And yet, from the title to the final words, Zhang makes it clear that no one can escape the burden of political involvement in modern China. In this first year after the breakdown of the united front between Communists and Nationalists, Zhang's words mirror the inner conflict experienced by many intellectuals of the May Fourth era:

"I don't like being involved in politics right now. In fact, I never did like playing an active role in politics. Politics isn't everything. Now, more than ever, I am convinced that politics is inherently inadequate. Furthermore, I am convinced that this thing called politics becomes invariably deflected in the wrong direction. The more people get invovled with it, the more messed up it becomes. The more people emphasize politics, the more diffuse it becomes. If you want to think about politics clearly, you have to be less entranced with the subject"(34–36).

After this polemical opening, Zhang goes on to urge readers—the so-called masses, in keeping with the current penchant for revolutionary language—to get involved with something other than politics: "Do science if you like to play games. Play at science instead of politics. Science is, after all, the best weapon in the fight for China's prosperity."

And yet, in spite of this playful language, Zhang is advocating science or scholarship not for its own sake but for the social utility of knowledge. In the end, neither science nor playing claims Zhang Shenfu's passion but, rather, the imminent danger of national disintegration. This brings Zhang back to the need for political engagement: "Since man is a social animal, it is impossible to avoid politics. China is in a critical situation. Who can be aloof at a moment such as this? . . . Now that the country is on the brink of destruction, now that the ruling powers have brought about ruin and poverty, there is especially a need to rise up and change the situation. There is also a need for people who are depressed by the situation. There is a need for those who cannot but become concerned with current affairs again.

"For all these reasons—although I have become deeply disillusioned by politics and, in fact, have sometimes been deeply exhausted, depleted by politics—I cannot help but become an observer of the current state of the Chinese revolution. . . . Yet nobody can live beyond politics. Therefore I still watch modern China's political situation. I am an observer. Maybe as an observer I can see things more clearly. Since I am not someone who is eager or happy to be lured by politics, I can see things more dispassionately than those in the middle of politics"(38–39).

The ideal of pure objectivity flowers anew in this hope for a dispassionate point of view toward politics. As with his philosophical stance, Zhang Shenfu found it difficult to define and to maintain dispassion, especially about politics.

And yet, in spite of its cool ardor, Zhang's essay was out of step with *Revolutionary Critique*. The editor of this magazine, Chen Gongpo, was a Beijing University graduate of the May Fourth era. He now served as president of Shanghai's Dalu University, an institution that offered refuge to a number of leftist intellectuals like Zhang Shenfu. Chen himself, however, was involved in the political reform of the Guomindang. He was in no position to make a political disclaimer. Every other prominent intellectual—including socialists like Xu Deheng and Zhou Gucheng, who were also at Dalu University—used the pages of *Revolutionary Critique* to discuss the positive value of political action. Only Zhang Shenfu's essay laments the burden of political consciousness. This lament remains an enduring theme throughout Zhang's life, but it is never so strong or so categorical as to prevent him from becoming repeatedly embroiled in the political issues of the day.

The plaint adds a note of melancholy to Zhang's various political commitments. In our 1981 conversation, as in the 1928 essay, Zhang Shenfu insists on speaking as a man who would have liked to live beyond politics. This voice seems to say, "If I were not Chinese, if I were not the heir of a Confucian obsession with political responsibility, if I were not Zhang Shenfu as known by

my good friend Xu Yin, I might have left the realm of the red dust. I might have
been the greatest philosopher in twentieth-century China!''

A Responsiveness to History

JUNE 16, 1980. Today is my last visit to Zhang Shenfu's house before leaving China. I talk with him for two hours in the company of his good friend Li
Jiansheng, the widow of Zhang Bojun, Zhang Shenfu's longtime political associate who is still disgraced. Our three-way conversation drifts back to the
1920s, when Zhang Shenfu, Li Jiansheng, and Zhang Bojun became involved
in the politics of a Third Party—an alternative to both the Nationalist and the
Communist parties that was being planned throughout 1927–28. Though the
Third Party never materialized into a significant political force, it united the
fate of these three individuals.

Today, Zhang and Li are looking back to their most intense period of political activism. They are asking themselves what went wrong. Their aged faces
wrinkle with self-mocking laughter. Li: "Really now, why did we intellectuals
feel so compelled to get involved in politics over and over again? You would
think we would have been chastised by the failures of 1927. The revolution
suffered its greatest defeat in 1927, yet we rallied to its defense in the very
moment it was falling apart."

Zhang looks at her, then at me, with a sweeping, helpless sort of smile: "We
are intellectuals, aren't we? What could we do but take the weight of the world
on our shoulders? That is what Chinese literati have been doing for ages. . . . We
have an addiction to social responsibility, you might say. . . . But it was right
to get involved. I still believe that. Even after the failure of 1927, we intellectuals tried to find our own path. We wanted to do something in spite of all that
defeat. I had seen through the shortcomings of Communist Party policies in
1925. The Communist Party had failed in its vision even before the White
Terror of 1927. You and I and Bojun and others tried to come up with a third
alternative, something between the Nationalists and the Communists. But we
were defeated by history I guess."

Zhang Shenfu's voice trails off, the smile gone. He seems lost as he looks
past his old friend. An awkward silence settles over the room as Li Jiansheng
and Zhang Shenfu go on thinking about their political failures.

APRIL 30, 1987. One of Zhang Shenfu's former students, the historian Zhao
Lisheng, is visiting me at Wesleyan University. In a university guest house, far
from China, Zhao takes me back to the 1930s, to the days when he first attended Zhang Shenfu's logic courses at Qinghua University: "Zhang Shenfu
was always political, you know. That is my most enduring impression of the
man. He was always drawn to current events. He was always trying to figure out

Zhang Shenfu in animated conversation with Li Jiansheng, widow of Zhang Bojun, in 1980.
(V. Schwarcz)

how intellectuals should respond to history. He was always on the side of the Communists, even when not a Party member. He never had a fiercely independent cast of mind like his friend Mr. Liang Shuming."

"Why are Chinese intellectuals so frequently attracted to history?" I ask the seventy-one-year-old man sitting next to me on the couch. He has already told me about his own suffering as a result of the Communist Party's anti-intellectual policies after 1949: Zhao Lisheng was made a rightist in 1957 and was then much persecuted during the Cultural Revolution of 1966–69. He is bitter about his ravaged life; he speaks about it in a high-pitched tone and with the vivid gestures of a Peking Opera actor.

"You are a historian," I go on, mindful of the professional scholar inside the amateur performer; "Can you perhaps help me understand Zhang Shenfu as part of a tradition of political activism among Chinese intellectuals?"

Zhao Lisheng stops to look at me hard. Then he laughs with a shrill echo: "You know Chinese poetry a bit? Do you know the Han dynasty poem about the abandoned wife?"

"No, I am not sure which you mean," I confess.

Zhao Lisheng takes a pen and piece of paper and writes from memory the following stanza in Chinese:

Before I die I have only this to say,

I only wish to be buried in your land.

So, even if I were to become a heart-broken flower

I could still bloom near your home, my lord.

Finishing with a flourish, Zhao looks at me to make sure I understand the characters on the page.

"Yes?" I say, sure of the words but not of their intent.

"Well, that is the psychology of Chinese intellectuals, you see." Zhao continues: "They keep on acting out the role of the abandoned wife. No matter how forgotten they are, no matter how abandoned and mistreated by political overlords, they feel a deep loyalty to them. They all want to die in or near the lord's home."

Then, no longer testing my grasp of Chinese language or history, he adds, with downcast eyes: "We Chinese intellectuals are a pathetic, feminized bunch. . . . We, the heirs of China's Confucian tradition, have become like the abandoned wife."

JUNE 19, 1925. History invades Zhang Shenfu's life with a vengeance. Six months after quitting the Communist Party, Zhang is pulled back into the maelstrom. His old loyalties and old attachments are catalyzed once again.

Zhang Shenfu, like all of China, is deeply shaken by news of a massacre in Shanghai: twelve students were killed during a large labor demonstration protesting the treatment of workers in Japanese- and British-owned textile factories. The shooting was carried out in the name of British authorities by Sikh mercenaries.

The geographical distance between Zhang Shenfu's home in Beijing and the events in Shanghai has vanished. His recently cultivated distance from the Chinese Communist Party diminishes as well. In a series of short meditations entitled "Imperialism and All That," Zhang reveals his profound disturbance over what is now called the massacre of Nanjing Road.[4] He is also aware that his compatriots have become swept up in a fervent anti-imperialist rhetoric fanned by Communist labor organizers. These essays are meant to sound an alarm—anti-imperialism is becoming a dangerous codeword for old-fashioned antiforeignism. Zhang Shenfu's goal is to ward off hysteria while sharing in this national outpouring of grief and rage. His meditations seek to make room for a distinctive form of political commitment and political commentary:

"I do not know whether my patriotism measures up to the degree required these days. I can't help feeling that the massacre that took place in Shanghai is not just China's humiliation but the humiliation of mankind. The responsibility for this occurrence must be placed on human nature and on a social system. If human nature and the social system do not change, such things will keep on happening. I too participated in one of the national demonstrations about these events. I took along a little flag I had made. My flag had two sides: on one side was written "Down with Imperialism!"; on the other, "Redeem the Dishonor of Mankind!" (1).

The anecdote about the flag situates Zhang Shenfu in a world of his own making. In June 1925 other graduates of the Beijing University *New Tide* Society —soft-spoken, literary men like Ye Shengtao, Zhu Ziqing, and Yu Pingbo—were writing poems and essays about the need to redeem Chinese shame and Chinese blood. Zhang Shenfu seems concerned with something else. His meditations about imperialism raise questions about the cause of the killings in Shanghai. For Zhang Shenfu, imperialism is not "a thing" that can be easily overthrown or destroyed but, rather, a "system of social relations" that brings dishonor to all mankind. It must be dissected and understood before it can be eliminated:

"Imperialism is not a simple matter of commercial, industrial, or even political domination. It is a system upheld through ideology and military might. . . . Chinese patriots who would face up to this complex system must start with a fundamental change in human nature. . . . and perhaps talk less of warring against imperialism. The Chinese people, I am afraid, are unprepared for war with foreign imperialists. They have no way to cope with modern warfare as described by J. Calliens in his work *A Defense of Chemical Warfare* or in T. B. S. Haldane's *The Future of War*" (2).

The reference to foreign texts in the midst of a nativist event is nothing new for Zhang Shenfu. Nor is the journal that brings to the public new meditations on imperialism. *Yu Si* (Spinners of Words) was an established magazine edited by *New Tide* member Sun Fuyuan, in collaboration with two May Fourth luminaries, Lu Xun and his brother, Zhou Zuoren. These writers had hoped to avoid ideological controversy and to focus their efforts on the creation of a new literature. But the May Thirtieth massacre in Shanghai overwhelmed their agenda, just as it did that of Zhang Shenfu. Although they had hoped to stay out of the throes of politics, history pulled them back into the fray.

Three days after the publication of "Imperialism and All That," Zhang Shenfu wrote another essay, entitled "The Establishment of a Third Kind of Culture." In it, he tried to spell out the need for a new worldview that would transcend old Chinese culture as well as modern, Western-capitalist civilization. Without abandoning the rhetoric of anti-imperialism—which was still monopolizing the ears and hearts of his compatriots—Zhang tried to describe a third kind of culture that would be both "rational and substantive." This new culture, Zhang claims, was "based on a materialist understanding of society. It is a culture that corresponds with actual historical conditions."[5]

These were vague, almost hollow words in the weeks after the Shanghai massacre, when the passions of patriotism were further heated by the blood of martyrs on Nanjing Road. During these same weeks Zhu Ziqing, a fellow member of New Tide, wrote the "Song of Blood," and Ye Shengtao, another New Tide colleague, wrote the "Flowers of Blood."[6] Zhang Shenfu, on the other hand, went on seeking a middle ground between reason and passion, between China's political predicament and the cultural necessities of the future. Critical thought rang louder in his ears than talk of bloodshed. Three years before Zhang Shenfu became actively involved in organizing a Third Party between the Nationalists and the Communists, he was already arguing for a third kind of culture. Both the Third Party and the third kind of culture met with failure. But not before Zhang Shenfu became convinced that his own mission lay in preparing China for a union of enlightened reason and revolutionary passion.

AUGUST 19, 1925. Zhang Shenfu writes an open letter to the literary scholar Zhou Zuoren.[7] The two men have known each other for more than five years (and would remain loyal friends for thirty). At this moment in 1925, though, there is a strain between them. Zhou is more active, more prominent politically. He is a public figure in protests against the new minister of education, Zhang Shizhao, who is trying to quiet a student movement at the Women's Normal University in Beijing. The more he tries to quell the disorder through administrative regulations, the greater the outcry against the Ministry of Education.

Yet Zhang Shenfu, who is disinclined to abandon a friend under attack, feels protective toward Zhang Shizhao, his old acquaintance from the May Fourth period. The public criticism of Zhang Shizhao increases during the weeks following the Shanghai massacre. Zhang Shenfu seeks to create and maintain a middle ground. He wants to reach out to Zhou Zuoren, without abandoning his loyalty to Zhang Shizhao. More important, he wants to unburden his thoughts to a writer who understands the loneliness of a cultural radical like himself:

"Mr. Kaiming," writes Zhang Shenfu, using Zhou Zuoren's given name, "My heart is heavy and very black these days. No sooner does one start to speak than destructive words pour out unavoidably. I am afraid I am incapable of maintaining the equanimity that you are capable of. But still I'd like to address a few words to you, maybe because I am so often disinclined toward speaking. Now I am trying to avoid being caught in the dichotomy between laughter and cursing. . . . Society, you see, Mr. Kaiming, has burdened me so that it is impossible to act or speak responsibly.

"You still describe yourself as belonging to something, as sharing in society. My own situation, by contrast, is different. I do not have any friends. . . . As to Bolshevism, I cannot but have deep feelings about it. But my relationship to the Communists has been reduced to almost nothing. . . . Still, I believe that China is close to becoming red someday. . . . At the same time, I am uncertain whether the Bolsheviks can, in fact, avert the extinction of our nation. . . . For myself, I am not at all patriotic. It's just that I find it more convenient to live in a place where I am used to the people, where others share my language, history, and thought. So I don't especially like to see our country overrun by others who don't share our language, our history" (1).

After this bleak, self-pitying beginning, Zhang Shenfu goes on in a more optimistic vein: "I believe that if we want to change the world, we must change human nature. I am working hard toward that goal, while being aware that we do not even understand human nature. Even if China were to become like Russia politically—and human nature remained unchanged—we would be in greater danger than we are today. If we want to be truly practical today, what is most necessary is the liberation of thought [*sixiang jiefang*]. For all these reasons, I am in sympathy with you, with your fight against the dictatorship of ideology.

"I know that I tend to brag a great deal about wanting to change the world, to change human nature and, thereby, to improve society. But there is no way to improve society today except to tell the truth. In other words, one should catalog and expose all human frailities. . . . What science is doing is nothing but this. . . . You and I talk about science. But what we really mean is the spirit of the scientific method. If we wanted to give it a name, we could call this 'pure objectivity' [*danchun keguan*]" (2).

Though pure objectivity remained Zhang Shenfu's philosophical goal for the decade to come, he was unable to clarify it much beyond the vague words of the summer of 1925. Political turmoil in the realm of red dust kept pulling Zhang back to ideological polemics.

Nonetheless, the longing for a genuine liberation of thought (a slogan still in use in post-Mao China) remained strong. In 1925 Zhang reached out to Zhou Zuoren because he knew Zhou shared his distaste for simplistic slogans. Unlike his more acerbic, more famous brother, Lu Xun (canonized posthumously by Mao Zedong as a "revolutionary leader on the cultural front"), Zhou Zuoren was interested in the complex prerequisites of cultural change. In his own work Zhou Zuoren explored a new approach to Chinese literary criticism through well-crafted, sophisticated essays. Like Zhang Shenfu, Zhou Zuoren was an avid reader in the fields of psychology and psychoanalysis. Like Zhang, Zhou looked to psychology to solve the problem of human nature.

AUGUST 21, 1925. Zhou Zuoren answers Zhang Shenfu's public letter: "Security guards are already putting down student demonstrators as I write this to you. So I must disagree with you about the minister of education Zhang Shizhao. For China's sake, he must step down. . . . Now, to respond to your other concerns. Like you I am a non-Party person. I have a deep dissatisfaction with partisan politics and have kept out of all factions. If I now take a stand against Zhang Shizhao, it is out of a deeper duty to distinguish right from wrong."[8]

Then, after clarifying the difference between Zhang Shenfu and himself, Zhou Zuoren goes on to affirm their common ground: "But I agree with you, we must not be deflected from the fundamental problems of human nature. Does that mean that we talk more about sex in public? Yes, I think we should. But there are too many imbeciles in the world who will oppose us. Too many imbeciles, except Russell, of course. Take you and me, for example. How can we talk on equal footing with all those imbeciles?" (2).

MARCH 14, 1926. Eight months after Zhou Zuoren's letter, Zhang Shenfu is talking back to the "imbeciles." More specifically, he is responding to a series of articles in the Beijing newspapers that criticized his political support for Zhang Shizhao by making allegations about his common-law marriage to Liu Qingyang. Zhang's answer appears is an essay entitled "Self-Vindication": "Recently I have been staying at home and doing some reading. I was appalled to read all the nonsense about Liu Qingyang and myself. . . . These articles tried to slander my relationship with Liu and the Communist Party through an attack on personal matters. . . . It is always so in our society: if you want to insult somebody, you must make some allegations about their relationship to the opposite sex. . . . You will first want to insinuate a great deal about how they have sex and then denounce their political position.

"But to set the record straight, the relationship between Liu Qingyang and me is nothing new. It is only in China, however, that it is not possible to ac-knowledge that a married man might be in love with his lover [Zhang Shenfu's second wife was still alive and the official consort at this time]. . . . In my mind, however, sexual intercourse, marriage, and love are three different things. . . . So all this stuff about 'common-law husband' and 'common-law wife' is just plain nonsense.

"For myself, I will not deny the facts: I was a Communist. I left the Com-munist Party because I realized I am not fit for collective life. I am an anarchist and a follower of Bertrand Russell. Nobody can break my will. My refuge remains critical thought."[9]

With these words, Zhang Shenfu restates the anarchist faith he had pro-claimed in his 1920 letter to the Young China Association. But there is some-thing new in his tone. His 1926 self-vindication goes beyond the indecisive words of 1920. It also strikes a different chord than the muted, lonely letter he wrote to Zhou Zuoren in 1925.

By spring 1926, Zhang Shenfu appears to have rediscovered a capacity for righteous indignation. He acknowledges his distance from and tempera-mental sympathy for the Communist Party, in which Liu Qingyang remains a prominent activist. Then he goes on to challenge Chinese social mores directly.

Less than a year after this self-vindication, however, Zhang Shenfu's choices narrowed dramatically. By summer 1927, Zhang Shenfu was swept up in yet another wave of political mobilization. Following the breakdown of the united front between the Communist and the Nationalist parties in April 1927, Zhang fled to Wuhan to defend revolution with all his rhetorical might.

MAY 22, 1927. Zhang Shenfu writes an essay entitled "Order and Discipline" for the *Wuhan People's Daily*, a newspaper he has just started in central China.[10]

Everything has changed since the outspoken days of 1926 in Beijing: Zhang Shenfu and Liu Qingyang have been forced out of the capital by a political persecution campaign directed against Communists. They have fled to Wuhan, where the Communists and certain left-wing Nationalists are trying to patch up the broken united front. Liu Qingyang is deeply involved in Party activities as head of the local Women's Bureau. Zhang is politically prominent as the editor of the *Wuhan People's Daily*, a revolutionary newspaper funded by the local warlord Tan Zhisheng.

On this day Zhang's newspaper enters the debate about the proper relationship between revolution and social order. This is not merely a theoretical problem for the various militants crowded into a city that sees itself as the last outpost of the revolution begun by Sun Yatsen. Zhang Shenfu's essay today reflects this effort to present a mature outlook on revolution. It tries to defend the need for law and order in the face of factional warfare. The more powerful Nationalists are threatening to bury the Communists with their superior firepower and their business connections in Shanghai. For the moment, though, the soon-to-be enemies of the Communist Party are still calling themselves revolutionaries.

Zhang Shenfu, the man who proclaimed his anarchist faith a year earlier, now tries to defend the agenda of political revolution in Leninist terms: "The revolution is no revolution without order, without discipline. Revolution is not a children's game. We revolutionaries are not, and must not appear to be, gangsters. To be sure, the revolution aims to destroy the old order and build a new order in its stead. What we are after now is revolutionary order. . . . If we want order, we must have more discipline first. Discipline and Party power are mutually dependent. It is our hope that those in power at the Central Government [Guomindang] are fully aware of this."

MAY 30, 1927. Zhang Shenfu writes another lead article for the *Wuhan People's Daily*, this one commemorating the Shanghai massacre of 1925. The ambiguity of tone that Zhang had sought to inject into public debate about imperialism two years earlier is now gone. In the changed and tense circumstances of Wuhan, Zhang dwells on his grief for those killed in 1925. This commemorative essay evokes the life-and-death struggle for revolution unfolding in Wuhan:

"Today is the memorial day for the May Thirtieth movement. It is a fitting time for us to reflect more deeply on its meaning. All of us know that many of our comrades have been killed because of imperialism, have been possessed by imperialism. So, we must fight to destroy imperialism. . . . In fighting against imperialism, we have suffered great losses. But the power of the people has grown ever stronger. More recently, the course of our revolution has floundered and failed many times. Many people who were once revolutionaries have now changed over to the counterrevolutionary front.

"So many of our worthy comrades have been killed—especially Mr. Li Shouchang [Li Dazhao]. This brave and thoughtful man has also been murdered. So today we commemorate comrades fallen in battle. Our losses since the May Thirtieth incident have been great indeed. This only shows us how difficult it really is to make revolution."[11]

Two years earlier Zhang Shenfu had refused to be drawn into simplistic slogans. He had rejected the Manichaean distinction between revolutionary and counterrevolutionary. But the altered circumstances of 1927 forced him to see the world and his role in it in starker colors.

During the early part of 1927, Zhang Shenfu and Liu Qingyang had become especially close to Li Dazhao. In March they even shared his hideout in the Soviet Embassy in Beijing—where he was finally arrested on April 6, 1927. By the time Li was executed on April 28, Zhang Shenfu and Liu Qingyang had made their secret getaway to Wuhan.

But the grief over the death of this old friend from the May Fourth era weighed heavily on Zhang Shenfu. It was part of the reason why he threw in his lot with the remaining revolutionaries in Wuhan. This political alliance cost him dearly, however, as did all the others he made before and after 1927.

JUNE 2, 1927. The *Wuhan People's Daily* is publishing a defense of Zhang Shenfu. The article, entitled "An Announcement Concerning Zhang Songnian," appears on the front page without any byline.[12] The author tries to shield Zhang from the increasing vehemence of Nationalist Party politicians. This defense is a response to direct attacks on Zhang Shenfu by Chen Baoyan, editor of the government's official newspaper, *Zhongyang ribao* (Central Government Daily).

"Mr. Zhang's articles have met with extremely harsh criticism from *Zhongyang ribao*. In times of crisis such as these, all revolutionary comrades should unite in a common cause. But the comrades at the central government daily have disregarded this goal and indulged in uncalled-for attacks against members of the revolutionary camp. We believe that *Zhongyang ribao* should hold on to higher standards. We, as revolutionaries, judge it to be more appro-priate to concentrate our energies on opposing counterrevolutionaries. It will be our policy from now on to overlook opposition from the government and suggest that all comrades direct their attack on those among our enemies who are truly counterrevolutionary."

This is the last appeal from the weak to the strong. By July 1927 the Nation-alists in Wuhan broke with the Communists and began a fierce suppression of the Communist Party in Hebei province. On July 27 Comintern representative Mikhail Borodin — Sun Yatsen's old friend and the nemesis of Jiang Kaishek — is forced to leave Wuhan and return to the Soviet Union.

At the same time, Zhang Shenfu and Liu Qingyang are on the move again. In the spring they had left their home in Beijing in secrecy. Now they leave Wuhan in the same way — in haste and fear. By the end of 1927 they are in Shanghai, among other friends dispirited by the war between Nationalists and Communists. Liu Qingyang drifts further away from the underground Commu-nist Party organization and begins a new life as wife and mother.

Zhang Shenfu joins Zhang Bojun and Li Jiansheng in planning a Third Party but by the end of 1928 withdraws from those discussions as well. For the next few years, Zhang Shenfu acts out the role of the "abandoned wife." He writes about and teaches philosophy, while never forsaking a longing to reenter the realm of political revolution that had spewed him out so unceremoniously in the summer of 1927.

There is a second chance for the abandoned wife: Zhang Shenfu rejoins the revolution in 1935–36.

Paying the Price

JUNE 8, 1980. Zhang Shenfu goes over stories he has told me before. Each repetition offers me a new glimpse or adds new significance to past events. Today Zhang speaks about his friendship with the "traitor" Zhou Zuoren, about his defense of Zhang Bojun in 1957, about his support of Zhang Shizhao in 1925–26. The only connecting thread appears to be a mood — a prideful sort of self-criticism: "I am too honest, too loyal to friends for my own good. I have a compulsive honesty. I always speak my mind. Then I get into trouble."

I listen and watch the early summer shadows dance on his aged face. I wonder why Zhang's melancholy never turns into remorse. Zhang does not regret his fidelities; he only grumbles about the price paid. The complaint becomes explicit when he recalls two disparate incidents from his political life: "I have paid dearly for my political involvements. Twice I have suffered aca-demic repression. In 1924, after coming back from France, I wanted to return to teach at Beijing University. But Hu Shi, the liberal philosopher-administrator, blocked my appointment. He was dead set against me because I was a known member of the Communist Party.

"In the summer of 1936 I again lost a position. This time, after five years at Qinghua University, I was fired. My contract for a sabbatical was not renewed because I had become too prominent in the National Salvation movement against Japanese aggression. Two professors in the political science department, Zhang Xiro and Qian Duansheng, launched a campaign against my reappointment. They claimed that I was teaching politics, not philosophy.

"They pointed to my arrest in 1936 as proof that I was not sticking to my academic responsibility. True, I was arrested in February 1936. I was kept in jail until May. But the charges against me were false. The claim that I was the ringleader of the Communist Party in North China was ridiculous. But time for rational distinctions between truth and falsehood had run out. I became a casualty of the escalating events. . . . Yes, I have been denied academic positions twice, jailed once for a long stretch. And still, I don't regret what I have done."

I search the lined face in front of me. I have heard the story of his being "too honest" before. But the details of his academic persecution are new. So is Zhang Shenfu's sense of personal injury.

Can he really deny that he was more involved with politics than philosophy in the mid-1930s? Does the desire to see himself as a great philosopher cloud his recollection of political activism? Zhang Shenfu clearly does not regret his prominence in the National Salvation Association after he was fired from Qinghua. Is he just expressing a wish that he might have had academic respectability along with political visibility?

FEBRUARY 15, 1982. Zhang Shenfu's former student Zhao Lisheng is completing a memoir about his student days at Qinghua. Entitled "Zhang Shenfu as I Knew Him," this essay is a personal tribute to a man still castigated in the annals of Communist historiography.[13] The draft re-creates the first impression that the politically outspoken professor made on his students the year before he was fired from Qinghua: "In 1934 we had a choice of three logic courses at Qinghua. The first was taught by Professor Jin Yuelin. This was a straightforward introduction to mathematical logic in keeping with Western methods. There were approximately fifty to sixty students in this class. Another course was taught by Shen Youding, also on mathematical logic. Almost nobody understood the subject, so there were only three people in the class: the professor, the shadows, and me. For in truth, I was the only student who showed up for this obscure class.

"The other logic course was taught by Mr. Zhang Shenfu. It was so crowded that people were sitting all over the windowsills. The course was supposedly on logic, but political commentary comes closer to the actual subject, because

Zhang Shenfu, professor of Western philosophy and mathematical logic at Qinghua University, circa 1934. (Courtesy of Zhang Shenfu)

Zhang Shenfu spent most of the class time attacking Jiang Kaishek and the Nationalist government. It was only during the last few minutes of the class that he would suddenly teach something about formal logic.

"One day, after taking attendance, Zhang Shenfu froze in front of the class. He stood absolutely still, holding up a piece of paper: 'I got this letter today,' he says and takes out a folded paper with a drawing on it. It shows a man resembling Zhang Shenfu surrounded by police with drawn pistols. They were firing bullets. Beneath the drawing was the following message: Long Live the Third Party.

" 'Who wrote this?' Zhang asks his class with unblinking eyes. 'Please stand up.'

"No one moved. Zhang Shenfu continues in a lowered tone of voice: 'Is it because I knew Mr. Deng Yanda, the founder of the "Third Party"? But I want you to know that I had met Mr. Jiang Kaishek before Deng Yanda in Moscow. So how can you presume to decide my party membership?'

" 'I know very well who wrote this. He is right here in this classroom. He just doesn't have the courage to stand up. As for me, I want you to know I don't fear death' " (7).

The memory of this moment comes alive for Zhao Lisheng when he reencounters Zhang Shenfu in 1979. Zhang is, by this time, broken by history. His student writes the commemorative essay to evoke a once-heroic image of his teacher. But the student and teacher both know that Zhang Shenfu was no hero. The mid-1930s, though tense, were a time when intellectuals tried on many personae. The political postures were just a fragment of the "fortress

Qian Zhongshu,
one of China's
foremost writers
and literary critics,
as a student at
Qinghua University,
circa 1935. The
inscription honors
his teacher Zhang
Shenfu. (Courtesy
of Zhang Shenfu)

besieged"—a metaphor used to describe this epoch by Qian Zhongshu, another of Zhang's students and admirers at Qinghua University.[14]

Yes, he did stand his ground in 1934—as he often had before and would after. Yes, he did teach more politics than logic and was arrested and fired as a result. It was not death that hounded Zhang Shenfu, however, but the irresistible appeal of political activism. In spite of his claim that he was interested solely in pure objectivism and Bertrand Russell, Zhang Shenfu was repeatedly swept up in historic events.

A couple of months following the vignette described in Zhao Lisheng's memoir—in the winter of 1935–36—Zhang is caught up in a new wave of student demonstrations. But unlike his actions during the May Fourth movement of 1919, Zhang Shenfu this time tries to combine dialectical materialism, a love affair with Sun Junquan (president of the Women's Normal University), and a critique of the Nationalist government's response to Japanese aggression.

MAY 25, 1980. Zhang Shenfu is recollecting his role in the December Ninth movement of 1935. This is a moment of great interest to Communist Party historians who view the student demonstrations of that winter as key to a resurgence of Communist influence in national politics. Some historians have gone as far as to claim that the student demonstrations were led by the underground Party organization in Beijing and were intended to prepare the ground for a second United Front between Nationalists and Communists.

Reading history backward, these conjectures might appear reasonable enough. But Zhang is musing about more contingent aspects of the December Ninth incident. He is fully aware that other intellectuals of his generation—most notably, his Beida schoolmate Xu Deheng—have gained much by presenting the Communist Party as the leader of the December Ninth movement. Zhang also knows that there is a lot of political capital to be gained by associating oneself with Communist leaders who were students in 1935. Zhang Shenfu knew many of those students in 1935. Zhang Shenfu knew many of those students personally. In other conversations, he has spoken to me at length about Yao Yilin, Zhang Youyu, Huang Hua, and Zhang Bingnan—all powerful men in the Party now.

But today Zhang Shenfu is in no mood for politically expedient boasting. Rather, with his head thrown back to welcome the afternoon sun pouring through the lace curtain, he recalls the actual day of the demonstration in 1935. He describes to me the spontaneous upheaval that he became part of almost by accident:

"On the afternoon of December 9, I was in a coffee shop with three others. Yao Yilin was there, too. I had known he was a member of the Communist underground ever since I helped transfer some funds to him from Sun Yatsen's widow, Song Qingling. Also with us were Miss Qiu Yiqi, a member of the recently formed student association, and, of course, Sun Junquan. Sun and I were almost inseparable by then, and our love affair was almost as well known as our political association. She had played an important role in mobilizing students against the government for weeks before the massive demonstration of December 9. The Japanese had for some time been showering leaflets over Beijing, calling for autonomy for North China. Their plans for aggression were all ready. But inside China, Nationalists still warred against Communists, Chinese against Chinese at this moment of national emergency. . . .

"On the actual day of the student marches, we went to a downtown coffee shop at Xidan. There we received progress reports about the delegation from Qinghua University that was slowly making its way to Tiananmen from the outskirts of town. When we saw them come by the coffee shop, they told us about the warlords' efforts to suppress the demonstration, about the wounding of one student and the arrest of many more. People advocating National Salvation were in trouble now.

"Three days later, I was just walking down the street, minding my own business, when I was stopped and interrogated by the police. I answered: 'I am just strolling. Can't you see?' That time they let me go free. But a couple of months later, on February 29, my luck ran out. I guess I was becoming too well known in organizing a National Salvation Association.

"They came to my city address to arrest me. Then they went to my house on the Qinghua campus to arrest Liu Qingyang. My oldest daughter ran to Sun Junquan for help, but Sun could do nothing. I stayed in jail until May 7, 1936.

The only help that I got was when Liang Shuming came to visit and persuaded my jailers to remove the chains from my legs.

"Those were very hard months for me. I can still hear my jailers calling out my name loudly, harshly: 'Zhang Songnian! Zhang Songnian.' I got to hate the sound of my own name so much that after being released I never used it again. Just Shenfu, to this day."

The coffee shop outing on December 9 and the jailers' shouts, like the classroom incident recollected by Zhao Lisheng, frame Zhang Shenfu in a movie of his own making. All these moments appear in grainy black and white—so unlike the flashy reds that color the recollection of Xu Deheng.

MAY 26, 1983. I am interviewing Xu Deheng in a resonant chamber of the Great Hall of the People. The cameras of newspaper men flash around this renowned octogenarian who is recollecting his role in December Ninth movement of 1935 in my presence. Mindful of the cameras and of posterity, Xu offers a heroic painting, an enlarged canvas full of Communist heroes: "The Commander of the Red Army, you see, had distributed a manifesto as early as August 1935 calling on us to unite and fight the Japanese. I agreed with that call and mobilized the teachers and students of Beijing. We started the movement. My wife and I were in the leadership. She is from Hunan and an early member of Chairman Mao's New Citizen Society. On December 9, we led the big demonstration while the police chased after us with water hoses. But we won! Nothing can stop history!"

Distracted by the bright camera lights, I listen to Xu Deheng. He has written about his role in the May Fourth movement of 1919 and the December Ninth movement of 1935 countless times. His memory is embroidered with Party-sanctioned heroes who are absent in Zhang Shenfu's version of the event of 1935.

Unlike Xu Deheng, Zhang is willing to recall himself as a bystander swept up in a spontaneously unfolding event. Zhang is less interested than Xu in justifying the Party's version of a Communist-organized student movement. Zhang Shenfu is content to let his mind roam over discrete incidents such as the one about the Xidan coffee shop. There is no need in Zhang's recollection for the added bravura of police and water hoses.

Other aged intellectuals I know in Beijing also share Zhang Shenfu's and Zhao Lisheng's style of rambling recollection. The literary scholar Wu Xiaoling, for example—who was a Yanjing University student at the time of the December Ninth movement—also insists on a contingent version of December 9. In a conversation the day after my interview with Xu Deheng, he tells me: "The movement was thoroughly spontaneous. There was very little organization on the actual day of December 9, by Communists or anyone else. I remember we just rushed out of the building to join a group from the Furen Women's College. We took anything that was around. A hat box with a stick through it became the placard of our delegation."

APRIL 30, 1980. Literary scholar Wang Yao is talking to me about his student days at Qinghua. Today he recalls being in the same prison with Zhang Shenfu during March 1936, following Zhang's arrest for activism in the National Salvation movement: "Zhang Shenfu made a deep impression on us students. We had heard about his brave political comments in class before the arrest. But now, here he was jailed like the rest of us. He was put away for a long period of time. I was in jail with him for just a few days. I think he was kept for three months.

"What I remember most clearly is how he shared the food and blankets brought by his family with us. One cold night he put his thick coat on me, saying, 'You're young. You need it more. . . .'

"When I got out of prison, there were public meetings where students gathered to welcome us back and protest on behalf of those still held in jail. Seventeen students remained behind bars, as well as one prominent professor and his wife—Zhang Shenfu and Liu Qingyang. It made a powerful impression on all of us that a highly placed intellectual was suffering like any other ordinary student. Later, when Liu Qingyang was released before Zhang Shenfu, she addressed our student meetings with the plain words of a devoted wife. She said that Zhang Shenfu liked fried dumplings, and so she was going to take them to him every day. As for the rest of us, she urged us to keep up the fight for national salvation."

MAY 27, 1936. The *Qinghua University Weekly* publishes a lead essay by Zhang Shenfu entitled "The Meaning of Human Life." The editor's introduction points out that Zhang wrote this essay while he was in prison: "It shows that Mr. Zhang did not lose sight of the scholar's life. This leads us to admire him deeply. Even when Mr. Zhang lost his freedom, he did not give way to negative despair. Instead, he presents us with a positive understanding of human life. He shows us that life is not a blind unfolding of existence but a conscious reflection and reaction to events. For this insight we are most grateful to Mr. Zhang."[15]

Zhang himself is considerably less hyperbolic in his definition of human existence. He opens the essay with a simple question, "Why live?" The text that follows is more modest in scope than its metaphysical title. After the introduction, with his philosopher's penchant for examining words, Zhang takes apart the terms *why*, *life*, *meaning*, and *is*. From the beginning to the end, he makes it clear that life is "simply for the living." To those who had hoped for some grand counsel about the meaning of life, Zhang Shenfu writes: "Go on living for the sake of life itself, purely and simply for the sake of life" (7).

Prison simplified and sharpened Zhang Shenfu's outlook greatly: "Perhaps there are some young people who raise the question of the meaning of human life—because they are unsatisfied with life as it is, or they have run into some difficulty. The true solution to their difficulties lies in struggle, in practice, in getting a clear view of the situation around them. . . . Therefore, I say, the meaning of life does not lie outside of life itself. It can only be found in struggle. Or to put it in a few concise words, it can be found in this formula: from struggle to life"(8–9).

Zhang writes out this formula in English. He then gives a Chinese equivalent: "If you ask me once more, Why struggle? I can only answer, For the sake of struggle, that's all. To say that life is for the sake of living, that human existence is for the sake of living might be deemed inadequate, even misunderstood by some. But it is important to understand better what lies behind the word *meaning* in the minds of those who keep on asking about the 'meaning of life.' For example, if you ask, What is wind? the answer is simply an explanation of how air currents become uneven. This can be said to be the meaning of wind. And so it is with life, too. The meaning [*yiyi*] of life is nothing but the definition [*yisi*] of life.

"All the different words for life—such as *fate*, *vital force*, and the like —seek to impose meaning from outside of living itself. . . . Whether we use the English word *life* or the German *Leben* or the French *vie*, they all define life without appeal to some external force or meaning. . . . Even the distinction in English between *subsistence* and *existence*, or in German between *Dasein* and *Sein*, only underscores the point that the meaning of life lies in living itself.

"Therefore I say that the answer to the question, What is life? is simply, Life is life. . . . To be sure, one day when mathematics and science will be more advanced, one day when the structure of life itself will be more apparent, then the goal of existence will be more apparent. Then perhaps we can progress more toward its attainment"(10–11).

In jail, the forty-three-year-old professor of philosophy from Qinghua stripped his thought to stark essentials. Struggle was to become Zhang Shenfu's rallying cry throughout the war years that followed. Convinced that the purpose of life was to be found only in a definition of existence itself, convinced that China (like individuals) had no choice but to struggle for its survival, Zhang Shenfu entered the political fray once again.

In summer 1936, after being forced to resign from Qinghua, Zhang Shenfu became free to devote himself to organizing the National Salvation Association. By 1937 he was one of its chief leaders in North China and one of the main architects of a New Enlightenment movement—a revival of May Fourth ideals in the context of popular mobilization for war with Japan.[16] As war with Japan seemed more inevitable, Zhang Shenfu became convinced that philosophy found its ultimate calling in national resistance. Enlightenment—an elusive goal of intellectuals since the May Fourth movement of 1919—now appeared on the verge of fulfillment on a mass scale.

War: An Opportunity for Philosophizing?

JUNE 11, 1981. We are nearing the end of our conversation about philosophy and politics. Zhang Shenfu has just made an impassioned appeal that "politics must never influence philosophy." I challenge him by pointing out the obvious: "You have been involved in politics all your life. You often justify politics with your philosophy. In 1928 you wrote about Sun Yatsen and logic—as if Sun's words were the culmination of philosophical wisdom. During the anti-Japanese war you wrote countless essays about war and philosophy—as if they went together naturally, as if they complemented each other."

Zhang Shenfu looks away from me for a moment. Is he recalling other times when his philosophy became impure in the realm of red dust? The pause is not long enough to catalog all the political movements he has been a part of or all the essays he has written in response to a particular political movement that seemed to need philosophical justification. When he looks back at me, his response is simple: "Well, I still believe that philosophy must not be influenced by politics. But politics, of course, cannot help but be influenced by philosophy."

APRIL 15, 1980. A conversation with Feng Youlan, Zhang Shenfu's colleague at Qinghua in the 1930s. One of China's best-known philosophers, Feng has also been treading his own difficult path between politics and philosophy. This visit has been difficult to arrange, because my host is still tarnished by political association with the so-called Gang of Four. Though Feng Youlan's house is less than two minutes from my dormitory on the Beijing University campus, I have been refused permission to see him many times on the grounds that he is "not well." Today's conversation has been arranged, finally, through some writers who are friends of Feng's novelist daughter.

Feng Youlan is almost the same age as Zhang Shenfu and is well preserved in his own way. Wearing a woolen cap, the robust old man faces me with clear, sharp eyes. Though his hearing is not greatly impaired, he is slow to respond to my questions. And even slower still to open up about his own views on the relationship between politics and philosophy.

Given the tense circumstances that surround this visit, there is no point in asking Feng Youlan how he was appointed by Jiang Kaishek as Teacher of the Nation during the war against Japan. There is even less likelihood that Feng will answer questions about his conversion to Marxism or his association with Maoists during the anti-Confucian campaign of the early 1970s.

I know that some intellectuals have labeled Feng Youlan *fengpai* (a follower

of the winds), a disparaging term for a thinker. It suggests the lack of an independent stance during a rapidly changing political climate.

The octogenarian in front of me has survived repeated waves of criticism
and persecution. I know it is premature to talk about the costs of survival. So
we talk about safer subjects: his philosophical training under John Dewey at
Columbia University during the May Fourth period and his leadership of the
philosophy department at Qinghua during the 1930s. Feng Youlan knew Zhang
Shenfu well in this later period, having recruited him into the department and
having contributed frequently to Zhang's newspaper column "Trends in World
Thought."

By 1936–37 the two men drifted in different directions. Feng Youlan stayed
at Qinghua after Zhang Shenfu was fired. He continued to work on Confucian
humanism, whereas Zhang moved closer to dialectical materialism. Feng became known as the chief proponent of *rensheng zhexue* (humanistic philosophy)
—a philosophy centered on the *whys* of existence. Zhang, by contrast, was
swept up in a different struggle. In 1937, when Zhang Shenfu became a cham-
pion of the New Enlightenment movement, Feng Youlan showed no signs of
interest. Today he tells me why: "Mr. Zhang Shenfu always had a more exalted, or rather, more utilitarian view of philosophy than myself. In my view,
philosophy has always been of very limited social use. In this, I have been very
different from Mr. Zhang. He was always convinced that life is better if it is
lived philosophically.

"The New Enlightenment movement was his way of spreading this creed far
and wide. But I always sensed a certain arrogance behind the movement—in
its determination to bring enlightenment and philosophy to the masses. I, by
contrast, believe that philosophy is to be found everywhere that there is human
life. Everyone has his or her own philosophy of life, and individuals do not
need any high and mighty philosopher to tell them so."

This is not the first time I hear about Zhang Shenfu's arrogance. Nor is it the
first time I am faced with an intellectual survivor who eschews his own compromise with politics by pointing to the world-sullied views of another. Still,
Feng Youlan's comments cast new light on Zhang Shenfu as a wartime philosopher. Through the eyes of a fellow professional, Zhang's philosophical
messianism now appears to be the result of choice and temperament, not simply of political necessity.

MAY 25, 1938. Zhang Shenfu has just published his essay "The Necessity
of Wartime Philosophy" in a new journal called *Wartime Culture* (*Zhanshi
wenhua*), of which Zhang is the editor. As in Wuhan in 1927, Zhang has obtained outside financial support—this time from Chen Cheng, chief of the
political department in Jiang Kaishek's Military Affairs Commission. Now that

China is officially at war with Japan, the Nationalists and the Communists are collaborating in a united front once again. Whereas Jiang Kaishek and the Nationalists were counterrevolutionaries before, they now assume the mantle of leadership in war-torn China. Zhang Shenfu, in turn, feels safe and secure in using Nationalist funds for his publication efforts.

Zhang's opening editorial statement in *Wartime Culture* makes it clear that the magazine has a distinct mission: "to prove that culture can and should be made into a powerful weapon in the war against Japan."[17] His essay on wartime philosophy justifies the new magazine's purposes on yet another level. It argues that philosophy in particular—not just culture in general—is a necessity in the current war effort: "The necessity of wartime philosophy is twofold: first, in terms of common sense and, second, in a more specific sense of the word. First, as commonly understood, philosophy teaches people to have an expanded sense of the universe. It endows human existence with a more noble perspective. It gives people an ideal for human experience by cutting through the problem of life and death, by forcing one to abandon the limited view of self-preservation. All this is a necessity in wartime."[18]

After this exalted definition of philosophy—one that put off professional philosophers, such as Feng Youlan—Zhang Shenfu makes an appeal to science: "Second, in the more specific sense of the word, wartime is a period in which extraordinary action is required, a time when a realistic view is essential. A philosophy of struggle during wartime can provide this by encouraging insight and realism.

"Philosophy as it is commonly understood is something that everyone has, something that everyone can understand. Philosophy in its specialized sense is a form of scientific critique. Modern philosophy, especially of the analytical school is indistinguishable from critical analysis itself. Ordinarily, philosophy is understood to be concerned with the fundamental questions of human experience. But more deeply understood, philosophy contemplates fundamental problems through a certain method—most noticeably, critical analysis."

Having warmed up to scientific philosophy, Zhang Shenfu now goes on to introduce his current faith, dialectical materialism: "Dialectical materialism may be considered one form of this scientific analysis. Philosophy, then, is the self-consciousness that lies beneath all learning. Those most knowledgeable about philosophy tend to be more self-conscious in their actions as well. And conversely, only a self-consciously lived existence can be considered a truly philosophical one."

Finally, lest all this appear too abstract, too remote to readers threatened by Japanese bombs, Zhang Shenfu adds: "Today is a time when we fight for final victory in the anti-Japanese war. We fight for the successful establishment of the nation. This is a time when all must be willing to sacrifice themselves for the people, for the country. . . . To do this, everyone must be able to see beyond the present, beyond oneself, and act in keeping with a higher ideal. For this we must have wartime philosophy—a concrete philosophy, a concrete educational policy, a culture that fosters science, the scientific method, and the scientific temperament. This is the most urgent task of the day" (23).

The ideology advanced in this essay bears out what Feng Youlan emphasized in our conversation in 1980: Zhang Shenfu was determined to use philosophy to uplift China. He was determined to spread enlightenment in order to promote self-sacrifice among the masses who had to endure and to win the war. Zhang's was indeed a messianic view of the philosopher's calling.

Zhang Shenfu was convinced that his salvationist creed was a scientific response to historical circumstances: by 1938 China had been at war with Japan for a full year. The central city of Wuhan was about to fall, and the Nationalist government about to move inland. A Nationalist politician from the War Office was financing Zhang's journal. Wartime philosophy was therefore to be Zhang Shenfu's contribution to the motherland in her hour of need.

What Zhang tended to overlook in all this, however, was his fatal attraction to the realm of red dust. War excited Zhang Shenfu; it promised to speed up a process of enlightenment that philosophers like himself had been working for since the May Fourth movement. War promised to solve the problem of the meaning of life that Zhang had confronted in 1936 while in jail. Before the outbreak of war, life was lived for the sake of living. Struggle was its means and end. With the onset of war, however, life appeared to acquire new, lofty moral ideals. War offered Zhang Shenfu a new opportunity for concrete philosophizing. He proceeded to position himself in a way that would take advantage of this great opportunity which, in keeping with his faith in dialectical materialism, he insisted on calling a necessity.

APRIL 10, 1939. Zhang Shenfu publishes an essay entitled "The New Enlightenment Movement and the New Life Movement" in the Chunqing edition of *Wartime Culture*.[19] The war and Zhang Shenfu are both one year older than when he set forth his initial, optimistic wartime philosophy.

After the fall of Wuhan, Zhang Shenfu tried, without success, to make his way to the Communist-held areas in the northwest. Intellectuals such as Chen Boda and Ai Siqi—who had been allied with Zhang Shenfu in 1937, during the heyday of the New Enlightenment movement—had already reached the border areas held by Mao Zedong. In 1939, unable to join them, Zhang had no choice but to head toward the Nationalist base in the southwest.

In Chunqing, the wartime capital of Jiang Kaishek, Zhang Shenfu had to adjust to new political realities. Chen Cheng, the patron of his magazine, remained on the Guomindang's Military Affairs Commission. Now, however, the commission needed more propaganda and less philosophy. Zhang Shenfu's essay of April 1939 is meant to satisfy this demand, while seeming to fulfill his own agenda for wartime philosophy. He is interested in a New Enlightenment movement that might spread critical, scientific analysis among the masses. Jiang Kaishek, on the other hand, is promoting the New Life movement in order to revive the old Confucian values of loyalty and obedience. Jiang wants to make the masses more subservient to the Guomindang Party and its wartime leader.

Zhang's task in the 1939 essay is to convince himself that the New Enlightenment movement and the New Life movement are identical in spirit and in goal: "The New Life movement advocated by Mr. Jiang and the New Enlightenment movement are, in their essence, not only compatible but identical. The most obvious point of convergence is that the New Life movement emphasizes science. This is precisely the most important requirement of the New Enlightenment movement.

"Mr. Jiang made this amply clear when he said how much he valued the spirit of science. In his own words, he stated: 'The basic meaning of the scientific spirit is to search truth from facts.' Mr. Jiang also states that the New Life movement must start from ritual [*li*]. But ritual, in turn, must accord with human nature, which is inherently rational. Therefore, I believe not only that ritual is an appropriate guide to human nature but that it has the same function as reason itself."

In identifying scientific reason with Confucian ritual Zhang Shenfu was distorting his hopes for a critical wartime philosophy. For a brief moment in 1939 it appeared as if Zhang was willing to overlook the major philosophical and political differences between Jiang Kaishek and himself. Zhang did not like Jiang when they first met in Moscow in 1923. But now there was little he could say against Jiang publicly. The year 1939 was gloomy, and Zhang responded with extreme, almost self-corrupting realism. He knew that the war against Japan was not going well for the Nationalists. Financial support of any kind was difficult to obtain and maintain in Chunqing. *Wartime Culture* was a way to stay alive. When a new source of support became available, Zhang Shenfu promptly returned to a more critical definition of wartime philosophy.

MAY 7, 1942. Zhang Shenfu is publishing an essay called "Science and Democracy" in *New China Daily*, the Communist-sponsored newspaper in Chunqing.[20] He is back in close contact with his old friend Zhou Enlai. Zhou is now the chief Chinese Communist Party representative in the Nationalist area for the duration of the war with Japan.

It was Zhou who found Zhang Shenfu employment with the Communist newspaper and who sanctioned a special weekly column on science to be edited by Zhang Shenfu. Now, on the occasion of the twenty-third anniversary of the May Fourth movement, Zhang reaffirms his old faith in science and democracy.

Once again, Zhang feels free to be critical of the Guomindang and is convinced that critical, scientific philosophy is of use in wartime China:

"Today China faces several challenges: outwardly, we face the challenge of the United Front and the war of resistance; inwardly, we must implement democracy. In all matters of education and thought we must promote a genuinely scientific outlook. This is the only genuine alternative for China. But some people continue to advocate a dictatorship for China without realizing that this undercuts the war effort and the future of China. In other words, if there is no democracy, there can be no popular support. Naturally, dictatorship cannot maintain itself in such conditions."

Having argued that democracy is possible, indeed necessary, in wartime China, Zhang goes on to science: "Furthermore, today's era is the era of science. Without science there is no way to carry on the task of national construction. Science and democracy are the two crowning achievements of Western civilization. There are also, by now, great goals recognized by everyone. In China, science and democracy began to be advocated during the May Fourth movement of 1919. They are still relevant—in fact, they are even more urgent now. Today China needs science to be genuinely democratic. Science needs to be full of progressive ideas that help the vast majority of the masses. In science there are no class distinctions, because everyone is equal. Science does not slight labor. Hence, in science there is no distinction between manual, skilled, or automated work."

Finally, having argued that science is a life tool for the masses, Zhang Shenfu comes back to his favorite subject—the link between democracy and philosophy: "Democracy, in turn, must be made more scientific through philosophy. Democracy cannot live where ignorance holds sway. Like science itself, democracy depends on reason. Simply put, science and democracy are the mutually independent, inseparable goals of philosophy. Both are needed in the war of resistance and for the sake of national construction. The formation of science and the implementation of democracy are the preconditions for carrying out the united front and the war of resistance."

In 1942, under Communist patronage, Zhang Shenfu is able to return to his more critical definition of scientific philosophy. In his 1939 essay Zhang had tried to identify his own philosophical outlook with that of Jiang Kaishek—all in the name of a loose concept of science. In this 1942 editorial for the *New China Daily*, however, he restates the old May Fourth link between science and democracy.

Jiang Kaishek did not have much interest in or tolerance for democracy. The Communists, by contrast—especially those stationed in the Nationalist areas during the anti-Japanese war—found it very useful to appeal to democracy. It gave them an opportunity to legitimate themselves, to get ready for a role in the postwar period. Zhang Shenfu, too, was useful. Like other critically minded intellectuals in Chunqing, he challenged the dictatorship of the Guomindang in the name of philosophy and the legacy of May Fourth.

For Zhang Shenfu, the Communists' newspaper and the personal friendship with Zhou Enlai offered a way out of a crippling dependence on Jiang Kaishek's subordinates, such as Chen Cheng. With a new source of livelihood and the reconciliation with Liu Qingyang (after breaking away from Sun Junquan and Dong Guisheng), Zhang Shenfu was ready to address old political issues in a new context. He became active in the nascent Democratic League and turned his philosophical attention to the shape of Chinese politics after the war.

Unfinished Business: Democracy

JUNE 9, 1981. We are looking over one of Zhang Shenfu's favorite photographs—a group gathering from November 1946. Zhang has showed me this picture before. Whenever he wants me to understand how close he was with Zhou Enlai and his wife, Deng Yingchao, after the war years in Chunqing, Zhang appeals to this fragment from 1946. Today I see another reason for Zhang's attachment to this photograph: it shows him in the center—a tall, striking figure—while Zhou Enlai and Deng Yingchao fade off to the far left.

"Those, those were exciting days for me! Without doubt, those were some of the most exhilarating months of my life. I had just gotten back to Beijing for the first time in eight years. No sooner did Liu Qingyang and I arrive back home from Chunqing in March 1946 than I began to fly back and forth to Nanjing to plan for the opening of the first National Consultative Conference.

"I was one of the main leaders of the Democratic League. I was rather prominent at the time. When I made statements about the future of China, about the need for constitutional government, reporters would come, listen to me, and print my words."

Having drifted away from the photograph in front of us, Zhang now returns to it with agitation: "Look, look at us, so full of hope for a peaceful resolution of the conflict between the Communists and the Nationalists. Here we are, all gathered together on the eve of the first National Consultative Conference in November 1946. The civil war still seemed avoidable then. Look, there are Zhou Enlai and Deng Yingchao looking so youthful. The short, Confucian gentleman in the long robe and long beard is Shen Junru, a legal scholar and prominent member of our Democratic League. I am wearing a heavy wool coat and stand next to my old friend Zhang Bojun. It was cold in Nanjing in November 1946."

Forty years later, in 1986, following Zhang Shenfu's death, the same photograph—much enlarged—hangs in the National History Museum in Beijing. I see it during a visit to an exhibition dealing with the history of the

Leaders of China's democratic parties on the eve of the first National Consultative Confer-
ence, Nanjing, November 1946. *From the left*: Zhou Enlai; Zhou's wife, Deng Yingchao;
Zhang Bojun; *fifth from left*, Zhang Shenfu; *center*, the bearded Shen Junru. (Courtesy of
Zhang Shenfu)

Democratic League—the first public presentation of the league's history since
1949. Now, ten years after the death of Mao, it is possible to acknowledge that
other political forces, such as the Democratic League, helped bring the Chinese Communists into power. Now that peasants and workers are no longer
seen as the sole moving force in history, a wide assortment of intellectuals is
being retrospectively rehabilitated.

The main criterion for rehabilitation in 1986 remains support for the Communist cause. At the entrance of the exhibit, this point is hammered home
through a large, contemporary oil painting that shows Zhou Enlai in intimate
communion with two old-fashioned gentlemen who were unfailing friends of
the Chinese Communist Party—Shen Junru, the legal scholar in long robes
who had passed the imperial exams, and Dong Biwu, an early associate of Sun
Yatsen and the Guomindang.

In contrast to this vivid evocation of an idealized past, the November 1946
photograph looks drab. It has none of the ardent colors of the modern painting.
It is framed with a photograph of the building that served as Communist Party
headquarters in 1946. The single caption that unites both images suggests that
the gathering in November 1946 took place at the Communist headquarters just

Contemporary oil painting of Zhou Enlai (*left*), Dong Biwu (*center*), and Shen Junru (*right*), leaders of the pro-Communist Democratic League. This painting was shown in 1986 at the National History Museum as part of the first exhibit dealing with the Democratic League after 1949. (V. Schwarcz)

before the departure of Zhou Enlai. Zhang Shenfu's name is mentioned in a list that starts with Zhou Enlai, from left to right.

For Zhang Shenfu the November 1946 photograph stood apart—the last glimpse of himself in the company of those who sought to shape the future of China. He had seen himself as central to that mission and had expected to play a significant role as a patriot in the national consultative process.

By 1946, however, the beginning of the end of that hope was already in sight. Zhang liked to recollect his active months flying back and forth between Beijing and Nanjing. But the National Consultative Congress that opened in Nanjing on November 15, 1946, was already a doomed affair: the Chinese Communist Party and the Democratic League boycotted the meeting set up by Nationalist authorities. On November 19, 1946, Zhou Enlai flew back to the Communist base in Yan'an. This signaled the collapse of the negotiations and the beginning of civil war. During the civil war, Zhang Shenfu remained central only in a worn-out photograph. And still he nurtured his own vision of what democratic politics *should* look like after the war.

OCTOBER 6, 1945. Zhang Shenfu is completing a two-page essay entitled "Logic and Politics" for the newly established magazine *Democracy*. Started in Chunqing by a May Fourth intellectual, the educator Tao Xingzhi, this publication aims to become the main organ of the Democratic League. It takes pride in publishing position papers by such prominent speakers as Zhang in the months following the war with Japan. In this first month, Zhang is eager to bridge philosophical logic with the urgent task of national construction: "The task of modern logic is to develop some lofty hypotheses for mankind. Naturally, different social groups under different historical conditions will develop varying hypotheses. Philosophy can put forth the loftiest notions about the human condition precisely because it takes as its task the development of the loftiest hypothesis about the activity of all humankind."[21]

As China struggles to make sense of the destruction of war, Zhang Shenfu offers his old May Fourth creed, dressed in a new, dialectical garb: "Scientific philosophy is particularly relevant under such conditions. In encourages a dialectical mode of thought that clarifies cause and effect and their mutually independent relationship. In society, too, there must be similar conditions for unification. National solidarity and the implementation of democracy are the premises needed for the postwar government. Without such preconditions, a united national government cannot be established."

Then, as if science in general were insufficient, Zhang makes yet another appeal to logic: "Modern logic can make a particularly useful contribution in furthering the cause of national construction because it is a scientific method that diminishes misunderstanding among various groups. Modern logic is extremely clear and open-minded. It encourages a habit of thought that does not hide anything but tries to verify everything" (5).

Although the war had just ended, Zhang Shenfu is clearly mindful of the coming conflict between Nationalists and Communists. He senses and tries to respond to the fragile peace that has dawned upon China in 1945. For the moment, he uses his prominence as a philosopher of logic to affect the political discussions within the Democratic League.

Zhang Shenfu's friend Zhang Bojun is also writing about democracy in 1946. Zhang Bojun's essay "National Unity and Democracy" appears in the same issue of the new magazine as "Logic and Politics." It restates Zhang Shenfu's sentiments but without philosophical flourishes, without the arrogant certainties of modern logic. Though the two men continue to be allied in a subdivision of the Democratic League known as the Worker-Peasant Democratic Party, their paths have started to diverge: Zhang Bojun becoming more active in and more pragmatic about politics, and Zhang Shenfu more and more philosophical, almost messianic about the mission of intellectuals.

MARCH 10, 1947. Zhang Shenfu has finished writing "The Livelihood of the People," a long essay that evokes one of the three cardinal principles of Sun Yatsen: people's nationalism, democracy, and people's livelihood. Zhang reminds the current Guomindang leaders that the legacy of their founding father remains unfinished and that much remains to be done to improve the people's livelihood in the postwar period:

"The anti-Japanese war ended a year and a half ago. But our country's people are still looking forward to the hoped-for but unrealized good days. Although many people talk endlessly about the livelihood of the people, few really care about it enough to take it truly to heart. Then there are those who have no time to think about the people's livelihood at all. All they care about is how to keep a firm hold on their own position of power. Some of these people are in the most powerful places in our country today. So we must put into practice the Chinese people's unique talent for self-restraint. But self-restraint has a limit, like our patience. We cannot be forbearing forever. So those in power should seriously consider what is to be done about the livelihood of the people."[22]

After these critical remarks addressed to the ruling party Zhang Shenfu goes on to do what he likes best—to give political advice: "If you want to improve the livelihood of the people, the first thing to do is to return to peace, then proceed to abolish the privileges of the comprador bourgeoisie and set our country's economy on a solid foundation of independence. To insure genuine peace in the nation, there is one immediate need, which can be summarized simply: implement democracy. This includes the democratization of politics and of economic life as well."

To eliminate all doubts about the simple rationality of his advice, Zhang Shenfu adds: "Every Chinese person understands the reason for our nation's backwardness. Everyone can see that we cannot go on as before, that a backward life is no life at all. So everyone must change the old outlook, put down arms, and recover spiritually. We need genuine freedom to develop the nation. We cannot have a few people be the ruling power of the nation. Rather, we must pool our wisdom and help one another toward active modernization."

By the time Zhang Shenfu published this essay, the Democratic League had been declared illegal by the Nationalist government. Zhang's ardent plea to open up the political process fell on deaf ears—on both the right and the left. Even as Zhang Shenfu tried to revive Sun Yatsen's concerns with national unity and balanced economic development, the Guomindang was preparing for war against the Communists.

In spite of Zhang Shenfu's one-man effort to pull back the Nationalists and the Communists from the brink of civil war, his call for a return to peace came just as the guns were loaded for their bloodiest battles. In the Democratic League factional struggle ripened to the point of internecine war. A power struggle for leadership in the Beijing branch of the league raged on between Liu Qingyang and the young historian-playwright Wu Han. Zhang Shenfu, of course, was associated with Liu and suportive of her. He too was bruised in this struggle.

And still, Zhang Shenfu continued to hope that reason would prevail. But the situation was deteriorating into violence and demagogic propaganda.

JULY 1948. Zhang Shenfu retreats somewhat from his faith in reasoned political discourse in an essay entitled "On China's Alternative."[23] Published both as a magazine article and as the lead essay in a privately printed booklet, this work presents Zhang's last effort to prescribe a solution for China's ills: "In the past six months, there has been a great deal of discussion about liberalism, about the middle path between Communists and Nationalists, about the problem of intellectuals. But there has also been much confusion, much muddled thinking that caused misunderstanding among various points of view.

"My own point of view is that we must do everything possible to end the present situation of national disaster. To accomplish this, we do not need liberalism—since it starts, all too often, with simple self-interest. Rather, we must struggle to implement democracy with its three preconditions: freedom, equality, and cooperation.

"It is also my conviction that there is only one real alternative in China today: revolution. Our current era is a revolutionary era, an era of science and democracy. Thus, only a revolutionary approach suits the current situation. Only a revolutionary approach will bring about a solution to our social and political problems"(1–4).

To make these vague proposals more concrete, Zhang adds: "I also believe that the middle classes, though not very active politically, must be protected, and their economic interests secured. Intellectuals, too, have a bright prospect in this revolutionary era—especially those who understand the trends of the time and are able to catch up with and shape future change. The intellectuals who are most precious at the moment are those who not only are experts in their field but can also make significant contributions beyond their own self-management."

In his conclusion, Zhang insists: "Intellectuals derive their knowledge from objective reality. There is no distinction between intellectual and manual labor. Therefore, intellectuals who are aware of this will identify with the laboring masses and will serve the people."

This point of view echoes Communist propaganda. But Zhang Shenfu is either unmindful of this or doesn't care: "The only alternative for our time, the only alternative for the nation, is to keep pace with the people, to advance on the road of revolution. This is also the only alternative for intellectuals, the only kind of life possible in the future"(13–14). Within three months of this call for revolution, Zhang Shenfu was attacked as an enemy of the revolution and of the people.

The proximate origins of his undoing may be found in summer 1948. At that time Zhang began to drift away from revolutionary camp—even though he was convinced that intellectuals had only one choice: to ally themselves with the revolution. By the end of that summer, most of the important members of the Democratic League had fled North China for Hong Kong. In this British colony, out of the reach of the Guomindang, leftist intellectuals called for the inevitable: a "people's victory." Realistically, they knew this was to be a Communist victory on the mainland.

The statements from Hong Kong sounded no different from Zhang Shenfu's, but they had the sponsorship of the Communist organization that was to assume power in China. Without such backing Zhang Shenfu, who had stayed behind in Beijing, faced the last month of the civil war more or less alone. By September 1948 Liu Qingyang had also left to cross the border into the Communist-held area of Shi Jia Zhuang.

Zhang Shenfu ended 1948 as he had started his political entanglement in the realm of the red dust: calling for revolution in a righteous and rational voice all his own.

6

FINAL REGRETS,

FINAL RETORTS

"Sometimes we have to wait for years," said Reb Tain, "before the minute which marked us finds its voice again. But then it speaks, and we cannot stop the flow of words."
—Edmond Jabès,
The Book of Yukel

SEPTEMBER 18, 1989. I have returned from a conference with other China scholars, where we debated the significance of what happened in Tiananmen Square. Troubling questions about the role of intellectuals in politics emerge in the wake of the Beijing spring and the June 4 crackdown. I am increasingly suspicious of the political ends to which the May Fourth movement of 1919 was put on the eve of its seventieth anniversary in China. Young students and seasoned intellectuals alike used the past to give themselves overly heroic personas in the present. To my mind, the unacknowledged echoes of the Cultural Revolution of 1966–69 were ignored in the form of euphoria about the event of 1919. The intellectuals' movement degenerated once again into mob politics. This devolution is an old dilemma for China— and for Zhang Shenfu.

Privately, I have been reassured about the safety of my friends in China. But in public, the merits of the student movement and the reasons for the Chinese government's cruel repression go unresolved. The cultural roots of Deng Xiaoping's autocracy remain obscure as I return to my work on Zhang Shenfu.

How can I justify this project at this time? I keep returning to Zhang Shenfu because he, unlike the vast question of autocracy in China, is a concrete puzzle for me. Our conversations are as vivid in my memory as the blood is on the streets of Beijing. Through the prism of those conversations I now try to understand China's convulsive reaction to intellectuals like Zhang Shenfu. His story, for me, foreshadows the tragedy in Tiananmen Square.

JUNE 2, 1980. The first day of summer is near as I round the corner from the White Tower Pagoda to Wang Fu Cang Lane. Zhang Shenfu waits for me at the open window. He has traded winter wool for a dark blue cotton jacket. It buttons to the side, mandarin style, and is cut long over blue trousers still puffy with long underwear.

Today I come to talk about how Zhang joined the Communist Party in 1920. But he drifts back to Liu Qingyang and ends up dwelling on the reasons for their separation in 1948. The more Zhang Shenfu recalls his love affairs and Liu's injured pride, the more regretful he becomes: "I wasn't quite fair to her, you know. She had been generous with me ever since our days in Paris. She cooked pork for me in spite of the fact that she was a Moslem. . . . I had done much to anger her during my affair with Sun Junquan, and later in Chunqing when I lived with that student, Dong Guisheng. . . . Still, maybe we could have worked all that out, if I had not written that one article in 1948. One act of foolishness snapped our thirty-year bond!"

"One foolish act?" I repeat, with a change in intonation. Zhang looks at me and registers my smile of disbelief. We had, after all, talked often before about their long separation in Chunqing, about the tension between Liu Qingyang's pragmatic politics and Zhang's ceaseless effort to rethink the foundations of human nature.

"Well, maybe not one single article. But that piece in 1948 is one of the few things I really regret about my life. That and my withdrawal from the Communist Party in 1925. I could have found perhaps other, less impulsive ways to express my views. Imagine, just imagine what my life would have been like if I had not been cast out of the rank of so-called revolutionaries! Ah, but what is the point of such regrets? And anyhow, I was always incapable of keeping my mouth shut. I have always said just what I think, no matter the consequences. I seem incapable of political conniving."

"Yes, yes, this old man is still full of foolishness," adds Zhang's wife, Guan Suowen, who has come in a few minutes earlier. She always joins us toward the end of the afternoon and appears particularly irritated when she hears the conversation move back again to Liu Qingyang. Being less attractive, less educated, less of a public woman than Liu, Guan has never reconciled herself to the special place her predecessor still holds in Zhang Shenfu's heart.

I now turn to Guan Suowen and expect the usual—some snippet of information that puts Liu Qingyang one peg below her, like last week's morsel: "Liu started out with bound feet, you know! I am the only one of Zhang's wives to be truly modern. I always had natural feet, you see."

But today Guan has a different tale: "Yes, yes, this old man cannot keep his mouth shut. He can never play by the rules of the game. Just last week, you see, they had a meeting of the Workers-Peasants Party. And he was as disobedient as ever. When everybody got up to talk about Chairman Mao, to weigh Mao's contribution to the revolution, this one here refused to call him chairman. That is sure to be noticed, you know. And can cause trouble still."

Zhang Shenfu laughs out loud, with the trace of contempt that greets most of Guan Suowen's comments to me. But he does not contradict the story, as he has done often before: "Yes, yes, I never could tow the line. Why start now?"

Zhang Shenfu's Foxtail

JUNE 9, 1981. I have been back in China only one week, though it seems longer. Because of our daily visits, Zhang and I are moving quickly through the details of his life. We have already cleared up much about his years in the Communist Party before 1925. Today we are up to the 1940s, circling the climax that changed his life—the circumstances behind one essay, "An Appeal for Peace," published in October 1948. This essay unleashed vehement Communist criticism against Zhang. For the first time, in the winter of 1948–49, he was called "an enemy of the people." This foreshadowed the name calling of the 1950s and 1960s. Though Zhang had strayed from the ranks of the Party many years earlier, it was only in 1948 that he was cast beyond the pale.

Today we near this sore point. I do not ask why but, rather, how he came to write the 1948 article. Zhang Shenfu adds bits of information that I did not know before: "I got paid three thousand yuan for that one article, you see. It was quite a lot of money in those days. Professors were not getting their salaries. Starvation was rampant; everyone had a food problem. Qu Anping, editor of the magazine *Guancha* (The Observer) in which my article appeared, was a very well known, very respected figure during that time. When he approached me about writing a piece for him, how could I refuse? His magazine had the largest circulation among the democratic-minded magazines of the time. And it paid authors immediately upon delivery of the manuscript. I think I was one of their highest paid contributors in 1948."

"You want to know more about Qu Anping? about *Guancha*?" Zhang says, reiterating questions I have asked. "Well, I knew Qu's reputation as an outspoken journalist of considerable integrity. He had edited a literary supplement for the Guomindang during the war in Chunqing. We traveled in different circles then—he with literary types like Liang Shiqiu, I with Zhou Enlai's group around *Xinhua ribao*. After the war, he settled in Shanghai, I in Beijing. He taught at Fudan University and started *Guancha*. I became involved with the struggle in the North China branch of the Democratic League.

"Our paths crossed briefly, when I submitted that article in 1948. Yes, I needed the money. But I also had a chance to make a point against the government of Jiang Kaishek. *Guancha* had been under attack by the Guomindang throughout 1948. They even accused Qu Anping of aiding the 'Communist bandits.' Such unfair accusations—only with slightly altered labels—would be heaped again on Qu Anping, Zhang Bojun, and me during the 1957 antirightist campaign. One has to wonder what, if anything, has changed over time.

"Anyway, in 1948 all those campaigns against us were yet to come. But Qu's magazine was already beginning to feel the heat because it published information about the government's losses during the civil war. Everyone was so weary of that war. Things looked especially bleak to me, stuck as I was in the capital in North China. So I wrote 'An Appeal for Peace.' A few months earlier the Communists themselves [who were losing battles in the civil war] had made such appeals. What I had no way of knowing was that the tide of war had turned in the countryside. The Communists were doing better and wanted to fight on for victory. A few weeks and a few hundred miles divided my article from the Communist view of the war."

OCTOBER 23, 1948. Zhang Shenfu's "An Appeal for Peace" appears on the front page of *Guancha*—the leading essay in an issue dedicated to the origins of the civil war and to news about the situation of civilians in the urban centers.[1] The issue has no cover sheet. The hasty, artless look of the magazine bespeaks its political persecution by the government. Time is clearly running out—with several warnings of suppression already given. Zhang Shenfu's word choice for the title ("Hu yu") evokes an ancient call to action. It is a rallying cry addressed to fellow intellectuals as well as a plea addressed to the menacing Guomindang.

Predictably, Zhang's essay opens with a logical, localized argument for peace: "Our most urgent task right now, negatively put, is to destroy the present. More positively, it is to restore peace. If the war is not promptly and legally ended and peace rapidly restored, it is quite certain that the entire nation—or at least the population in the northeast and North China plain or, more specifically, in the cities of the northeast and the North China plain—cannot survive. Then our country will have been drained of its existence. Our last bit of integrity will be gone, thrown out, wasted" (1).

The seeming logic of "if A then B" does not quite convey the urgent cry of an intellectual worried about the imminent demise of his nation. The grief and pain, however, are there—right beneath the logic. And by the second paragraph, grief, pain, and logic give way to self-blame. Zhang's appeal, it now becomes apparent, is a call to conscience for fellow intellectuals. He appeals to a diminishing audience. Most of his political colleagues in the Democratic League have already left Beijing for Hong Kong or the interior. So Zhang's words seek out the few remaining "book readers" (*dushu ren*).

With this old-fashioned term for intellectuals (who, by the 1940s, were calling one another by the more common term *zhishi fenzi*, literally "knowledgeable elements"), Zhang tells book readers left in the Nationalist areas: "We have made a big mistake. We have failed to distinguish between what is true and what is false. We have been incapable of realizing what can succeed and what is irretrievably lost." Then Zhang Shenfu elaborates his own vision of how the civil war can be ended and peace restored. He offers a characteristically simple formula:

"What I advocate here is a slogan that is openly acknowledged by everyone in the nation. That is, 'Democracy, Peace, Unity.' The order of these slogans is telling: First there must be democracy—only then can there be peace. First there must be peace—only then can there be unity. In other words: with democratization, there will be peace. With peace, there will come unity. I believe that circumstances today must necessarily follow this order. . . . To be sure, in appealing for peace, in calling for the restoration of peace, we are calling for a genuine peace, a long-term peace, a peace that is truly for the sake of the nation, for the sake of our people.

"Chaos cannot put an end to chaos. Revolution cannot put an end to revolution. If both sides claim to be warring for the sake of peace, this only serves to confuse the situation, to make matters more dangerous all around. If both sides want peace, then warring must stop immediately. No side should continue to fight!" (2).

Zhang's article appears alongside other essays on the current state of the civil war, all of which share his conviction that the nation wants peace, that war must end. Zhang's first essay differs because it is more impassioned, less mindful of the actual details of the war than the other essays, which are full of news items about Guomindang losses and atrocities.

None of the essays in this October 23 issue of *Guancha* dwells on the rapid pace of Communist victory. None reports the October 15 seizure of Jinzhou, a major city in Manchuria, by the Peoples Liberation Army (PLA). Zhang Shenfu's essay, in particular, does not mention the capture of one hundred thousand Nationalist soldiers in Jinzhou. In fact, on October 19, the PLA had taken Changchun, the capital of Chilin province. And on October 23—the day that Zhang Shenfu's "Appeal for Peace" appeared in *Guancha*—the PLA occupied Zhongzhou, capital of the central Chinese province of Henan.

An intellectual who presumed to speak to and for the book readers of the nation thus ended up misreading the winds of war. Calling for peace, Zhang tried once more to use logic to persuade a nation and a government about to enter the final conflagration of civil war.

Two months after the publication of "An Appeal for Peace," *Guancha* was shut down by a government order that accused the journal of "continued attack on the policy of the Nationalist government," of "ridiculing the army of the government," and of "making propaganda for the Communists and troubling the spirit of the nation."[2] Zhang Shenfu had also "troubled the spirits of the nation." Because of his October 23 essay, he had the dubious honor of being singled out for attack by members of his own Democratic League.

NOVEMBER 15, 1948. The Hong Kong–based central committee of the Democratic League expels Zhang Shenfu from membership. There are echoes here of the February 1923 meeting in Billancourt, France, where Zhang Shenfu had been expelled, in absentia, from the Chinese Communist Youth Party.

In 1948, as in 1923, a radical coalition of intellectuals far from Zhang Shenfu casts him out and disowns his role as founding father. But there is a new twist to this expulsion. In 1923 the Comintern had forced the Youth Party to revoke its decision and to reinstate Zhang Shenfu. In 1948, by contrast, the force behind the group in Hong Kong—the Chinese Communist Party—took power on the Chinese mainland in 1949. With this victory, the Hong Kong verdict remained in effect. Over time, it acquired the weight of unquestionable truth.

The record of the November 15, 1948, meeting in Hong Kong has been preserved in the Democratic League archives. Brief and schematic, it opens with a simple statement: "Zhang Shenfu, a member of our League, having violated our political principles several times, is now dismissed from membership." Two simple reasons are listed in the paragraphs that follow:

1. On January 2, Zhang Shenfu signed a statement about upcoming elections for the legislature in the *World Daily News* jointly with certain Guomindang reactionaries. . . . This is tantamount to admitting that the puppet Nationalist government and the Nationalist Constitution are legal.

2. In his article "An Appeal for Peace," published recently in *Guancha*, Zhang Shenfu accepted the so-called constitutional government of Jiang Kaishek. Thereby, he supported Jiang's principle of political suppression and slandering of the People's Liberation Army as bandits.

As can be seen from Zhang Shenfu's actions and words, he has now taken the antipeople, antidemocratic road. Therefore, in keeping with the political principles and established procedures of the Democratic League, we expel him from our alliance.[3]

Established procedures were ill defined in the midst of the Chinese civil war. Both in Hong Kong in 1948 and in Billancourt in 1923, Chinese intellectuals were literally inventing procedures. In both settings they tried to keep up with what they perceived to be a revolution at hand.

The major difference between 1948 and 1923 is the growing propensity for political name calling. In 1923 young students in Europe did not like Zhang Shenfu's haughty, "autocratic" ways of telling them what to do, and they said so. By 1948, however, Zhang was being attacked in the name of the sacred, transcendent authority of the people. Having been declared "anti-people" he became a nonentity. Dehumanized, he became dispensable.

Here in Hong Kong, half a decade before the antirightist campaign of 1957 and almost two decades before the Cultural Revolution, intellectuals began to label one another with names that would mean imprisonment and death for many of them after 1949.

DECEMBER 16, 1948. The *People's Daily*, the Communist Party's official newspaper, is publishing a lead article headlined "The Democratic League Gives Voice to the Current Situation," followed by "The League reaffirms its determination to struggle for democracy by dismissing such servile sellouts as the traitor Zhang Shenfu."[4]

In one month Zhang Shenfu has gone from being a local enemy of the people to being a nationally proclaimed traitor. The *People's Daily* underscores the escalation of the charges by expanding the ranks of Zhang Shenfu's accusers. Now it quotes the most prominent members of the Democratic League —the old Confucian gentleman Shen Junru and Zhang Shenfu's own friends, Zhang Bojun among them. Zhang Bojun and Shen Junru are portrayed as the leaders of the campaign to purge Zhang Shenfu's "traitorous influence for the sake of the democratic struggle."

After an initial report about the internal struggles of the Democratic League, the *People's Daily* goes on to elaborate its own version of what makes Zhang Shenfu a traitor: "Now that the Nanjing-based autocratic clique cannot hold on to any important cities, now that it begs for help from the United States, they have made so-called scholars like Zhang Shenfu publish appeals for peace. Although Zhang Shenfu was once a member of the Democratic League, he now defiles the people's liberation war as an irrational risk. His published appeal for peace supports the authority of the Nanjing government by asking it to become more constitutional, less militaristic. By doing so Zhang Shenfu revealed his true face."

As if this were not enough, the *People's Daily* goes to link Zhang's "sins" to the national crisis at hand: "In sum, a democratic China cannot exist until the reactionary rule is eliminated. A peaceful new China cannot exist until the source of civil war and all obstacles to peace are wiped out. If we try to reconcile with the enemy, we will never achieve permanent peace but only help them to recover from their failures. Therefore, all those who want to stand on the side of the people, all those who are truly patriotic, should share these same principles. Only those who want to serve the reactionaries have a different point of view."

Thus, by December 16, 1948, the sphere of acceptable points of view had narrowed to one: that of the soon-to-be victorious Communist Party. Although the article about the expulsion of Zhang Shenfu still claimed to speak in the name of the Democratic League, in the name of intellectuals like Shen Junru and Zhang Bojun, the iron fist inside the democratic glove was unmistakable.

For the moment, though, Zhang Shenfu—who was living, writing, and teaching in unliberated Beijing—was untouched by the vehemence of the *People's Daily*. On the other hand, Liu Qingyang, who had moved into the Communist-liberated areas with her children one month earlier, had no such freedom.

On December 26, ten days after the article labeling Zhang a traitor of democracy, the *People's Daily* carried, on the back page, a divorce announcement entitled "Zhang Shenfu betrays democracy, makes war on behalf of tigers: Liu Qingyang Reprimands Severely": "According to Hong Kong sources, Liu Qingyang wrote a letter to the Democratic League pleading with Shen Junru and Zhang Bojun to express her urgent rage at how Zhang Shenfu's thought had sunk so low as to betray the standpoint of the people. In this letter she states her intention to break all private and public relationships with Zhang Shenfu."[5]

Breaking relations became a common practice during the antirightist campaign of 1957–58 and during the Cultural Revolution of 1966–69. To save oneself, to prove that one was truly on the side of the people, spouses and children would repeatedly break family ties after 1949. Liu Qingyang was among the first to feel the burden of this demand on the eve of liberation. In denouncing her common-law husband and lover, she dutifully restated all the accusations against him as traitor, enemy of the people and accomplice of tyrants, or as the *People's Daily* vividly put it, as the "servile head of vicious tigers."

LATE WINTER 1948. Demonology continues to thrive in Hong Kong. Zhang Shenfu continues to remain the chief villain in an essay by the writer Meng Chao entitled "Zhang Shenfu's Foxtail."[6] One of the founders of the short-lived Sun Society in Shanghai in 1928, Meng has been making a name for himself in left-wing literary circles through acerbic essays about the evils of life under the Guomindang.

For a brief period during the anti-Japanese war, Meng Chao moved in the company of dramatist Xia Yan and experimented with pure literary theories in a journal called *Wild Grasses*. By 1948, however, Xia Yan and Meng Chao had to prove their left-wing credentials all over again. Attacking Zhang Shenfu served this purpose. Eighteen years later, during the Cultural Revolution, Meng Chao himself would be attacked as a "vicious promoter of poisonous weeds."[7] In 1948 Meng had begun the process of hurling political accusations against a fellow intellectual with the following words: "Whenever revolution develops rapidly, the devils who have been hiding within the ranks of the people's revolution expose themselves. During such times, they cannot cover up their foxtails any more. This is precisely what is happening now. Just as the people's army is winning one glorious victory after another, a searchlight forces Zhang Shenfu to expose his real self. The people can now see plainly the banner that he has been holding up all these years. His 'Appeal for Peace' is an apt confession. The disguise of democracy has finally fallen off, revealing his true, traitorous identity."[8]

In the name of the people, Meng Chao goes on to assail Zhang Shenfu's concern for the fate of the urban population victimized by civil war: "Zhang Shenfu uses the untenable situation of the people's lives in the Guomindang areas to spread a poisonous gas among us. Although he uses vague words, it is clear that he wants to shore up the stability of the reactionary regime, to give the reactionaries a chance to fight back. But the people's power today is a hundred times greater than that of the Guomindang, and their days are numbered. Zhang Shenfu is thus pouring cold water on the revolutionary fire, even though he fails to say so directly. Although it is true that the final goal of revolution is peace, the traitor Zhang Shenfu is not willing to admit the logic that only when the reactionary government collapses will there be genuine peace."

Knowing the tools of intellectual discourse well, Meng Chao accuses Zhang of being too skilled at this business: "Zhang Shenfu talks about the people, but really he is just a tool of the reactionaries. He has special weapons, soft ropes, and a knifelike tongue. He writes shamelessly about the need to distinguish right from wrong, success from failure. But he confounds black and white by denying the crimes of the reactionary regime. He claims to preach 'Democracy, Peace, and Unity,' but he denies that the reactionary regime is an obstacle to all of these. Now that U.S. imperialists like Ambassador Leighton Stewart manipulate backstage while Guomindang officials and generals sit up front, Zhang Shenfu is not giving a solo performance. His is a duet, or rather a trio. Peace will come only after the fall of the reactionary regime, after we set up a new Consultative Conference—one that will not include thugs and traitors like Zhang Shenfu."

Finally, as if sensing that this murderous indictment of one of his own kind might bring blame on all intellectuals, Meng Chao adds: "Maybe some people will start spreading rumors that there is now a divergence in the revolutionary ranks since we are liquidating Zhang Shenfu from our camp. This is no concern of ours. This kind of liquidation is nothing but a healthy activity that reinforces the solidarities developed during the anti-Japanese war—when we got rid of another traitor, Wang Jingwei. Now we expose Zhang Shenfu's foxtail and drive him out to his true masters"(45–46).

Twenty years later the Cultural Revolution in fact tried to liquidate the intellectual class. But Meng Chao's 1948 essay shows how early the process actually began. Once named a traitor, an intellectual was no longer human. He was sentenced to figurative—then later, actual—death.

DECEMBER 1, 1948. In Beijing, far from the *People's Daily* and his accusers in Hong Kong, Zhang Shenfu publishes his last article before the Communist's final victory of October 1949. A premonition that this may be the swan song of independent-minded intellectuals leads Zhang to title this essay "Reason and Madness."[9] It appears in *Free Criticism (Ziyou pipan)*—one of the last journals of nonpartisan opinion published in Beijing after the suppression of *Guancha*.

Free Criticism had already risen to Zhang Shenfu's defense one month earlier. In a long, investigative article on the history of the split within the Democratic League, the magazine tried to prove how faithful Zhang Shenfu had been to the original aims of the organization founded in February 1941.[10] This essay detailed Zhang Shenfu's leading role in the National Salvation groups that were brought into the democratic alliance in 1943. It also exposed the controversies that had riddled the loose alliance of small groups and parties since 1946. The split within the league was attributed to the war between the Nationalists and the Communists and not to Zhang Shenfu's ideas.

To clarify the controversy, the article gave Zhang Shenfu the last word in defending himself against the charges that led to his expulsion on November 15, 1948: "I am not surprised by this decision, nor do I give it undue importance. I know Shen Junru and Zhang Bojun to be respectable and reasonable intellectuals. Others in Hong Kong are not that way at all. Such a decision must have been reached only when Shen and Zhang were not present. In appealing for peace, I tried to promote the case of democracy. Although this is almost impossible in the present circumstance, I must keep on trying. Ever since I joined the revolution at the age of eighteen, I have been faithful to my own beliefs—that cannot be changed by any pressure from opportunists."

One month later, in December 1948, Zhang Shenfu's self-defense took a different form. By then he no longer cared to clear his own name. Rather, he joined in an effort to salvage the philosophical reputation of his mentor, Bertrand Russell.

Zhang Shenfu's December 1948 article is oddly narrow and cool-headed. It is, on the surface, a simple defense of Bertrand Russell, who had been labeled a bourgeois idealist by young, self-styled dialectical materialists in the Communist Party. Zhang Shenfu rallies to Russell's cause and thereby makes his most impassioned defense of rationalism:

"The most precious thing in the world today is reason and the most dangerous is irrationalism. And yet, madness is far more popular in the modern world than reason. Now, everyone who is well read should know that Russell is a thinker who ardently supports rationality. To be sure, his statement that dialectical materialism is the God of Soviet Marxists was not exactly reasonable. Nonetheless, we should not deny Russell's great contributions to rationalist philosophy

because he once scolded Soviet Marxists. Genuine philosophy cannot be suppressed, killed, or done away with, in spite of ill-founded criticism of Russell
by dogmatic dialectical materialists."[11]

By defending Russell and rationality Zhang Shenfu made a last effort to
clear his own name. In the final months before Communist victory, he tried to
preserve a space for critical thought in a world torn by guns and dogma. When
he said that genuine philosophy could not be killed, Zhang was expressing a
hope. He wanted to persuade himself that thought as such might be spared
during the coming liberation. The events of the 1950s and 1960s, however,
proved him wrong.

Ninety-Five Percent Correct

JANUARY 21, 1980. I have been coming to Zhang Shenfu's house every two
weeks since our first meeting in the National Library in November 1979. This
month he has invited me to come more often, because I am getting ready to
leave for Hong Kong. Zhang has let me know that he wants some books, especially volume two of Russell's autobiography. "I want to hear the man's story
from his own mouth. Other versions, like the Clark biography I have read, are
full of distortions."

The closer we get to the people who matter to him personally, the more
animated Zhang Shenfu's conversation becomes. He is most excited when talking about Bertrand Russell, Liu Qingyang, and mathematical logic. But once
in a while, Zhang delivers himself of bits of political rancor. Today, a most
poignant unburdening: "I have been politically repressed you know. The pain
of political repression [zhengzhi yali] has been great for me. . . . But not just
for me. The whole nation has suffered as well. . . . They have prevented me
from saying anything or publishing anything since 1949. . . . Mao held a personal grudge against me all these years. He never forgot that I once scolded him
when he worked under me at the Beida Library during May Fourth. After
liberation he went around telling some people that 'Zhang Shenfu is insuffer-
ably bossy.' He could never forgive or forget the fact that once I made him
rewrite a bunch of acquisition cards. A petty, vengeful man. And so, I have
been silenced and repressed."

I look at the wrinkled face, at the sparkling eyes half hidden by afternoon
shadows. The features might tell me more than what I am hearing. The words,
though spoken with deep feeling, don't quite jibe with what I know, with what
both of us know. Zhang Shenfu did write some things after 1949. So I ask: "But
what about the essay you published last spring commemorating the sixtieth anniversary of the May Fourth movement? That was one of the ways I found out that
you were alive, one of the clues I used to trace you at the National Library."

"Oh that! That was just a little, insignificant piece. The first time I could say something publicly in thirty years!"

"But weren't you made a rightist in 1957? What was the reason for that? You must have said something in public to earn that label, to become the subject of a public campaign against you."

"Oh, I suppose I did say some things in public—I can't remember what anymore. They were rounding up victims by the hundreds. I was swept up in the process. And all that because I allowed myself to be dragged back into politics by my old friend Zhang Bojun. I met him in the street in 1957, and he invited me back into the Workers-Peasants Party. I couldn't refuse and so ended up in the same trouble as him."

JUNE 7, 1981. Our first private conversation since my return to China four days ago. The warm welcome that greeted me at Zhang Shenfu's birthday celebration yesterday carries over into our conversation today. I have kept my promise to come back, and Zhang is clearly grateful.

Yesterday, in the presence of his friends and family, he was shining with pride when he received my gift—a copy of the index-card file annotating each of his articles that I have collected over the past three years. The overflowing delight in having some of his past recovered did not, however, blind him to the pain that covered the eyes of Li Jiansheng. As she fingered the index cards, Li kept murmuring: "There is not even half of this left from my husband's writings. His name remains sullied. Zhang Bojun remains [even in the more tolerant era of Deng Xiaoping] one of the four big criminals of 1957."

With Li Jiansheng's face fresh in mind, with the cards now stacked in front of us on the little table, I ask Zhang Shenfu about the 1950s. Contrary to what I heard and thought a year ago, Zhang was not totally silenced in the 1950s. I show him two entries—the short article from 1955 about the writer Hu Feng and a longer article from 1957 on the May Fourth movement.

"It is embarrassing, you know, to even look at that junk from 1955. It comes from a reign of terror against intellectuals. I did not know much about the literary critic Hu Feng. He was made a symbol, a warning to us all. No one was allowed to stay on the sidelines of the movement to condemn his bourgeois thought. They came to the National Library and pretty much requisitioned that piece from me."

"The 1957 article—now, that is altogether different. I remember that one well. I had just come out of the hospital after a long illness. It was spring and a new breeze of freedom was blowing through the political world as well. I joined in those discussions because I really believed that the spirit of May Fourth, the spirit of liberalization, was finally coming to fruition in China. But I was wrong. That is exactly what got me in trouble. When everyone was

attacking Zhang Bojun in June 1957, I spoke up for him. I said that his suggestions for political reform were not all wrong. I went so far as to say that they
were 95 percent right. . . . Well, that sealed my fate. I was made into a rightist."

JUNE 7, 1955. Zhang Shenfu publishes a two-column, essay in *Guangming
ribao*, the Communist Party newspaper directed at intellectuals. It is entitled
"Wrongdoers Filled with Ten Thousand Evils Such as Hu Feng Must Be Severely Punished." The newspaper identifies the author not only by name but by
institutional affiliation as well: "Beijing National Library Research Fellow
—Zhang Shenfu."

   This is Zhang's first public statement since 1949. A man who had been the
target of vicious name calling seven years earlier is now forced to add his voice
to yet another anti-intellectual campaign. In 1955, as in 1948, demonology
prevails. Here, too, a script is being dictated to prominent intellectuals. Mutual
incriminations are forcibly published under the intellectuals' own names. In
1948–49 Zhang Shenfu's lover and friends were writing about the need to
"severely punish the traitor Zhang Shenfu." Now Zhang is forced to use almost identical language to pillory as reactionary and bourgeois the poet-writer
Hu Feng.

   In 1948 Zhang had been relatively untouched by acrimonious labels because
he was far from Hong Kong. The Chinese political world was falling apart in the
last months of the civil war, and no one yet had the power to make the labels stick,
to extract blood for them. By 1955, however, everything had changed. China
was united and intellectuals were forced to follow the one voice of the Party.

   Zhang Shenfu was still safe. One of the most influential Communist leaders, Beijing's mayor Peng Zhen, had helped Zhang get a job in the National
Library. In 1949 Peng—who had come to know and respect Zhang in 1936
during his underground work with patriotic students and professors in Beijing
—warned Zhang Shenfu against going back to teach philosophy at Beida.[12]
With the Democratic League's name-smearing campaign still in mind, Peng
told Zhang to expect only the same if he returned to his old alma mater. The
National Library was a low-profile refuge that gave Zhang Shenfu a chance to
be near his beloved books all day.

   In the heat of the nationwide campaign against Hu Feng, however, not even
the National Library was safe. The winds of repression touched Zhang Shenfu
as well. What began as the purge of one intellectual, who had dared to suggest
that Marxism might best be understood through concrete experience rather than
through enforced political study, now blossomed into a full-blown reign of
terror against all intellectuals. Everyone had to be whipped into line. All intellectuals had to expunge from themselves the bourgeois tendencies supposedly
embodied in Hu Feng.

Zhang Shenfu greeting an old friend, Peng Zhen, former mayor of Beijing and recently rehabilitated leader of the Chinese Communist Party, in 1985. Behind Zhang Shenfu stands his youngest daughter, Zhang Yanni. (Courtesy of Zhang Yanni)

Zhang Shenfu had managed to stay out of the campaign through most of the winter and spring of 1955. But by June his position as senior research fellow at the National Library required him to display a "correct attitude":

"After reading the three sets of materials about the Hu Feng counterrevolutionary campaign, one cannot but feel the kind of rage that shakes man and heaven alike. . . . Especially from the third set of materials, we can see how many of those in the Hu Feng gang are evil spies sent by the United States and Jiang Kaishek. This is not surprising. Hu Feng's gang has been counterrevolutionary all along. They only pretended to be progressive artists, Marxists, revolutionary writers. In fact they are so evil as to be hardly considered human at all. For the sake of our people, for the sake of democratic power, and for the sake of socialist construction we must ask that Hu Feng and his gang be punished ruthlessly."[13]

Having waited until the last possible minute—until the third and last set of materials about Hu Feng came out in summer 1955—Zhang Shenfu is, finally, drawn in to the fray. He discharged his duty with this minimal piece of writing, though it did not give him peace of mind. An intellectual who had been called everything from a conniving foe to a vicious tiger, Zhang is now forced to join the chorus denying the humanity of Hu Feng and his so-called gang. A man who has known what it is to be falsely accused of being a "reactionary in the service of Jiang Kiashek" now has to smear another Marxist with similar labels.

It is no surprise, then, that Zhang Shenfu responded with unbridled enthusi-asm when the climate for intellectuals appeared to change in spring 1957.

APRIL 27, 1957. A major essay by Zhang Shenfu, entitled "Develop the Spirit of May Fourth: Open Up," appears in the *Guangming ribao*. In this newspaper managed by his old friend Zhang Bojun and edited by Qu Anping —the man who inadvertently opened the floodgate of criticism against Zhang Shenfu in 1948—Zhang speaks his mind once again.

Zhang Shenfu's essay on the spirit of May Fourth appears as the main article in a special column dedicated to the Hundred Flowers campaign. "Let a hun-dred flowers bloom, let a hundred schools contend" is a slogan used by Mao Zedong to sanction more intellectual debate. It enables Zhang Shenfu to make yet another impassioned plea for intellectual pluralism.

From May 1937 onward, Zhang Shenfu had used the commemorations of the May Fourth movement of 1919 to develop his political commentary. He wrote essays to advance his ideas about intellectual emancipation in China: One essay, published in May 1937, had advocated new enlightenment and the advancement of critical thought among the masses. In May 1942, during the Sino-Japanese war, Zhang's commemorative essay returned to the subject of an unfinished enlightenment movement. In May 1948, just a couple of months before the debacle occasioned by an "Appeal for Peace," Zhang Shenfu and Liu Qingyang, both contributed articles about May Fourth to the Beijing University journal.[14] In all these essays, as in 1957, Zhang argued that the spirit of May Fourth lay in one word: *fang*, literally, to open up. Zhang's call for pluralism during the civil war, however, had a different connotation after 1949, when one-party rule was institutionalized in the People's Republic. Not surprisingly, Zhang began his 1957 appeal for intellectual emancipation with a required tribute to Communist Party chairman Mao Zedong: "These last few days, the weather has warmed up a great deal. And just at this time, too, I have come out of the hospital after a long illness. Now I find that although my contacts remain few, the newspapers tell me that the [political] climate is quite different as well.

"With the weather warming up, with my illness healed, with the political climate more airy, how can one not feel elated? How can one avoid feeling truly happy? Last year, too, I became excited when I heard about the call 'Let a hundred flowers bloom, let a hundred schools contend!' For a while, from July to September [1956] people were warmed up by the climate of discussion. Then a cold current blew once again.

"In the current Hundred Flowers, Chairman Mao has said that we should not hold back. This is like a spring thunder that releases the warm currents once again. Anyone concerned with the fate of our nation cannot but appreciate the wise leadership of Chairman Mao."[15]

Having paid the expected tribute to the Party chief who had the power to set the temperature for the nation's intellectual climate, Zhang Shenfu presses beyond Mao's words. He recalls having been prevented from publishing an article on the emancipation of thought in winter 1956. Then, with rancor put aside, he describes the reasons for China's intellectual backwardness:

"China's march toward science has not been easy. We have not reached a high level of achievement in the sciences because we have not dared to do what it takes: look up to intellectuals, take good care of them and let them speak their minds freely. . . . We know from Chinese history that learning flourished most during the so-called Hundred Schools period. This was similar to the situation in ancient Greece and other Western countries. Whenever the Hundred Schools were crushed, learning declined as well. This happened in China after the Han dynasty and in Europe during the Middle Ages."

Zhang Shenfu's concern, of course, was not intellectual history in general, or even the development of Chinese science. Rather, he wanted to present his own views in the current debate about the fate of Chinese Marxism. More precisely, he wanted to probe the reasons for its dogmatic stagnation: "Marxism itself should be developed through discussion and on the basis of our own concrete situation. Vigilance in ideology is necessary, but we must not become oversensitive. Confucius understood this and so does Chairman Mao. . . . Taking all this into account, there should not be any limits on what people say or think. Because Marxism is in a leadership position in our country, and because we are in favor of genuine openness, it is harmful for certain leaders to use one stroke of the club to destroy those people who just open their mouths to speak. Don't be afraid! Neither the people nor the leaders should be afraid to speak their minds!"

From Marxism, Zhang Shenfu jumps to praise his favorite official of the day—Luo Longji, a senior leader of the Democratic League: "For the past half a year I have found the speeches of Mr. Luo Longji on the problem of intellectuals most clear. Mr. Luo talks about the ancient scholars [shi] and their passive way of helping to administer the nation by 'cooking small dishes.' His point is that these scholars failed to recognize that they themselves were being cooked in these small dishes. Traditionally Chinese intellectuals who did not cooperate with authorities practiced passive resistance. Today's intellectuals, however, are learning how to resist more openly. And I believe that there is nothing that should not be open to debate. As long as our speech is not against the constitution, we should be free to say anything."

At the end of his article, to protect himself against the eventuality of yet another cold wind, Zhang Shenfu added: "Maybe all this strikes people as too naïve. Not having been out of the hospital very long, I have been dazzled by the bright new light. I have not yet accustomed myself to many things outside. If my words are inadequate, I ask for special forgiveness."

Forgiveness is precisely what Zhang Shenfu did not get in summer 1957. After the brief spell of tolerance that warmed China in April 1957, Mao Zedong launched the antirightist campaign. It all began to unravel with a June 8 editorial in the *People's Daily*, in which outspoken proponents of intellectual and political liberation, most notably Luo Longji and Zhang Bojun, were accused of being rightists. They were labeled as criminals who sought to overturn the rule of the Chinese Communist Party.

A year and a half of debate about pluralism ended in bitter disappointment. Zhang Shenfu, having been forced to add his voice to the 1955 campaign against Hu Feng, knew that the charges of political traitorship now being heaped on critical intellectuals were also false. He was powerless to turn back Mao's tide. But he could, and did, speak his own mind this time.

JUNE 14, 1957. The *Guangming ribao*—the same newspaper that welcomed Zhang's essay in April—now carries a long front-page editorial entitled "Draw a Clear Boundary Against Rightist Elements." In unequivocal words the editorial urges intellectuals to redeem themselves by thoroughly repudiating the "Luo Longji–Zhang Bojun reactionary clique." These two are labeled the most evil of the rightists. Nine years before the Cultural Revolution made the disowning of one's family and friends a criterion of political virtue, the editorial states: "Anyone who upholds socialism, anyone who is a genuine patriot and who is a true friend of the Communist Party must now draw a clear, unequivocal, unfeeling boundary against the rightist elements."[16]

On page 2, the newspaper features an article about a June 12 meeting that began to purge the leadership of the Workers-Peasants Party. The title, printed in the same bold type as the editorial, is "Many People Criticize Zhang Bojun's Erroneous Thought." The subtitle, more modest in display, adds: "Zhang Shenfu puts forth a different opinion stating that Zhang Bojun did not commit a fundamental error."

Below these titles are six long columns dedicated to comments that prove how Zhang Bojun's proposals for political reform were intended to overthrow the Communist Party's democratic centralism. Near the end, the article includes one short paragraph on Zhang Shenfu: "Zhang Shenfu said that Zhang Bojun tends to speak out a bit too carelessly, that he tends to speak without adequate reflection. He said that Zhang Bojun's position is not 100 percent correct, only 95 percent correct. In reference to Zhang Bojun's suggestions for setting up institutions for political reform, Zhang Shenfu said that this is a proposal still worth considering."[17]

Nowhere in Zhang Shenfu's long political career was he so obviously out of step with prevalent currents as at the June 12 meeting. Faced with the demand by the Communist Party that intellectuals save their own skins by condemning

exemplary reactionaries like Luo Longji and Zhang Bojun, Zhang Shenfu refused to comply. He used hard, bitter irony when he declared that in public
memory Zhang Bojun was "not 100 percent correct."

"Only 95 percent correct" sealed Zhang Shenfu's fate as a rightist, but it
also enabled him to keep faith with his deepest convictions. Zhang had managed to tell the truth as he saw it. This has been his core creed from the May
Fourth period onward. By July 1921, while in Paris, he had already written an
essay entitled "Tell the Truth!" In it, Zhang Shenfu argued that China needed
to found a "Truth-Speaking Party," at the very moment when Mao Zedong and
his colleagues were inaugurating the first Chinese Communist Party Congress
in Shanghai.[18]

By 1957 the Communist Party founded in Shanghai, which never valued
truth telling very much, seemed to have an open aversion to it. The Party now
demanded that intellectuals lie, especially about their own values and capabilities.

The requirement that intellectuals incriminate each other and themselves
grew more acute in summer 1957. On July 15 both Luo Longji and Zhang
Bojun delivered abject self-criticisms. Luo, the thinker whom Zhang had written about so enthusiastically in April, was forced to accuse himself of every
possible crime against the people and the Communist Party. The very defense
of intellectuals that so appealed to Zhang Shenfu in the early spring was a
source of guilt by the summer: "It is true," Luo wrote, "that I was sympathetic
with the intellectuals and that I had always wanted to speak a couple of good
words to make them happy. This was the root of my mistake."[19]

Zhang Bojun's confession, entitled "I Bow My Head and Admit My Guilt
Before the People," was even more self-deprecating than Luo Longji's because
Zhang's political mistakes were assumed to be greater: "I am an offender guilty
of serious political mistakes. . . . With all my heart I accept and thank you for
the denunciations and exposures in the last few days. They brought to light my
absurd words and actions. . . . I have a deep feeling that in reprimanding and criticizing me, the people of our country are rescuing me and are giving me a chance
of rebirth. I wish to express my heartfelt thanks once again to the whole nation."[20]

Zhang Shenfu refused to join in such rescue efforts as long as possible. In
the end, he too was made a rightist, though he never became such a prominent
people's enemy as his old friend Zhang Bojun. Unable to say anything in public, Zhang Shenfu returned to his library work. The next wave of anti-intellectual
frenzy—the Cultural Revolution of 1966–69—found him as reluctant as ever
to incriminate himself and others.

JUNE 16, 1980. Zhang Shenfu and Li Jiansheng are laughing as they recollect their political foibles. The late afternoon sun casts dancing shadows over
the tired eyes of these two old friends who now recount for me the "foolish-

ness" that led them to hope for an independent Third Party after the outbreak of White Terror in 1927. They are asking themselves aloud what impels intellectuals to continue speaking out when the power of the gun and of autocratic parties is so much greater than their "puny voices."

The talk about puny voices leads me to ask about the Cultural Revolution. Zhang Shenfu leans his head back, without the customary gurgle of laughter this time. He looks away before he answers me: "I had it pretty easy during those years of terror. Nothing but a few months of enforced living at the library offices where the Red Guards interrogated me endlessly. It wasn't so bad at all when I compare my fate to that of others. Bojun, my friend, died of an untreated illness during those years of cruelty."

Zhang casts a gaze of pity toward Li Jiansheng. Then he goes on: "My old friend Liang Shuming was beaten over and over again. Red Guards came to his house, forced him to kneel, and whipped him. They burned his books. I tried to visit him whenever possible. He was such a broken old man."

Zhang's last words bring Li Jiansheng back to life somehow. She comes out of her silent grieving and starts to tell me with an animated voice: "You see, that is Zhang Shenfu's true character. No matter how outcast a person may be, he will not disown his friends. He was that way with me and Bojun.

"I'll never forget an early spring day in 1958 when we ran into each other across the street form Beihai Park. I had grown accustomed to most people crossing to the other side when they saw us coming. But not Zhang Shenfu. He made a point of walking toward us, to shake Bojun's hands warmly, to ask about his health and mine. You cannot imagine the comfort of that gesture in those cold, cold days."

AUGUST 15, 1986. I am back in the conference room of the Beijing National Library. Seven years after I first met Zhang Shenfu here and two months after his death, I am meeting with four of his colleagues. Zheng Jiaoxun is the oldest among them and has known Zhang Shenfu since the late 1910s. Li Deming, the next most senior man in the room, was Zhang Shenfu's assistant and secretary from the early 1950s on. In front of me are seated Huang Dengpei and Cai Xiangming, two young researchers who were assigned to library work just before the outbreak of the Cultural Revolution in 1966.

To my surprise, these very different men have all agreed to share with me their recollections of Zhang Shenfu. Perhaps his recent death and the positive official verdict on his life have loosened tongues held silent for two decades.

Zheng Jiaoxun talks first and most easily about his early association with Zhang Shenfu: "I got to know Mr. Zhang quite well in the Sturm und Drang [*Kuangbiao zhoukan*] literary society in Shanghai. Zhang Shenfu used to submit articles on Russell and Wittgenstein."

Li Deming is introduced next as the "son of an eminent botany professor with a Yale Ph.D." Mr. Li is considerably more reserved than the others. I wonder if this is because—as I have learned from Zhang's daughter earlier in the day—Li was involved in accusing Zhang Shenfu as a rightist in 1957.

I try to ask Li Deming about his recollections of the mid-1950s: "Let's just forget that. Let's not dwell on those tangled times. We have come to pay homage to Mr. Zhang. . . . My deepest, most enduring impression of him is that he was so well qualified for his library job. He could read so many languages and knew books so well."

The two young men, Cai and Huang, are the liveliest and talk the longest. In 1965 Cai was assigned to the library's German department, Huang to the English section; both worked in "close, daily contact" with Zhang Shenfu during the year before the Cultural Revolution. Now they trip over each other in the rush to tell me how the Cultural Revolution "taught us so much about Zhang Shenfu":

Cai: "I never heard about Zhang Shenfu until I was assigned here and then not very much until the Cultural Revolution broke out. Then, suddenly, there was an outpouring of materials, posters detailing the activities of this quiet, efficient old man."

Huang: "Yes, yes, we knew almost nothing about Zhang before the Cultural Revolution. Of course, we would have liked to ask. But no one on the staff dared to tell us about him, because he was condemned as a rightist. Some of the older people around here surely must have known about his accomplishments, about how he introduced Premier Zhou Enlai into the Communist Party in Paris. But no one told us a thing."

Then Huang goes on: "As members of the Red Guard, you see, we were involved in gathering documents about Zhang Shenfu. When we began to interrogate him and read his self-confessions, we began to learn about the man for the first time. It was a strange way to learn, to be sure, but I did. I learned more about philosophy and political developments before 1949 while attacking Zhang Shenfu than in my entire education before. . . . I remember most vividly a part of his diary we put up on posters. This included an imaginary conversation with a woman. Even in those years, Zhang Shenfu seemed wrapped up in his own world and did not give a damn about anyone."

Cai: "When it was all over, I remember Zhang Shenfu sending me a big bunch of cards listing the books he thought the Library should acquire. Even in the last days of the Cultural Revolution he rummaged through the old booksellers in Beijing. Whenever he saw something he thought we needed, he would write up a card. That is why our collection on philosophy is one of the best in the world—all because of Zhang Shenfu."

SEPTEMBER 21, 1967. With Red Guards looking over his shoulder, Zhang Shenfu is completing the final draft of his self-criticism entitled "My Education, Professions, and Activities." Neither the title nor the content is particularly abject in this chronicle of his life from 1904 to the present. When appropriate, he dwells on his role in the founding of the Chinese Communist Party and on his intimate contacts with such public heroes as Li Dazhao. However, he manages not to disparage other friends, such as Chen Duxiu and Liang Shuming. He tells simply and factually the story of how he introduced Zhou Enlai into the Communist Party in Paris in 1921, as well as how he came to write "An Appeal for Peace" in 1948.

Self-blame is more noticeable in the post-1949 portion of the chronology. Here Zhang Shenfu, in keeping with required sins, confesses to a tendency toward "individual heroism": "I always liked to see the limelight, to show off, to consider myself a wise hero without whom nothing could be done."[21]

The record goes on chronologically and objectively through 1957 and includes his defense of Zhang Bojun as "95 percent correct." Bringing the story up to 1965, Zhang confesses half-heartedly: "It was not exactly that I did not read the works of Chairman Mao. I was very familiar with them. It was not that I did not cherish them or did not enjoy reading them. Rather, although I thought they were important and precious, I did not read them attentively enough. Rereading them two years later, I realize their real meaning and value. I realize that every sentence of Chairman Mao's work is the truth."

In the end, however, Zhang Shenfu manages to privilege the voice of his own memory over the "truth" of Mao's sacred texts. In the conclusion of his self-review he manages to imply about himself what he had said aloud about Zhang Bojun in 1957. He almost comes out and says "I am 95 percent correct": "Most of this year, 1967, I have been sick again. And still almost every day people from other institutions come to seek me out at the library to ask questions about the history I have lived through, about people I knew in the December Ninth movement of 1935. Although these interviews are not good for my health, I still feel happy when I do them. I try my best to help these interviewers. I was told that I have been of more help to them than others because I have a good memory" (32–33).

True, Lively, and Moderate

JUNE 8, 1981. I am fifteen minutes late for my first taped interview with Zhang since my return to China last week. He brushes off my apology about a bus delay with a warm greeting. Eager to continue our conversation, he is unfazed when I ask to attach a microphone to his jacket.

I start by inquiring about Li Jiansheng. She seemed withdrawn at Zhang's birthday party two days ago, as if nursing some inner hurt: "It is all because she

The rehabilitated Zhang Shenfu in 1981, striking a formal pose in front of his house, which has been decorated for "superior cleanliness" in a neighborhood hygiene campaign. (V. Schwarcz)

has been frustrated in obtaining a rehabilitation for Zhang Bojun, you know. The higher-ups just won't relent. They have given her better housing. They forgave the daughter for the crimes of the father. But they insist on the validity of those crimes. I guess they need a few prominent evildoers, especially dead ones, to prove to themselves that the entire antirightist campaign of 1957 was not all wrong. They try to put Li Jiansheng off by telling her that the country cannot afford a full rehabilitation for Zhang Bojun.

"Me? Well, I suppose I have been more fortunate. I was never one of the big rightists. When I was finally rehabilitated in 1979, though, it was in a backward sort of way. A Party delegation came to my house and told me that after reviewing my case they decided that it was Qu Anping—the editor of *Guangming ribao* [during the time Zhang Bojun was manager in 1957]—who made the statement 'Zhang Bojun is 95 percent correct.'

"I know what I said. But what could I do? I was rehabilitated through a lie.

Guan Suowen,
Zhang Shenfu's
fourth wife,
shortly before
their marriage in
1955. (Courtesy
of Guan Suowen)

An accusation against me, an accusation that was unfair in the first place, was removed by pinning it on an other man, a dead man."

"Oh, don't sound so ungrateful, so critical," chimes in Guan Suowen as she brings in some sweets. "We were lucky to get 400 yuan back pay for reparations. Of course, the country does not have enough money to pay back all those who have been wronged in 1957. . . . And it was good, too, to have your salary restored. It helps these days to have the 240 yuan a month."

The country, like money, is something tangible for Guan. She appreciates both, in keeping with Party-mandated gratitude. Unlike Zhang Shenfu, she tries hard to please those who want to rehabilitate his reputation, no matter what the cost in truth. Almost every day now she welcomes some Party historian or other who seeks an interview with Zhang Shenfu.

Since his rehabilitation in 1979, Zhang has become an important new source for a revisionist history of the Chinese Communist Party. Whereas Mao Zedong and his view previously reigned supreme, Zhou Enlai has now moved to center stage. Zhang Shenfu is key to this latest refurbishing of the revolutionary pantheon.

FEBRUARY 9, 1987. Zhang Shenfu's political rehabilitation reaches its climax the year after his death. The Democratic League's (Communist-controlled) newspaper, Unity (*Tuanjie bao*), carries an article entitled "The Man Who Introduced Zhou Enlai into the Chinese Communist Party—Zhang Shenfu."[22] It retells, without much change, Zhang's own version of his political career. Its content differs little from the chronology that Zhang prepared for the Red Guards in 1967. The tone, however, is new. It is conciliatory, full of praise of Zhang

Shenfu. Here, one of the Democratic League's leaders—ostracized in 1948—is reclaimed as the political mentor of China's much-venerated, loudly mourned premier.

The conclusion emphasizes Zhang's closeness to the public idol: "Comrade Zhou Enlai was always very concerned about Zhang Shenfu. The two men were bound from beginning to end by a deep personal friendship" (2). The rest of the article confirms the conclusion by detailing Zhang Shenfu's links with the Communist Party. These links are not new to the reading public. During the eleven years following Mao's death in 1976, Zhang Shenfu was transformed from a forgotten founder of Chinese Communist Party cells into the chief voice for Party-sponsored recollections of Zhou Enlai. Zhang's public rehabilitation was thus nearly complete.

Public rehabilitation, however, is not the same as self-rehabilitation. And the latter is precisely what Zhang Shenfu sought during the last decade of his life. This is what he was after in our conversations. Like the story of Qu Anping, his public rehabilitation was based on half-truths. Too much had been left out or changed by politics.

In his own eyes, Zhang Shenfu remained first and foremost a philosopher. This is what he emphasized to me on Wang Fu Cang Lane. This is what he took pride in when he completed his long essay "My Admiration for and Understanding of Russell" in February 1983—an essay that was not published in his lifetime. Like his complex interest in Confucius, his vision of himself as a philosopher remains buried in brief newspaper announcements, such as the one in November 1985 that notes Zhang's participation in the founding of a new National Confucius Research Institute.[23]

The challenge to survive as a thinker had to be carried on behind the scenes of political rhetoric. Zhang Shenfu persevered in his task when politicians had no interest in thought and even when his health failed.

APRIL 14, 1980. Zhang Shenfu's physician is leaving as I come in today. She has given him shots "for recurring dizziness." When I enter the small sitting room, his welcome is warm but the outstretched hand is weak. Zhang's eyes are clouded as we begin talk, but they grow brighter by the end of the visit. I begin with questions about his time in Göttingen. He insists that we talk about his philosophy: "For the past few months, as you know, I have been trying to summarize my philosophical standpoint. Talking with you has stimulated me to ask myself new questions. So I have begun to write a philosophical statement, something I call 'My Worldview.' I have been trying to analyze my own life perspective and examine my mistakes, shortcomings, and achievements more objectively. I want to use my life, the evolution of my own worldview, as a mirror for China.

Zhang Shenfu making a speech at the opening of the National Confucius Research Institute in Beijing, 1985. (Courtesy of Zhang Yanni)

"The goal of this process of analysis and reflection is to state my core beliefs. To come up with the simplest words for what life is about, how to treat others properly. I think I have finally come up with three words that say it all: true [*shi*], lively [*huo*], and moderate [*zhong*]."

At this point, Zhang chuckles loudly with self-gratification—as if he had found a treasure. His old obsession with condensing thought into verbal morsels has triumphed once again. Then, he reaches for my notebook: "Here, I will write these three little words for you. Shi, you know, has been a central article of my faith from the May Fourth period on. I always wrote about the importance of truth, about the tendency of people to mask it from themselves. I even wrote for a newspaper called *Truth* in the 1930s. Truth was what I was always aiming for in my philosophy of encompassing objectivity.

"Huo, now that word is so simple at first glance—just a synonym for living. But what I mean is something deeper, something closer to dialectical materialism, something about the constancy of change and the need to always adjust to it. Not like the deadening dogmatism that Mao propagated at the end of his day. That was no genuine or lively Marxism.

"Zhong, this is the golden mean—one of the oldest concepts in Confucian thought. It is the core of the wisdom of Chinese philosophy as far as I am concerned. It is so important to understand what real moderation is and what its

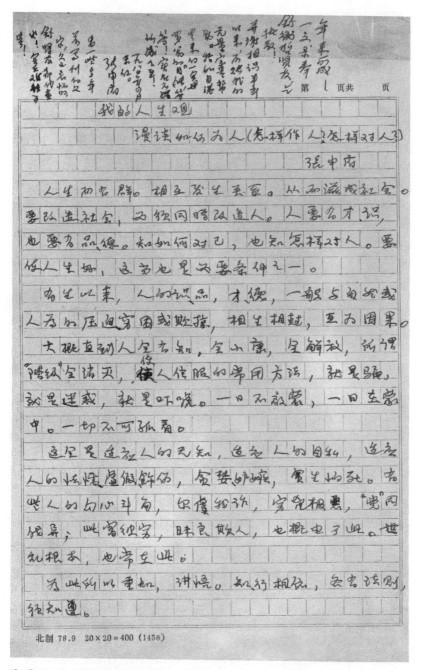

The first page of Zhang Shenfu's manuscript "My Worldview," which he inscribed to me in 1980.

current implication is, especially now, when our country is just recovering from
another bout of extremism. I have been a temperamental moderate all my life. I
have always managed somehow not to be consumed by radical passions. For
myself, I have found that when things went haywire, I just let things shake off
me. I remain unaffected [*buzaihu*].''

At the end of our conversation today, Zhang Shenfu gets up slowly to walk
into his study. Motioning to me to wait, he shuffles back with a manuscript in
his hand: "Here, this is for you. The current version of 'My Worldview.' ''

I look down at the seven pages of handwritten characters with gratitude and
amazement. In the midst of his failing health, Zhang has managed to copy for
me, in his own hand, the fruit of this spring's reflections. The shaky but legible
characters testify to the huge effort. I thank him for this gift. Then he insists on
inscribing the manuscript for me. With an even more unsteady hand he writes
at the top, above the title: "During the course of this year, as I wrote the article,
my worthy friend Shu Hengzhe [my Chinese name] provided much appreciated
aid. I especially want to thank her for her immeasurable, precious help to
me—such as bringing from Hong Kong a full edition of Russell's autobiography. There are also certain articles of mine that I wrote many years ago and
cannot even remember. But my worthy friend had found them all. It is truly
difficult to express appreciation for this fully."

JULY 1982. Zhang Shenfu's philosophical testament finally appears in print.
It is published by a recently founded journal, *Research in the History of
Chinese Philosophy*. The English table of contents lists Zhang's essay under
the title "Gains from Reading." In Chinese his column is entitled *Xinde*
—literally, profits of the heart. The editor introduces the new column as
follows: "With this issue we are inaugurating a new column, *Xinde*, to give
an opportunity for scholars, especially those of an older generation, to express their own views, to pass on the fruits of their lifelong meditations. These
are strictly individual reflections and hence cannot conform to any precon-
ceived notions, nor can they be considered to reflect the point of view of the
editors."[24]

This disclaimer is followed by Zhang's retitled article. The printed version
of the work no longer bears the personal questions of the subtitle. Two years
ago Zhang Shenfu gave me a draft called "My Worldview: How to be fully
human? How to behave toward others?" Now the article is simply called "Shi,
huo, zhong"—"True, Lively, and Moderate."

Below the title are some other changes from Zhang's manuscript: in a passage where he argues for the importance of realism (shi) as an antidote to
Maoist excesses, the editors have omitted a few words. Whereas in 1980 Zhang
wrote, "In today's world extreme idealism and extreme leftist tendencies have

often prevailed. Therefore realism is an urgent necessity," the article published in 1982 simply states that "realism has concrete significance today" (78).

In other places, Zhang Shenfu's utopian Marxism has been toned down. His pleas for scientific philosophy are similarly rephrased. And yet, in spite of these omissions and transmutations, Zhang's reflections are faithfully preserved. His characteristic mix of classical Chinese allusions with Marxist epigrams is well preserved. Through this mingling, Zhang manages to convey something of what he stands for. Beneath the jumble of words from different epochs I hear the voice of an old man trying to sum up his life and to admonish his contemporaries: "Only after you have acquired keen insight into your own character and capabilities can you begin to understand others. You must know not only how to behave toward others but also how to be considerate of their different ways of thinking. . . . Before you place the blame on someone else you must first examine yourself thoroughly. Before you criticize someone you must undertake a thorough process of self-examination.

"You must know your own limits, have a clear grasp of the current situation and of your own weakness. When you are faced with a problem that has no solution, with a situation that cannot be resolved or handled with reason, it is best to adopt a live-and-let-live, a buzaihu outlook. Otherwise, you will be tempted to do something beyond your capability. It is important not to be willful, opinionated, or imperious. But at the same time one must not lose self-confidence or be discouraged" (78).

This general advice addressed to some absent and abstract reader summarizes a life in which Zhang Shenfu paid dearly for being willful, opinionated, and imperious. This is also a lifetime during which he never lost confidence in the integrity of his own point of view.

Not surprisingly, Zhang concludes his essay with a poetical tribute to the three pillars of his credo. Using a playful repetition of words—echoing the style of his earliest essays in *Thought as Such*, as well as the language of the Daoist classic *The Way and Its Power*—Zhang writes: "To understand real rest is never to rest. Real change is endless change. Real happiness is not the happiness that comes too soon. Real contentment comes from a concrete grasp of shi, huo, zhong. This is a knowledge that comes only in practice, and only gradually" (95).

With the essay "True, Lively, and Moderate" Zhang Shenfu managed to rehabilitate himself in his own eyes. Nothing that he did or published after his political rehabilitation in 1979 ever pleased him as much as the fact that he had managed to complete a philosophical testament and had it published before he died.

He never said so, but I believe that this essay contained the most fitting epitaph for Zhang Shenfu's long life: "Real change is endless change. . . . Real contentment comes from a concrete grasp of shi, huo, zhong."

POSTSCRIPT TO AN

ENIGMATIC LIFE

"Fair and foul are
near of kin,
And fair needs
foul," I cried.
. . . .
"For nothing can
be sole or whole
That has not
been rent."
—W. B. Yeats,
"Crazy Jane Talks
with the Bishop"

JULY 2, 1986. Zhang Shenfu died on June 20. At ninety-three, his lungs refused oxygen from without. The official cause of death: "Pulmonary failure."

The news reaches me two weeks later through a letter from his daughter Zhang Yanni. She writes: "At five in the afternoon of the 20th, in spite of the doctors' efforts, my father passed away. . . . During his last days, high officials from the Ministry of Culture, from the Beijing National Library, from the People's Consultative Conference, and from the Democratic League showed ceaseless concern through calls to the hospital and to the family. Final arrangements for the official memorial are being handled by the Beijing National Library in cooperation with the State Documents Publication Office. It will be held in early July. All of us here look forward to your forthcoming biography of Zhang Shenfu. It will make an important contribution to the history of contemporary China."

I have been expecting such a letter. Yet when it arrives, it leaves me hollow. The letter sounds like an article from the *People's Daily*. Why does the daughter's voice—a young woman who has been my friend and helpmate for seven years—sound so compromised today? Why do I hear appreciation of my "forthcoming biography of Zhang Shenfu" as perfunctory at best and a warning to stay within the parameters of the Party convention at worst?

I know well that her future and the future of her aged mother hinges on the goodwill of the high officials she names in the letter. Publicly rehabilitated, Zhang Shenfu attained respectability and comfort for the whole family in a world where everything from new plumbing to a job assignment depends on the favor of well-placed bureaucrats.

Still, rancor rises within me. Zhang's death threatens to flatten the story of his life. If his own daughter's account sounds sterilized, what hope is there that others will recall its fullness? What will be the fate of the grainy, messy details in the life of a Communist who loved mathematical logic and a feminist who betrayed the women closest to him? Will the tale about the man who introduced Zhou Enlai into the Communist Party be the only one to last, the only one to merit attention? I want to cry out with "Crazy Jane"

Zhang Shenfu in
1975, before his
political rehabili-
tation as a rightist.
(Courtesy of
Zhang Shenfu)

against the mythmakers: "'Fair and foul are near of kin, / And fair needs foul'"!

But who will listen? All this was clearer when Zhang was alive. I felt empowered by him, then licensed by him to write about both fair and foul. But now a memorializing machinery seems to have been set in motion, starting with this letter from Zhang Yanni. Representatives of the Communist Party, the Democratic League, the Beijing National Library, and the State Documents Publication Office will authorize Zhang's life in the foreseeable future. There is nothing for me to do but wait until another story can be fitted into the interstices of public memory.

JULY 13, 1986. The *People's Daily* publishes the official announcement of Zhang Shenfu's death. Its title suggests the final, public verdict on his life: "Comrade Zhang Shenfu passes away in the capital: Well-known democratic patriot was an old friend of our Party."[1]

The two-column life history elaborates a political narrative. Zhang is shown to have earned the coveted title of comrade through his work in founding the Communist Party and introducing Zhou Enlai into it. His scholarly contributions during the May Fourth period and the 1930s are noted in passing in this chronicle that dwells on his "patriotic" activities before and after his "withdrawal" from the Communist Party in 1925.

Zhang Shenfu's role in the December Ninth movement of 1935, in the National Salvation Association of the late 1930s, and in the Democratic League of the 1940s is factually recapitulated. When the chronicle gets to 1949, the editorial embroidering becomes more apparent: "Comrade Zhang Shenfu fully supported the leadership of the Chinese Communist Party and ardently loved socialism. In the course of his work at the Beijing National Library he made certain contributions. After the smashing of the Gang of Four, comrade Zhang Shenfu attended the National People's Congress and did a great deal of work to promote the policy of the united front."

Retrospectively, Zhang Shenfu is remembered as a bridge between Communists and other forces in Chinese society. The other gulfs he tried to cross —between Russell and Confucius, between objective philosophizing and political commitment—are forgotten for the moment.

JULY 15, 1986. The Hong Kong–based *Huasheng bao* (The Voice of China) also publishes an obituary of Zhang Shenfu in an attempt to present the other side of the politician commemorated by the *People's Daily* in Beijing. Here Zhang wears yet another public face, not that of comrade but of "a pioneer in intellectual life and an exemplar for scholars."[2]

The article consists of interview notes by Zou Shifang, a journalist who met Zhang Shenfu shortly before his death. Zou talks about his time and conversation with the aged philosopher and how deeply impressed he was by the scholarship and integrity of the man who introduced Zhou Enlai into the Communist Party. This story also dwells on Zhang's early association with such famous May Fourth leftists as Chen Duxiu and Li Dazhao.

After detailing Zhang Shenfu's credentials as political luminary, the article goes on to talk about the old man's fierce attachment to the philosophical credo of shi, huo, zhong: "Indeed, Zhang Shenfu's entire scholarly manner may be characterized as true, lively, and moderate. . . . He never touched cigarettes or alcohol. He was clean and tidy all his life. He loved books. During the Cultural Revolution his books were not touched by the Red Guards because of Zhou Enlai's protection. Now he still sits among his books. He is a book himself—a book that is worthy of study and reflection."

Zhang Shenfu, an exemplary book? Like the image of Zhang as patriotic comrade, this one strikes me as a flat version of the man I talked with for five years on Wang Fu Cang Lane. To my mind, Zhang was too eccentric to fit into the category of exemplary intellectual.

I react similarly to another passage in the interview by Zou Shifang: "Zhang Yanni told me there is a foreign scholar abroad who is already writing a long biography of Zhang Shenfu. We, his kin, should do our best to catch up."

Am I in a race between kin and foreign friends? I hope not. Someday, no doubt, a Chinese scholar will tell his or her version of Zhang Shenfu's life. For now, I search for a form that does justice to my dialogues with Zhang Shenfu.

JULY 20, 1986. Zhang Shenfu's absence weighs more and more heavily on me. Without his words of encouragement, without his laughter in my ears, how am I to go on with our story?

While he was alive, our dialogues were enlivened by the tension between my questions and his desire to keep on musing about his life. The public world, to be sure, had its own agenda: Was Zhang important in the founding of the Communist Party or not? Was he a model of scholarly integrity or not? Was he a patriotic revolutionary or not?

But these did not matter to me. As soon as I stepped across the threshold of the inner courtyard on Wang Fu Cang Lane, I was extricated from the demands of public historiography. I was free to listen to and to look at Zhang Shenfu in my own way.

Over the five years that we talked he became the underbelly of China's history for me. The convolutions of his life—like the silences that surrounded it in the official annals of the revolution—taught me a great deal about the frailties of memory. Zhang was like a broken mirror through which I glimpsed the fragmented reality of China in revolution.

But not anymore. With his death, the bits have scattered too far. Any piece might be mistaken for the whole. How to go on with the story? I know that I must stay away from false unities, especially those offered by political history and systematic philosophy. They do not fit Zhang's life or our conversations. And so I come back to Yeats: " 'For nothing can be sole or whole / That has not been rent.' "

Now the fabric of my contact with Zhang Shenfu has been rent, and I am left with the pieces. I take two such remembrances from my wall: two photographs. In a large frame, the blowup of the famous boat photograph with Zhou Enlai—famous because Zhou's image long ago had been singled out from its murky context and removed.

Like the airbrushed photograph that begins Milan Kundera's *The Book of Laughter and Forgetting*, this photograph has become for me an emblem of the repressed memory that passes for Party history. At the head of the boat sits Zhang Shenfu, the faded dandy. Out of focus, he alone faces the others. Needless glasses adorn an overserious face. His long hair is parted faddishly in the middle. He wears the finest, best-fitting European tie of the three young men on the boat. He strikes me as a romantic consciously posing for an image. I might have wanted to stop and talk with him on a Paris street, more out of curiosity about his manner than for what he might tell me of China.

Then, a sixty-year leap to one of the first photographs I took of Zhang Shenfu during spring 1980. My camera was poorly set, so the picture evokes a shadowy image. This is one of my favorites among dozens of close-ups I have of Zhang Shenfu.

Half of Zhang's face is covered by darkness; the other half is bathed by the sunlight streaming in from the window above. His hair is short and grey now. The glasses are gone. The strong hooked nose is more pronounced than in the 1920s, more naked, more mischievous somehow. The wrinkles that surround his eyes bear witness to his advanced age. They also assert Zhang's hard-won right to question, to laugh at the world. The tightly drawn mouth is a counter-point to the tape recorder on the table—the symbol of our covenant, our commitment to dialogue. Zhang's hand rests half on the table, half off. He is holding back, while holding on. My teacup in the foreground is a sign that I am still a guest, no matter how much I imagine myself to be the long-awaited friend and collaborator.

Now there are no more pictures to be taken. This is part of what it means to be alone. No more camera opportunities to record Zhang Shenfu's life or my relationship to it. Words will have to do. Yet words are so thin, so empty in these weeks after his death. No doubt the passage of time, the carrying out of a pledge I made to record our dialogues will flesh out the words once again. Some words, anyhow.

For now, however, all I can do is to record the chasm between the life (the unfolding, the distorted, the unwhole but living life) and the words that weave the web around it. It is on that chasm, there all along but painfully apparent today, that I build my book about Zhang Shenfu.

NOTES

Introduction: The Laughing Voice of Zhang Shenfu

1. Zhang Shenfu's manuscript "Wo de jiaoyu, zhiye, huodong" (My education, professions, and activities) was completed on September 21, 1967. It was the third and final version of his autobiography commissioned and supervised by Red Guards during his detention at the offices of the National Beijing Library in the summer and autumn of 1967. I obtained a copy of all three drafts twenty years after they were composed, in summer 1987.

2. For a preliminary discussion of Zhang Shenfu's role in contemporary Party historiography see Vera Schwarcz, "Out of Historical Amnesia: An Eclectic and Nearly Forgotten Chinese Communist in Europe," *Modern China* 1, no. 2 (April 1987): 177–225. For a more detailed discussion of the didactic intent of traditional Chinese—especially Confucian —history, see Dennis Twitchett, "Problems in Chinese Bibliography," in *Confucian Personalities* (Stanford, 1962), and Stephen Owen, *Remembrances: The Experience of the Past in Classical Chinese Literature* (Cambridge, 1986).

3. For a thoughtful discussion of the origins and implications of the zizan form of autobiography, see Pei-yi Wu, "Varieties of the Chinese Self," in *Designs of Selfhood*, ed. Vytantas Kovalis (New York, 1984), esp. 119–22.

4. For a detailed description of how the past is used in contemporary oral history in the People's Republic of China see Bruce Stave, "The Chinese Puzzle: In Search of Oral History in the People's Republic of China," *International Journal of Oral History* 6, no. 3 (November 1985): 156–61.

5. For a scathing indictment of Zhou Enlai's "bending"—compromising—temperament see Simon Leys, "The Path of an Empty Boat: Zhou Enlai," in *Burning Forest* (New York, 1986), 152–58.

6. Zhang Shenfu, "Zhongguo gongchandang jianli qianhou qingkuang de huiyi" (Recollections of the circumstances before and after the founding of the Chinese Communist Party), in *Yida qianhou* (Before and after the first Party Congress), vol. 2 (Beijing, 1980), 558.

7. Zhang Shenfu, "Wo de jiaoyu," 25.

8. J. K. Shryock, *The Study of Human Abilities: The Ren Wu Chi of Liu Shao* (New Haven, 1937), 2.

9. Ibid., 104.

Chapter 1: The Making of a Bookish Rebel

1. In late middle age, Ji Yun (1724–1805) rose once again to national prominence as chief editor of the largest collection of literature ever attempted in Chinese history. Under orders from the Qian Long emperor, Ji gathered hundreds of scholars and thousands of texts to compile the *Siku quanshu*, the *Complete Library in Four Branches of Literature*. This project had a double agenda: to systematize and to censor anti-Manchu references from the entire Chinese literary heritage. See "Chi Yun," in Arthur Hummel, ed., *Eminent Chinese of the Ch'ing Period* (Taipei, 1970), 120–23.

2. Zhang Shenfu, "Yi guanjun yu Wuchang chengnei panbing jiaoxie mianzui xi" (Urgent proclamation by military officials to the rebel forces inside the city of Wuhan about how to surrender arms and avoid punishment), unpublished school essay, ca. 1910.

3. For a fuller discussion of Liang Shuming's friendship with Guo Renlin, as well as the fuller content of Liang Shuming's memoirs, see Guy Alitto, *The Last Confucian: Liang Shu-ming and the Chinese Dilemma of Modernity* (Berkeley, 1979).

4. Liang Shuming, "Jiuyuan jueyi lun" (On tracing the origin and solving doubts), *Dongfang zazhi*, no. 13 (May–July 1916): 5–7.

5. Zhang Shenfu, "Nü shuxuejia Guwalusike furen renzhuan" (A biography of the female mathematician Kovalevsky), *Funü zazhi* 1, no. 2 (February 1915): 2–4.

6. Alitto, *The Last Confucian*, 50–51.

7. Zhang Shenfu spoke to me at length about Li Guangyu on January 20, 1980. He also wrote about this old schoolmate and their joint journey to France in 1920. See Zhang Shenfu, "Jiandang chuqi de yixie qingkuang" (Certain circumstances surrounding the early period of Party founding), in *Yida qianhou*, vol. 2 (Beijing, 1980), 222.

8. Zhang Shenfu, "Quan du zazhi" (A plea for reading magazines), *Xin qingnian* 5, no. 4 (October 1918): 433–34.

9. Chen Duxiu, "Women jiujing ying bu yinggai aiguo?" (Should we be patriotic after all?), *Duxiu wencun* (Collected works of Chen Duxiu), vol. 1 (Shanghai, 1922), 648–49.

10. Chi (pen name of Zhang Shenfu), "Guo" (The state), *Shaonian Zhongguo*, pt. 1 (January 15, 1920): 318–20.

11. Zhang Shenfu, "Weiji sixiang" (Dangerous thought), *Xin qingnian* 6, no. 5 (May 1919): 552–54.

12. Liang Shuming, "Lun xuesheng shijian" (On the students' episode), *Meizhou pinglun* (May 18, 1915), 4.

13. Chi, "Ziyou yu zhixu" (Freedom and order), pts. 1, 2, *Meizhou pinglun* (July 13 and 27, 1919): 1–2; 2.

Chapter 2: Libertine and Liberationist

1. Founded in August 1922, *Shaonian* borrowed its French subtitle *La Jeunesse* from the prestigious *Xin qingnian* (New Youth) started in China in 1916 by Chen Duxiu. The European-based publication was a much smaller, more improvised enterprise than the publication that circulated throughout China from 1916 to 1926. The hand-lettered *Shaonian* did not reach beyond the small circle of Chinese Communists in Europe. The name was changed to *Chi guang* (Red Light) in the beginning of 1924; a year later the journal was defunct.

2. Zhang Shenfu, "Nan-nü wenti bucheng wenti de jiejue" (An unproblematic solution to the man-woman problem), *Shaonian* (*La Jeunesse*) (October 1922): 20–23.

3. The story of Bertrand Russell's marriages to Alys Smith, Dora Black, Helen Patricia Spence, and Edith Finch is well told in Ronald Clark, *The Life of Bertrand Russell* (New York: Alfred Knopf, 1976), and in Russell's *Autobiography*, 3 vols. (New York, 1967–69).

4. Brian Harrison, "Bertrand Russell: The False Consciousness of a Feminist," *Russell* 4, no. 1 (Summer 1984): 158.

5. Bertrand Russell, letter to Zhang Shenfu, November 10, 1920, Russell Archives, McMaster University Library, Hamilton, Ontario (hereinafter RAMUL).

6. This photograph is reproduced in Clark, *The Life of Bertrand Russell*, ix, with the date given incorrectly as 1921.

7. Russell, letter to Zhang, November 10, 1920, RAMUL.

8. Zhang Shenfu, "Ji bianzhe" (Letter to the editor), *Chenbao* (November 13, 1920), 4.

9. Bertrand Russell, "The Place of Sex Among Human Values," in *The Basic Writings of Bertrand Russell* (New York, 1961), 352–53.

10. Zhang Shenfu, "Jiehun yu furen" (Marriage and women), *Meizhou pinglun* (February 2, 1919), 2.

11. Zhang Shenfu, "Jiaqu you liyou ma?" (Is marriage rational?), *Meizhou pinglun* (February 9, 1919), 3.

12. Zhang Shenfu, "Nan-nü wenti" (The man-woman problem), *Xin qingnian* 6, no. 3 (March 15, 1919).

13. Henrik Ibsen, *Four Major Plays*, translated by Rolf Fjelde (New York, 1965), 111. For a full discussion of the "Nora-complex" in China, see Vera Schwarcz "Ibsen's Nora: The Promise and the Trap," *Bulletin of Concerned Asian Scholars* (March 1975): 3–5.

14. Zhang Shenfu, "Nan-nü wenti," 321.

15. Zhang Shenfu, "Nüzi jiefang da budang (The great unfairness of women's liberation), *Shaonian Zhongguo* (October 1919).

16. This photograph, along with others discussed in this book, has been preserved in Zhang Shenfu's personal library at 29 Wang Fu Cang Lane, Beijing. When Zhang was forced to move to the southwest during the war with Japan in the period from 1937 to 1945, he left this collection in the care of trusted servants.

17. Christina Gillmartin, "Mobilizing Women: The Early Experience of the Chinese Communist Party, 1920–1927," (Ph.D. diss., University of Pennsylvania, 1986), 90–93.

18. Li Cangming, "Nüjie xianxingzhe: Ji Liu Qingyang tongzhi" (A pioneer in women's work: Remembering comrade Liu Qingyang," in *Beijing nüjie* (Outstanding women of Beijing) (Beijing, 1987), 16.

19. "Liu Qingyang tongzhi zhuidao hui zai Beijing juxing" (Memorial service for Comrade Liu Qingyang held in Beijing), *Renmin ribao* (August 3, 1979), 4.

20. In 1974 Zhou Enlai was the indirect target of the widespread anti-Confucius study campaign enforced throughout China.

21. Li Cangming, "Nüjie xianxingzhe," 16.

22. Liu Qingyang was the offspring of Moslems who were ethnically Chinese. Called *hui*, just like their coreligionists in northwest China, these Moslems are descendants of the earliest converts to Islam, who settled in the Chinese heartland and intermarried with Chinese. Despite this prolonged assimilation, Chinese Moslems have maintained fidelity to the dietary laws of Islam. Tianjin, a major port in Northeast China, has been a long-standing center of Chinese Moslems.

23. "Juewu de xuanyuan" (Manifesto of the Enlightenment Society), in *Wusi shiqi de shetuan* (Study societies of the May Fourth era), vol. 2 (Beijing, 1979), 302–03.

24. Zhang Shenfu, "Zhongguo gongchandang jinlai qianhou qingkuang de huiyi" (Recollections of the circumstances before and after the founding of the Chinese Communist Party), in *Yida qianhou*, vol. 2 (Beijing, 1980), 548.

25. Li Cangming, "Nüjie xianxingzhe," 51.

26. Claude Cadart and Chen Yingxiang, *L'Envol du communisme en Chine: Mémoires de Peng Shuzhi* (Paris, 1983).

27. Li Cangming, "Nüjie xianxingzhe," 22.

28. Liu Qingyang, "Zhencao yu jiefu" (Purity and chastity), *Funu ribao* (March 6, 1924), 4.

29. Ibid., (March 7, 1924), 4.

30. Ibid., (March 8, 1924), 3-4.

31. Liu Qingyang, "Wuhu! Zhenshizhe!" (Alas! The truth seekers!), *Chenbao fukan* (September 26, 1924), 2-3.

32. Yun Daiying, "Funü yundong" (The women's movement), *Zhongguo qingnian* (March 7, 1925), 287-90.

33. Both Yu Feibin's *Xingyu de weisheng*, published in 1925, and Cheng Hao's *Renlei de xing shenghuo*, published in 1927, are discussed in Chen Dongyuan's *Zhongguo funü shenghuo shi* (A history of the life of Chinese women) (Shanghai, 1928).

34. Zhang Shenfu, "Xing de yishu tong xing de ziyou" (The art of sex and sexual freedom), in *Suosi* (Shanghai, 1931), 216.

35. Zhang Shenfu, "Funü yu geming" (Women and revolution), in *Suosi*, 220-24.

36. Zhang Shenfu, "Nan-nü de xiangyu" (The mutual understanding between men and women), in *Suosi*, 225-31.

37. Zhang Shenfu's longest exposition of the philosophers of the Vienna School appeared in installment no. 19 of "Xu suosi" (Thought as Such Continued), *Dagong bao* (January 5, 1933).

38. Hebi, "Jiashi wo shi nüzi de hua" (If I were a woman), *Dagong bao* (April 27, 1933), 4.

39. Zhang Shenfu, "Da Hebi" (Answering Hebi), *Dagong bao* (April 27, 1933), 4.

40. Sun Junquan, letter to Zhang Shenfu, November 7, 1937, preserved in Zhang Shenfu's personal collection at 29 Wang Fu Cang Lane) (hereinafter ZSPC).

41. Dong Guisheng, letter to Zhang Shenfu, June 10, 1938, ZSPC.

42. Zhang Shenfu, letter to Dong Guisheng, March 6, 1939, ZSPC.

43. Dong Guisheng, letter to Zhang Shenfu, May 23, 1939, ZSPC.

44. For further discussion of Zhang Shenfu's role in the Democratic League, including his expulsion after the organization became allied with the Communist Party, see chapter 5.

45. Zhang Shenfu, "Xianfa yu funü (Women and the constitution), *Duli yu minzhu* (March 1944), 43.

46. "Zhang Shenfu beipan minzhu wei hu zuo zhan: Liu Qingyang yanyu chize (Zhang Shenfu betrays democracy, makes war on behalf of tigers: Liu Qingyang reprimands severely), *Renmin ribao* (December 26, 1948), 4.

47. Katherine Tait, "Russell and Feminism," *Russell*, nos. 29-32 (1978): 9. For Dora Black's view of how Russell treated women, see Dora Russell, *The Tamarisk Tree* (London, 1975), 290-94.

Chapter 3: An Eccentric and Almost Forgotten Communist

1. Ed Hammond, *The Coming of Grace: A Pictorial Biography of Zhou Enlai* (New York, 1980), 34.

2. The Great Leap Forward of 1958-60 was a nationwide mobilization to achieve "pure communism" inspired by Mao Zedong's critique of Soviet-style socialism. The Great Leap ended with a series of natural and man-made disasters. This mobilization of the countryside followed the Hundred Flowers movement of 1957 and Mao's disenchantment with critically minded intellectuals. Zhang Shenfu's role and fate during the Hundred Flowers campaign is discussed in chapter 6.

3. Zhou Enlai, "Lun zhishi fenzi de wenti" (On the question of intellectuals), in *Zhou Enlai* *xuanji* (Beijing, 1982), 357.

4. Zhang Shenfu, "Jiandang chuqi de yixie qingkuang" (Certain circumstances surrounding the Party's founding), in *Yida qianhou*, vol. 2 (Beijing, 1980), 220–26.

5. In 1920 Lenin and the Comintern sent Grigori Voitinsky to China with a Chinese radical named Yang Mingzhao. Upon consulting a Russian emigrant who taught the Russian language at Beijing University, Voitinsky and Yang agreed that the university's Marxist librarian Li Dazhao would be most receptive to the idea of starting a Communist organization in China.

6. Zhou Zhixin, "Beijing gongchandang xiaozu" (The Beijing cell of the Chinese Communist Party), *Renmin ribao* (October 6, 1980), 4, emphasis mine.

7. Zhang Shenfu, "Jiandang chuqi," 222.

8. Zhang Shenfu, "Gei Shaonian Zhongguo xuehui de xin" (Letter to the Young China Association, September 20, 1920), in *Yida qianhou*, vol. 1, 144–45.

9. For a further discussion of the role of anarchism and socialism in the early CCP, see Arif Dirlik, "Ideology and Organization in the May Fourth Movement," *Republican China* (November 1986): 3–19.

10. Zhang Gongyang, "Zongguo gongchandang lu Ou zhibu" (The European branch of the Chinese Communist Party), *Renmin ribao* (August 22, 1980), 4.

11. Zhang Shenfu, "Zhang Shenfu tan lu Ou dangtuan zuzhi huodong qingkuang" (Zhang Shenfu speaks about the circumstances surrounding Party organizing in Europe), *Tianjin wenshi ziliao*, no. 15 (May 1981), 89.

12. For an alternative to the self-aggrandizing memory that surfaced in Zhang Shenfu's recollections of his role in the founding of the CCP see Hanna Krall's *Shielding the Flame* (New York, 1977). In this extraordinary narrative, Dr. Marek Edelman, the last surviving leader of the Warsaw Ghetto uprising, consistently refuses to enlarge his own or his comrades' role in one of the key moments of twentieth-century history. Unlike Zhang Shenfu, who was a momentary witness to the birth of a movement that became victorious in 1949, Edelman played a major role in the Jewish resistance, a heroic yet defeated effort that he recounts with a deep sense of vulnerability and loss.

13. Zhang Yanni, "Zong shuji songlaile xian lizhi" (The General Secretary sent fresh lichi fruit), *Zhoujie bao* (November 2, 1985), 6.

14. "Zhang Shenfu tongzhi zai Beijing jieshi" (Comrade Zhang Shenfu passed away in Beijing), *Renmin ribao* (July 13, 1986), 4.

15. For a full discussion of the Société Franco-Chinoise d'Education—founded in 1916 by A. Aulard, professor at the Sorbonne, and Cai Yuanpei, president of the National Beijing University (who became active in setting up the Sino-French Institute for Chinese students at the University of Lyon)—see Geneviève Barman and Nicole Dulioust, *Etudiants-ouvriers chinois en France, 1920–1940* (Paris, 1981), xi.

16. Liu Ye, Zhu Yuhe, and Zhao Yuanbi, "Lu Ou Zhongguo dangtuan de jianli jingguo" (The organizational origins of Chinese Communism in Europe), *Dangshi yanjiu* (February 1981): 87–92.

17. Barman and Dulioust, *Etudiants-ouvriers*, xi–xvii.

18. For a discussion of the slogans, participants, and issues involved in the 1921 demonstration see John Kong-cheong Leung, "The Chinese Worker Student Movement," (Ph.D. diss., Brown University, 1982), 400–22.

19. For a discussion of the intellectual biography of Zhao Shiyan, see Marilyn Levine, *"The Found Generation: Chinese Communism in Europe, 1919–1925,"* (Ph.D. diss., University of Chicago, 1985).

20. Liu Ye, Zhu Yuhe, and Zhao Yuanbi, "Lu Ou Zhongguo dangtuan," 89.

21. Zhang Shenfu, "Ying Fa gongchandang—Zhongguo gaizao" (The British and French Communist parties and China's reforms), *Xin qingnian* 9, no. 3 (July 1921): 1–2.

22. Zhang Shenfu, "Zhang Shenfu tan lu Ou," 89.

23. Wu Qi, "Zhou Enlai tongzhi qingnian shidai zai Fa De liangguo de geming huodong" (Comrade Zhou Enlai's revolutionary activities in France and Germany during his youth), *Tianjin wenshi ziliao* (May 1981): 139.

24. Bertrand Russell, letter to Jean Nicod, November 11, 1920, RAMUL.

25. Zhang Shenfu, "Ying Fa gongchandang," 3.

26. Zhang Shenfu, "Nan-nü wenti bucheng wenti de jiejue" (An unproblematic solution to the man-woman problem), *Shaonian* (October 1922), 22.

27. R (Zhang Shenfu), "Zhongguo gongchandang yu qi muqian de zhengce" (The Chinese Communist Party and its future policies) and "Gongchan shaonian yundong de buzuo" (The proceedings of the Young Communist International), *Shaonian* (October 1922), 4, 33–36.

28. Zhang Shenfu, "Gongchan shaonian," 34.

29. Zheng Chaolin, interview with Zhang Yanni (Zhang Shenfu's daughter), November 12, 1986, Shanghai. I was given a full transcript of this interview by Miss Zhang. The same story is told, without the vivid dialogue, in "Zheng Chaolin tan Zhao Shiyan he lu Ou zhibu" (Zheng Chaolin talks about Zhao Shiyan and the European branch of the CCP), in *Yida qianhou*, vol. 2 (Beijing, 1980), 535–36.

30. Ibid.

31. Ibid.

32. Ibid.

33. Ren Zhuoxuan (born 1895) arrived in France in 1920, stayed five years, and returned to China through Moscow. After Zhang's departure from Europe, Ren directed the European headquarters of CCP. He also joined the staff of *Shaonian* in 1923 and worked for the journal under the direction of Zhou Enlai. Left for dead on a Nationalist execution ground in 1927, he made peace with his captors and reemerged in 1928 as a GMD theoretician, using the pen name Ye Qing. Part of this history is retold in Conrad Brandt, *The French-Returned Elite in the Chinese Communist Party* (Hong Kong: Hong Kong University Press, 1961).

34. Zhang Shenfu, "Chouban Huangpu junxiao diandi" (Some bits about the founding of the Whampoa Military Academy), in *Huangpu junxiao* (Beijing, 1984), 97–100.

35. "Zhang Shenfu tongzhi zai Beijing jieshi" (Comrade Zhang Shenfu passed away in Beijing), *Renmin ribao* (July 13, 1986), 4.

36. I have already discussed this conversation in the introduction, in the context of Zhang's self-portrait through a history project.

37. Zhang Shenfu, "Zongguo gongchandang jianli qianhou qingkuang de huiyi (Recollections of the circumstances before and after the founding of the Chinese Communist Party), in *Yida qianhou*, vol. 2, 548–54.

38. Zhang Shenfu, "Shuo shihua" (Straight talk), *Xin qingnian* 9, no. 3 (July 1921): 2.

Chapter 4: Between Russell and Confucius

1. Zhang Shenfu, "Xuyan" (Introduction), in *Suosi* (Thought as such) (Shanghai, 1931), 1–4.

2. Zhang Shenfu, letter to Bertrand Russell, November 9, 1920, RAMUL.

3. Suzanne Ogden, "The Sage in the Inkpot: Bertrand Russell and China's Social Reconstruction in the 1920s," *Modern Asian Studies* 16, no. 4 (1982): 533–34.

4. Ronald Clark, *The Life of Bertrand Russell* (New York: Knopf, 1976), p. 389. On this page Zhang (Chang Sung-nien) is the only member of the Beijing University faculty named as "responsible for Russell's visit," while Liang Qichao is not mentioned in the biography at all.

5. Bertrand Russell, "A Free Man's Worship," in *Basic Writings of Bertrand Russell* (New York, 1961), 68. For a fuller discussion of Russell's spiritual crises, see Bertrand Russell "My Religious Reminiscences," ibid., 31–36, and Clark, *Bertrand Russell*, 93–96.

6. Zhang Songnian (Shenfu), "Ziyou ren de chongbai" (A free man's worship), *Shijie* (January 15, 1928), 2.

7. Zhang Shenfu, "Wo dui Luosu de zanpei yu liaojie" (My admiration for and understanding of Bertrand Russell), unpublished manuscript, completed March 2, 1983. In August 1986 Zhang Yanni, Zhang's daughter, presented me with a copy of this manuscript and described the circumstances of its composition.

8. Clark, *Bertrand Russell*, 153–54.

9. Zhang Shenfu, "Wo dui Luosu," 3.

10. In 1919–20 Zhang Shenfu (sometimes using a pen name) wrote about or translated the following articles by Russell:

> Zhang Songnian, "Lian duoshi: Zhexue shuxue guanxi shi lunyin" (Reflections under a stone roof: Outline of a history of the relationship between philosophy and mathematics), *Xinchao* (February and April 1919).
>
> Chi, "Women suo neng zuode" (translation of Russell's "What We Can Do"), *Meizhou pinglun* 17 (April 13, 1919).
>
> Zhang Songnian, "Jingshen duli xuanyan" (translation of "Déclaration d'indépendance de l'esprit"), *Xin qingnian* 7, no. 1 (December 1919).
>
> Zhang Chi, "Guo" (translation of Russell's "The State"), *Shaonian Zhongguo* 1, no. 7 (January 15, 1920).
>
> Zhang Songnian, "Luosu yu renkou wenti" (Russell and the population problem), *Xin qingnian* 7, no. 4 (March 1920).
>
> Zhang Songnian, "Luosu" (Russell [extensive biographical and philosophical introduction to a special issue on Bertrand Russell]), *Xin qingnian* 8, no. 2 (October 1920).
>
> Zhang Songnian, "Meng yu shishi" (translation and introduction to Russell's "Dreams and Facts"), *Xin qingnian* 8, no. 2 (October 1920).
>
> Zhang Songnian, "Minzhu yu geming" (translation of and introduction to Russell's "Democracy and Revolution"), *Xin qingnian* 8, nos. 2, 3 (October and November 1920).
>
> Zhang Songnian, "Zhexue li de kexue fa" (translation of and introduction to Russell's "On the Scientific Method in Philosophy"), *Xin qingnian* 8, no. 2 (October 1920).
>
> Zhang Songnian, "Shibian Luosu jikan zhuzuo mulu" (A tentative bibliography of Bertrand Russell's published writings), *Xin qingnian* 8, nos. 3, 4 (November and December 1920).

11. The last letter from Russell to Zhang Shenfu in the Russell archives at McMaster University is dated September 17, 1962. It is a response to Zhang's congratulations on Russell's ninetieth birthday. In 1962 China was undergoing a brief period of political liberalization during which Zhou Enlai could, and did, acknowledge his political debt to Zhang Shenfu. Zhang thus felt free to contact his Western mentor. With the outbreak of the Cultural Revolution in 1966, the possibility of correspondence with Russell ended. In his September 17, 1962, letter to Zhang Shenfu, Russell writes:

> "It was very rewarding for me to receive your thoughtful and kind letter. I am enclosing to you a copy of a program given to me on the occasion of my ninetieth birthday, which I value and should wish you to have. I am also sending you a copy of my 'History of the World in Epitome', which I hope you will like. . . .
>
> "I should very much like to see you again to discuss all that has happened in the years since we last met. Naturally those who write about one have their own particular weltanschaung [sic] which affects their vision of oneself. I am not publishing my autobiography until my death, because there is so much that affects contemporary events, and because there is much that I am hoping to add to it.
>
> "The danger of nuclear war is overwhelming and terrifying, and I feel that I must do anything I am able to prevent it. . . .
>
> "I hope that you will write again, because it was a source of pleasure for me to hear from you."

12. Zhang Shenfu, "Wo dui Luosu," 7.

13. Sun Dunheng, "Zhang Shenfu jiaoshou zai Qinghua" (Professor Zhang Shenfu's years at Qinghua), *Beijing wenshi ziliao* (January 1988), 30–31.

14. Zhang Shenfu, "Zhu Luosu qishi" (To Russell, on his seventieth), *Xinhua ribao* (May 21, 1942), 4.

15. Zhang Shenfu, "Luosu: Xiandai shengcun zui weida de zhexuejia" (Russell: The greatest philosopher alive today), *Xinwen pinglun* (April 12, 1946), 16.

16. Zhang Shenfu, "Wo dui Luosu," 2.

17. Bertrand Russell, letter to Zhang Shenfu (Chang Shen-fu), November 10, 1920, RAMUL.

18. Zhang Shenfu, letter to Bertrand Russell, November 10, 1920, RAMUL, emphasis added.

19. Maurice Friedman, *To Deny Our Nothingness: Contemporary Images of Man* (New York, 1967), 363.

20. Zhang Shenfu, "Ji bianzhe" (letter to the editor), *Chenbao* (March 16, 1920), 4.

21. Zhang Shenfu, "Ji bianzhe" (letter to the editor), *Chenbao* (October 30, 1920), 4.

22. Zhang Shenfu, "Luosu" (Russell), *Xin qingnian* 8, no. 2 (October 1920): 1.

23. Liang Shuming, "Dui Luosu zhi buman" (My reservations about Russell), in *Shuming sahou wenlu* (Liang Shuming's writings after the age of thirty) (Shanghai, 1930; reprint, Taiwan, 1971), 103–10.

24. Zhang Shenfu, "Guanyu Luosu" (About Russell), *Qinghua zhoukan* (May 1, 1931), 8–9.

25. Bertrand Russell's early essay "Self-Appreciation" is discussed at length from a critical perspective by Sidney Hook, "The Philosopher as a Young Man," *New York Times Book Review* (January 29, 1984), 7–8.

26. Bertrand Russell, *The Problem of China* (London, 1922), 38.

27. Zhang Shenfu, "Zun Kong jiudeliao Zhongguo ma?" (Can worship of Confucius save China?), *Qinghua zhoubao* (November 12, 1934), 7.

28. Zhang Shenfu, "Xu suosi, 4" (Thought as such continued), in *Suosi* (Beijing, 1986), 135.

29. Zhang Shenfu, "Xu suosi, 101" (Thought as such continued), in *Suosi* (1986), 195.

30. For a translation of the "Doctrine of the Mean" see James Legge, *The Chinese Classics*, vol. 1 (London, 1861), 269.

31. Zhang Shenfu, "Chun keguan fa" (The method of pure objectivity), in *Suosi* (Shanghai, 1931), 195–99.

32. Zhang Shenfu "Suosi: Jingsheng yu wuzhi" (Thought as such: Spirit and matter), *Jingbao fukan* (March 26, 1925), 3.

33. Zhang Shenfu, "Chun keguan fa," 198.

34. Zhang Shenfu, "Xu suosi, 6" (Thought as such continued, no. 6), in *Suosi* (1986), 139.

35. Ibid., 140.

Chapter 5: In the Realm of Red Dust

1. See Zhang Songnian (Zhang Shenfu), "Zhongshan xiansheng yu luoji" (Mr. Sun Yatsen and logic), *Zongli danchen jinian kan* (Commemorating the premier's [Sun Yatsen's] birthday) (November 12, 1928), 7–9, and "Weiwulun de zhongyao" (The importance of dialectical materialism), in *Duli yu minzhu* (Independence and democracy) (Chunqing, 1945), 89–96.

2. The impact of Mencius on the consciousness of Chinese intellectuals is discussed with critical insight in a key work by the noted twentieth-century historian Qian Mu, *Zhongguo zhishi fenzi* (Chinese intellectuals) (Hong Kong, 1951), esp. 28–33.

3. TSS (Zhang Shenfu), "Wo duiyu Zhongguo geming" (My attitude toward the Chinese revolution), *Geming pinglun*, no. 6 (June 1928).

4. (Zhang) Shenfu, "Diguo zhuyi deng" (Imperialism and all that), *Yusi*, no. 35 (June 19, 1925).

5. (Zhang) Shenfu, "Di san wenhua zhi jianshe" (The establishment of a third kind of culture), *Jingbao fukan* (June 22, 1925), 2.

6. The May Thirtieth movement of 1925 and its exhilarating impact on the consciousness of May Fourth intellectuals is discussed in Vera Schwarcz, *The Chinese Enlightenment* (Berkeley, 1986), esp. 145–50. For views of the Shanghai massacre of 1925 that contrasted with those of Zhang Shenfu, see Zhu Ziqing, "Xuege" (Song of blood), *Xiaoshuo yuebao* 16, no. 7 (July 1925); and Ye Shengtao (Ye Shaojun), "Wuyue sanshiyi ri zhi jiyu zhong" (In the midst of the May 31 downpour), *Xiaoshuo yuebao* 16, no. 7 (July 1925).

7. Zhang Songnian (Shenfu), "Bao Kaiming xiansheng" (An address to Mr. Kaiming), *Jingbao fukan* (August 19, 1925), 1–2.

8. Zhou Zuoren, "Da Zhang Songnian xiansheng shu" (A letter in response to Mr. Zhang Songnian), *Jingbao fukan* (August 21, 1925), 1.

9. Zhang Songnian (Shenfu), "Zibai" (Self-vindication), *Jingbao fukan* (March 14, 1926), 6–7.

10. (Zhang) Shenfu, "Zhixu yu jilu" (Order and discipline), *Wuhan minbao* (May 22, 1927), 1.

11. (Zhang) Shenfu, "Wusa jinian dao nanbei sinan tongzhi" (Commemorating May 30 and grieving for comrades slain in the north and south), *Wuhan minbao* (May 30, 1927), 4.

12. "Zhang Songnian qishi" (An announcement concerning Zhang Shenfu), *Wuhan minbao* (June 2, 1927), 1.

13. Zhao Lisheng, "Wo suo zhidao de Zhang Shenfu" (Zhang Shenfu as I know him), (draft manuscript, dated February 15, 1982), 7. This essay was drafted as a film script, capturing three moments in the life of Zhang Shenfu (in 1934, 1950, and 1979) that Zhao Lisheng believed show the victimization of Zhang Shenfu by the Communist Party. Published eight years later—under the title "Ji Zhang Shenfu Xiansheng" (Recording Mr. Zhang Shenfu), *Wenshi ziliao*, no. 12 (September 1990)—the revised version of the essay has lost the dramatic form and strongly voiced commentary of the original.

14. Qian Zhongshu, in his novel *Fortress Besieged*, parodies a character named Chu Shenming in words that portray Zhang Shenfu quite directly: "When Ch'u went abroad, for the sake of convenience, he had to wear glasses, and so it happened that his attitude toward women gradually changed. Though he loathed women and could smell them three doors away, he desired them, which was why his nose was so sharp. His mind was filled with them. If he came upon the expression *a posteriori* in mathematical logic, he would think of 'posterior,' and when he came across the mark 'X' he would think of a kiss. Luckily he had never made a careful study of Plato's dialogues with Timaeus; otherwise he would be dazed by every 'X' mark" (Ch'ien Chung-shu, *Fortress Besieged*, trans. J. Kelley and N. K. Mao [Bloomington: Indiana University Press, 1979], 84).

15. Zhang Shenfu, "Rensheng de yiyi" (The meaning of human life), *Qinghua zhoukan* (May 27, 1936), 6.

16. For a fuller discussion of the New Enlightenment movement of 1937–39, see Schwarcz, *Chinese Enlightenment*, 229–41.

17. Zhang Shenfu, "Fakan ci" (Statement of publication), *Zhanshi wenhua* (May 25, 1938), 1.

18. Zhang Shenfu, "Zhanshi zhexue de biyao" (The necessity of wartime philosophy), *Zhanshi wenhua* (May 25, 1938), 21–22.

19. Zhang Shenfu, "Xin qimeng yundong yu xin shenghuo yundong" (The new enlightenment movement and the new life movement), *Zhanshi wenhua* (April 10, 1939), 3–4.

20. Zhang Shenfu, "Kexue yu minzhu" (Science and democracy), *Xinhua ribao* (May 7, 1942), 4.

21. Zhang Shenfu, "Luoji yu zhengzhi" (Logic and politics), *Minzhu* (October 6, 1945), 4.

22. Zhang Shenfu, "Minsheng" (The livelihood of the people), *Minsheng yuekan* (March 10, 1943), 11.

23. Zhang Shenfu, "Lun Zhongguo de qulu" (On China's alternatives), *Zhongguo jianshe* (July 1948): 130–33; also reprinted in a booklet privately printed by Zhang Shenfu, *Women de qulu* (Our alternatives) (August 1948), 1–4.

Chapter 6: Final Regrets, Final Retorts

1. Zhang Shenfu, "Huyu heping" (An appeal for peace), *Guancha* (October 23, 1948).

2. The origins and the suppression of *Guancha* are discussed at length in Noel Castalino's "Les intellectuals non-engagés et l'opinion publique en Chine, 1945–1949" (thesis, Ecoles des Etudes en Sciences Sociales, Paris, 1983), 200–318. The Guomindang decree of December 23, 1948, ordering the suppression of *Guancha* is quoted by Castalino on p. 313.

3. "Zhongguo minzhu tongmeng kaichu Zhang Shenfu mengjie jueyi an" (Record of the session expelling Zhang Shenfu from the Democratic League), in *Zhongguo minzhu tongmeng* *lishi wenxian, 1941–1949* (Essays on the history of the Chinese Democratic League, 1941–1949) (Beijing, 1983), 484.

4. "Minmeng zongbu fayan shengming: Kaichu minzhu pantu Zhang Shenfu," (The Central Committee of the Democratic League speaks out decisively: Expels Zhang Shenfu, a traitor of democracy), *Renmin ribao* (December 16, 1948), 3.

5. "Zhang Shenfu beipan minzhu wei hu zuo zhan: Liu Qingyang yanyu chize" (Zhang Shenfu betrays democracy, makes war on behalf of tigers: Liu Qingyang reprimands severely) *Renmin ribao* (December 26, 1948), 4.

6. Meng Chao, "Zhang Shenfu de huli weiba" (Zhang Shenfu's foxtail), in Xia Yan, ed. *Lun duzi* (Concerning the gut) (Hong Kong, 1948), 41–46.

7. "Meng Chao," in Li Liming, *Zhongguo xiandai liubai zuojia xiaozhuan* (Brief biographies of six hundred modern Chinese writers) (Hong Kong, 1977), 224.

8. Meng Chao, "Zhang Shenfu," 43.

9. Zhang Shenfu, "Lixing yu kuangwang" (Reason and madness), *Ziyou pipan* (December 1, 1948), 12.

10. "Minmeng chengfen de jiehe yu tade fenlie" (The coming together, organization, and split within the Democratic League), *Ziyou pipan* (November 10, 1948), 12.

11. Zhang Shenfu, "Lixing yu kuangwang," 12.

12. Peng Zhen became mayor of Beijing after liberation and a prominent victim of the Cultural Revolution of 1966–69. His prescient advice to Zhang Shenfu not to return to teaching philosophy at Beijing University was confirmed in interviews with Zhang Dainian and Xu Yin, as well as by the repeated anti-intellectual campaigns that ravaged China's most famous university throughout the 1950s and 1960s.

13. Zhang Shenfu, "Bixu yancheng Hu Feng zhe qun wan'e lietu" (It is necessary to severely chastise the countless evils of Hu Feng and his traitorous clique), *Guangming ribao* (June 7, 1955), 3.

14. The following are Zhang Shenfu's most noted essays commemorating the May Fourth movement of 1919: Zhang Shenfu, "Wusi jinian yu xin qimeng yundong" (Commemorating May Fourth and the New Enlightenment movement), *Beiping xinbao* (May 2, 1937); Zhang Shenfu, "Wusi dangnian yu jinri" (May Fourth then and now), *Qunzhong* (May 1, 1942); "Wusi: Huiyi, ganxiang, zhanwang" (May Fourth: Memories, feelings, future hopes), *Beida banyue kan* (May 1, 1948); Zhang Shenfu, "Wusi yundong de jinxi" (The May Fourth movement: Its past and present), *Xin wenxue shiliao* (May 1979).

15. Zhang Shenfu, "Fayang wusi jingsheng: Fang!" (Develop the spirit of May Fourth: Open up!), *Guangming ribao* (April 27, 1957), 3.

16. "Tong youpai fenzi huaqing jiexian" (Draw a clear boundary against rightist elements), *Guangming ribao* (June 14, 1957), 1.

17. "Zai gongnong minzhudang zhongyang weiyuanhui zuotan huishang xuduo ren pipan Zhang Bojun de cuowu sixiang: Zhang Shenfu te yu yiyi renwei Zhang Bojun meiyou fan yuanzexing de cuowu" (At the conference meeting of the central committee of the Workers-Peasants Democracy Party many people criticize Zhang Bojun's erroneous thought: Zhang Shenfu puts forth another opinion stating that Zhang Bojun did not commit any errors of principle), *Guangming ribao* (June 14, 1957), 2.

18. Zhang Shenfu, "Shuo shihua" (Tell the truth), *Xin qingnian* 9, no. 3 (July 1921): 1–2.

19. Luo Longji (Luo Lung-chi), "My Preliminary Examination, July 15, 1957," in *Commu-*

nist China, 1955–1959: Policy Documents with Analysis (Cambridge, Mass., 1962), 335.

20. Zhang Bojun (Chang Po-chun), "I Bow My Head and Admit My Guilt Before the People, July 15, 1957," in *Communist China*, 337–38.

21. Zhang Shenfu, "Wode jiaoyu, zhiye, huodong" (My education, professions, and activities), unpublished manuscript, September 21, 1967, 12, ZSPC.

22. Wang Mingzhen, "Zhou Enlai de rudang jieshao ren Zhang Shenfu" (The man who introduced Zhou Enlai into the Chinese Communist Party—Zhang Shenfu), *Tuanjie bao* (February 9, 1987).

23. "Zhonghua Kongzi yanjiusuo jinxing xueshu zuotanhui" (China's Confucius Research Institute organizes a scholarly meeting), *Renmin ribao* (November 18, 1985).

24. Zhang Shenfu, "Shi, huo, zhong" (True, lively, moderate), *Zhongguo zhexueshi yanjiu* (July 1982), 77.

Postscript to an Enigmatic Life

1. "Zhang Shenfu tongzhi zai jing jieshi: Zhuming aiguo minzhu renshi, wo dang de lao pengyou" (Comrade Zhang Shenfu passes away in the capital: Well-known democratic patriot was an old friend of our party), *Renmin ribao* (July 13, 1986), 4.

2. Zhou Shifang, "Xuejie qisu, wenjiang kaimo: Fang quanguo zhengxie weiyuan zhuming zhexuejia Zhang Shenfu xiansheng" (A venerable figure in the scholarly world, a pathbreaking writer: A visit with national consultative conference representative and well-known philosopher Zhang Shenfu), *Huasheng bao* (July 15, 1986), 3.

WORKS BY

ZHANG SHENFU

This chronological bibliography lists works written by Zhang under his given name, Zhang Songnian; his literary name, Zhang Shenfu; and various pen names, which are indicated by parentheses.

"Yi guanjun yu Wuchang chengnei panbing jiaoxie mianzui xi" (Urgent proclamation by military officials to the rebel forces inside the city of Wuhan about how to surrender arms and avoid punishment). Unpublished school essay, ca. 1910.

"Nü shuxuejia Guwalusike furen renzhuan" (A biography of the female mathematician Kovalevsky). *Funü zazhi* 1:2 (February 1915).

(Chi) "Suigan lu" (Random reflections). *Meizhou pinglun* (February 2, 1918).

"Zhang Shenfu zhi Hu Shi" (Zhang Shenfu's letter to Hu Shi, May 5, 1918). In *Hu Shi laiwang shuxian xuan*, vol. 1 (Selected letters to and from Hu Shi), 3 vols. Beijing, 1980.

"Quan du zazhi" (A plea for reading magazines). *Xin qingnian* 5:4 (October 1918).

(Chi) "Suigan lu" (Random reflections). *Meizhou pinglun* (December 29, 1918). 1918).

(Chi) "Suigan lu" (Random reflections). *Meizhou pinglun* (December 29, 1918)

"Jiehun yu furen" (Marriage and women). *Meizhou pinglun* (February 2, 1919).

"Jiaqu you liyou ma?" (Is marriage rational?). *Meizhou pinglun* (February 9, 1919).

"Nan-nü wenti" (The man-woman problem). *Xin qingnian* 6:3 (March 15, 1919).

"Lian duoshi: Zhexue shuxue guanxi shi lunyin" (Reflections under a stone roof: Outline of a history of the relationship between philosophy and mathematics). *Xinchao* (February and April 1919).

"Zhongguo shuxue yuanliu kaolüe shiyu" (A schematic investigation of the origins of Chinese mathematics). *Beida yuekan* (April 1919).

(Chi) "Women suo neng zuode" (translation of "What We Can Do" by Bertrand Russell). *Meizhou pinglun* (April 13, 1919).

"Weiji sixiang" (Dangerous thought). *Xin qingnian* 6:5 (May 1919).

(Chi) "Ziyou yu zhixu" (Freedom and order). Pts. 1, 2. *Meizhou pinglun* (July

13 and 27, 1919).

"Nüzi jiefang da budang (The great unfairness of women's liberation). *Shaonian Zhongguo* (October 1919).

"Jingshen duli xuanyan" (translation of "Déclaration d'indépendance de l'esprit"). *Xin qingnian* 7:1 (December 1919).

"Lodan" (Rodin). *Xin qingnian* 7:2 (January 1920).

(Chi) "Guo" (translation of "The State" by Bertrand Russell). Pts. 1, 2. *Shaonian Zhongguo* 1:7, 2:3 (January 15 and September 15, 1920).

"Jindai xinlixue" (Modern psychology). *Xin qingnian* 7:3 (February 1920).

"Kexue li de yi geming" (A revolution in science). *Shaonian shijie* (March 1920).

"Luosu yu renkou wenti" (Russell and the population problem). *Xin qingnian* 7:4 (March 1920)

"Ji bianzhe" (Letter to the editor). *Chenbao* (March 16, 1920).

(Zhang Chi) "Dapo xianzhuang cai you jinbu!" (Destroy the present, only then can there be progress!). *Laodong jie* (September 19, 1920).

"Gei Shaonian Zhongguo xuehui de xin" (A letter to the Young China Association). *Shaonian zhongguo* (September 20, 1920).

"Luosu" (Russell—an extensive biographical and philosophical introduction to a special issue on Bertrand Russell). *Xin qingnian* 8:2 (October 1920)

"Meng yu shishi" (translation of "Dreams and Facts" by Bertrand Russell). *Xin qingnian* 8:2 (October 1920).

"Minzhu yu geming" (translation of "Democracy and Revolution" by Bertrand Russell). *Xin qingnian* 8:2, 3 (October and November 1920).

"Zhexue li de kexue fa" (translation of "On the Scientific Method in Philosophy" by Bertrand Russell). *Xin qingnian* 8:2 (October 1920).

"Ji bianzhe" (Letter to the editor). *Chenbao* (October 30, 1920).

"Shibian Luosu jikan zhuzuo mulu" (A tentative bibliography of Bertrand Russell's published writings). *Xin qingnian* 8:3, 4 (November and December 1920).

"Ji bianzhe" (Letter to the editor). *Chenbao* (November 13, 1920).

"Ying Fa gongchandang—Zhongguo gaizao" (The British and French Communist parties and China's reforms). *Xin qingnian* 9:3 (July 1921).

"Tongxin" (Letter to the editor). *Xin qingnian* 9:3 (July 1921).

"Shuo shihua" (Straight talk). *Xin qingnian* 9:3 (July 1921).

"Bali tongxin: Ge di laodong yundong xianzhuang" (Letter from Paris: The labor movement situation in various countries). Pts. 1, 2. *Chenbao* (November 9 and 15, 1921).

(Chi) "Suigan lu" (Random reflections). *Xin qingnian* 9:6 (July 1922).

"Bali zhi tongxin" (Letter from Paris). *Xin qingnian* 9:6 (July 1922).

(R) "Nan-nü wenti bucheng wenti de jiejue" (An unproblematic solution to the man-woman problem). *Shaonian* (October 1922).

(R) "Zhongguo gongchandang yu qi muqian de zhengce" (The Chinese Communist Party and its future policies). *Shaonian* (October 1922).

(R) "Jinri gongchandang zhi zhendi he zai?" (Wherein lies the true interest of the Communist Party?). *Shaonian* (October 1922).

(R) "Gongchan shaonian yundong de buzuo" (The proceedings of the Young Communist International). *Shaonian* (October 1922).

(R) "Hu Shi deng zhi zhengzhi zhuzhang yu women" (Our relationship to the political point of view of Hu Shi and others). *Shaonian* (October 1922).

"Lun dongzhuan" (translation of "On Motion" by Bertrand Russell). *Zhiyi xuncan* (February 14, 1923).

"Suosi: Jingsheng yu wuzhi" (Thought as such: Spirit and matter). *Jingbao fukan* (March 26, 1925).

"Suosi: Zhaoshu" (Thought as such: Forgiving). *Jingbao fukan* (March 30, 1925).

"Suosi: Fan jindou" (Thought as such: To turn a somersault). *Jingbao fukan* (April 1, 1925).

"Suosi: Liangbian" (Thought as such: Both sides). *Jingbao fukan* (April 4, 1925).

"Suosi: Jieshi" (Thought as such: Between the facts). *Jingbao fukan* (May 28, 1925).

"Suosi: Shengji" (Thought as such: Livelihood). *Jingbao fukan* (September 1, 1925).

"Diguo zhuyi deng" (Imperialism and all that). *Yusi* (June 19, 1925).

"Di san wenhua zhi jianshe" (The establishment of a third kind of culture). *Jingbao fukan* (June 22, 1925).

"Bao Kaiming xiansheng" (An address to Mr. Kaiming). *Jingbao fukan* (August 19, 1925).

"Shuxue yu zhexue" (Mathematics and philosophy). *Jingbao fukan* (September 14, 1925).

"Shuxue yu zhexue pian de jiaozheng" (A correction of the article on mathematics and philosophy). *Jingbao fukan* (September 15, 1925).

"Wu qiongxiao yu Ding Xilin" (The infinitesimal and Ding Xilin). *Jingbao fukan* (December 7, 1925).

"Wuwei de feihua" (Unspeakable rubbish). *Jingbao fukan* (December 19, 1925).

"Nüshi dashi zhi yu" (The repercussions of the events at the Women's Normal University). *Jingbao fukan* (December 27, 1925).

"Zhongyu tou yi piao" (Finally an election). *Jingbao fukan* (February 10, 1926).

"Zibai" (Self-vindication). *Jingbao fukan* (March 14, 1926).

"Luosi xiansheng zhi zhexue" (translation of "The Philosophy of Mr. Bertrand Russell" by C. E. M. Joad). *Zhongda jikan* (March 15, 1926).

"Ziran yu ren" (translation of "Nature and Man" by Bertrand Russell) *Zhongda jikan* (June 15, 1926).

Xiandai zhexue yinlun (translation of *Introduction to Modern Philosophy* by C. E. M. Joad). Shanghai, 1926.

"Zhongguo geming zhi yuce" (translation of "The Future of the Chinese Revolution" by Joseph Stalin). *Zhongyang fukan* (March 31, 1927).

"Geming wenhua shi shenma?" (What is revolutionary culture?). *Zhongyang fukan* (April 4, 1927).

"Zhixu yu jilu" (Order and discipline). *Wuhan minbao* (May 22, 1927).

"Ying Su duanjiao jianzhi bu de dajing xiaoguai" (The breakdown in relations between Britain and the Soviet Union is no surprise). *Wuhan minbao* (May 29, 1927).

"Wusa jinian dao nanbei sinian tongzhi" (Commemorating May 30 and grieving for comrades slain in the north and south). *Wuhan minbao* (May 30, 1927).

"Guanyu Xu Kexiang" (Concerning Xu Kexiang). *Wuhan minbao* (June 17, 1927).

"Huanying di si ci laodong daibiao dahui" (Greetings to the Fourth Labor Congress). *Wuhan minbao* (June 19, 1927).

"Kexue shi mixin ma?" (translation of "Is Science a Superstition?" by Bertrand Russell). *Minduo* (July 1, 1927).

"Yiwei de yiwei" (translation of "The Meaning of Meaning" by Bertrand Russell). *Minduo* (August 2, 1927).

(Song Ning) "Lun fanyi" (On translation). *Beixin* (November 1, 1927).

(Song Ning) "Xiaoren guo" (A nation of mean folk). *Beixin* (November 16, 1927).

(Song Ning) "Lun zixiang maodun" (On self-contradiction). *Beixin* (December 1, 1927).

"Ming li lun" (translation of *Tractatus Logico-Philosophicus* by Ludwig Wittgenstein). *Zhexue pinglun* (December 1927).

"Ziyou ren de chongbai" (A free man's worship). *Shijie* (January 15, 1928).

(Song Ning) "Yi zhi ban jie" (Half-knowing). *Beixin* (January 16, 1928).

"Shenma shi wuzhi" (translation of "What is Matter?" by Bertrand Russell). *Shijie zhoubao* (January 1928).

"Luosu lun yuanzi xinshuo" (Russell on the new atomic theory). *Dongfang zazhi* (March 25, 1928).

"Luosu lun yuanzi xinshuo jiaohou buji" (Additional remarks on Russell's new atomic theory). *Dongfang zazhi* (April 15, 1928).

"Xiangdui lun yu zhexue" (translation of "Relativism and Philosophy" by Bertrand Russell). *Shijie* (June 10, 1928).

"Xiandai wuli kexue de quxiang" (The direction of contemporary physics). *Dongfang zazhi* (June 10, 1928).

(TSS) "Wo duiyu Zhongguo geming" (My attitude toward the Chinese revolution). *Geming pinglun* (June 1928).

"Zhongshan xiansheng yu luoji" (Mr. Sun Yatsen and logic). *Zongli danchen jinian kan* (November 12, 1928).

"Luosu de yanyi lun" (Russell's theory of deduction). *Zhexue pinglun* (August 1930).

"Yuyan yu yiwei" (translation of "Language and Meaning" by Bertrand Russell). *Zhexue pinglun* (December 1930).

"Guanyu Luosu" (About Russell). *Qinghua zhoukan* (May 1, 1931).

Suosi (Thought as such). Shanghai, 1931.

"Gan" (Emotions). *Qinghua zhoukan* (April 2, 1932).

"Zhong gan" (Strong emotions). *Qinghua zhoukan* (May 14, 1932).

"Jidan yu ji: Yingxiong yu shishi" (The chicken and the egg: Heroes and their times). *Dagong bao* (September 17, 1932).

"Shi, li yu shishi" (Facts, reason, and circumstance). *Dagong bao* (March 9, 1933).

"Shuli luoji yu luoji de fazhan" (Mathematical logic and the development of logic). *Dagong bao* (June 22, 1933).

"Keguan yu weiwu" (Objectivity and materialism). *Dagong bao* (November 16, 1933).

"Zhe yi nian" (This year). *Dagong bao* (January 11, 1934).

"Fangfa" (Methodology). *Dagong bao* (February 8, 1934).

"Lun dongzhuan" (On motion). *Dagong bao* (March 22, 1934).

"Zun Kong jiudeliao Zhongguo ma?" (Can worship of Confucius save China?). *Qinghua zhoubao* (November 12, 1934).

"Wo dui wenxue de sange xiwang" (My three hopes for literature). In Zheng Zhenduo, ed., *Wo yu wenxue* (Literature and me). Shanghai, 1934.

"Xiandai zhexue de zhuchao" (The main trend in contemporary philosophy). *Qinghua zhoukan* (December 17, 1934).

"Du shu: Zenma du? Du shema?" (Reading books: How to read? What to read?). *Dushu jikan* (April 15, 1935).

"Rensheng de yiyi" (The meaning of human life). *Qinghua zhoukan* (May 27, 1936).

"Yao you ni ziji" (You must have your own self). *Shibao* (May 1936).

"Fei kexue sixiang" (Unscientific thinking). *Qinghua zhoukan* (June 3, 1936).

"Jiexi de jiexi" (The analysis of analysis). *Qinghua zhoukan* (June 9, 1936).

"Renjian xianhua" (People's idle talk). *Renren zhoubao* (October 24, 1936).

"Luoman Luolan yu Luosu" (Romain Rolland and Russell). *Renren zhoubao* (October 31, 1936).

"Jiuwang yundong shang de queqian" (The shortcomings of the movement for national salvation). *Renren zhoubao* (October 31, 1936).

"Rensheng zhexue" (Philosophy of living). *Shijie dongtai* (November 1936).

"Zhexue yu jiuzhi" (Philosophy and national salvation). *Renren zhoubao* (November 14, 1936).

"Women shizai zhidao shenma na?" (translation of "What Do We Understand After All?" by Bertrand Russell). *Renren zhoubao* (November 21, 1936).

"Ouzhou shi yi ge chenggong zhe ma?" (translation of "Is Europe a Success?" by Bertrand Russell). *Renren zhoubao* (November 21, 1936).

"Kexue yu minzhu" (Science and democracy). *Minzheng bao* (December 13, 1936).

"Zhexueshi shang de shibian de gongli" (Principles of periodization in the history of philosophy). *Shijie dongtai* (December 1936).

"Ansidan de rensheng guan" (Einstein's worldview). *Renren zhoubao* (December 25, 1936).

"Wusi jinian yu xin qimeng yundong" (Commemorating May Fourth and the new enlightenment movement). *Beiping xinbao* (May 2, 1937).

Shenma shi xin qimeng yundong?" (What is the new enlightenment movement?). *Xianshi yuebao* (June 1937).

"Shi!" (Truth!). *Beiping xinbao* (July 12, 1937).

"Zhanshi shenghuo, zhanshi jiaoyu, xin qimeng yundong, xin qingnian yundong" (Wartime living, wartime education, the new enlightenment movement, and a new youth movement). *Shishi leibian tekan* (December 10, 1937).

"Jingsheng dongyuan de faduan" (The development of spiritual mobilization). *Zhangzheng xunkan* (January 18, 1938).

Wo xiangxin Zhongguo (I believe in China). Shanghai, 1938.

"Fakan ci" (Statement of publication). *Zhanshi wenhua* (May 25, 1938).

"Wusi jiangyan hui" (Roundtable discussion about May Fourth). *Zhanshi wenhua* (May 25, 1938).

"Kangzhan jianguo wenhua de jianli faduan" (The establishment and development of a culture of national resistance). *Zhanshi wenhua* (May 25, 1938).

"Zhanshi zhexue de biyao" (The necessity of wartime philosophy). *Zhanshi wenhua* (May 25, 1938).

"Xin qimeng yundong yu puji jiaoyu yundong" (The new enlightenment movement and the movement for mass education). *Zhanshi wenhua* (June 10, 1938).

"Yige wenhua dongyuan de jinji xianyi (An urgent proposal for cultural mobilization). *Zhanshi wenhua* (June 10, 1938).

"Women yinggai ruhe bao guojia" (How we should report on the nation). *Zhanshi wenhua* (June 25, 1938).

"Bian houji" (Editor's postface). *Zhanshi wenhua* (June 25, 1938).

"Kangzhan yinian de wenhua" (One year of wartime culture). *Zhanshi wenhua* (July 25, 1938).

"Shi, wu yu xin" (Events, matter, and mind). *Zhexue pinglun* (September 30, 1938).

"Wei shizhu weiji qing zhengfu geng zuo yanming qieshi zhi biaoshi chedi shishi zhi gaibian" (A plea for the urgent, thorough, prompt, and comprehensive reform of the government). *Zhanshi wenhua* (November 10, 1938).

"Yi nianlai de Ying Mei quban jie" (British and American publications of the past year). *Zhanshi wenhua* (November 10, 1938).

"Zhanshi wenhua yinggai zenyang zai fazhan" (How to make wartime culture develop further). *Zhanshi wenhua* (January 10, 1939).

"Jiaoyu yu geming" (Education and revolution). *Zhanshi wenhua* (February 10, 1939).

"Sanmin zhuyi yanjiuyuan sheli de jianyi" (Proposal for the establishment of a research institute for the study of the three people's principles). *Zhanshi wenhua* (February 10, 1939).

"Lun Zhongguo hua" (On sinification). *Zhanshi wenhua* (February 10, 1939).

"Xing yi zhi nan de zhendi" (How true that action is easy but knowing difficult). *Zhanshi wenhua* (February 10, 1939).

"Xin qimeng yundong yu xin shenghuo yundong" (The new enlightenment movement and the new life movement). *Zhanshi wenhua* (April 10, 1939).

"Xin qimeng yundong yu qingnian yundong" (The new enlightenment movement and the youth movement). *Zhanshi wenhua* (April 10, 1939).

"Luosu de xinshu" (New books by Russell). *Zhanshi wenhua* (April 10, 1939).

"Guomin jingsheng zong dongyuan de luoji jiexi fafan" (An introduction to the logical analysis of a national spiritual mobilization). *Zhanshi wenhua* (April 10, 1939).

Shenma shi xin qimeng yundong? (What is the new enlightenment movement?). Chonqing, 1939.

"Wei shenma fan qinlue? Fan qinlue de zhexue" (Why resist invasion? Resistance philosophy). *Zhanshi zhexue* (December 15, 1939).

"Cai xiansheng de yisheng yu women yingdang zenyang daonian ta" (Mr. Cai Yuanpei's life and how we should honor his memory). *Xin Shu bao* (March 24, 1940).

"Yi jiaoyu zongzhi" (The purpose of meaningful education). *Zhongguo jiaoyu* (August 1940).

"Kexue yundong yu xin qimeng yundong" (The science movement and the new enlightment movement). *Zhongguo jiaoyu* (September 1940).

"Bianzhengfa yu jixie zhuyi de duibi" (Dialectics compared to a mechanistic view). *Zhongguo jiaoyu* (October 1940).

"Zong shu wo dui qingniande xiwang" (Restating once more my hopes for youth). *Zhanshi qingnian* (November 1, 1940).

"Renxing doushi" (A tenacious warrior). *Xinhua ribao* (January 5, 1941).

"Zhu Xinhua san zhou nian" (On the occasion of the third anniversary of Xinhua). *Xinhua ribao* (January 11, 1941).

"Sulian de shu" (Books from the Soviet Union). *Zhongguo jiaoyu* (January 1941).

"Zenyang kaizhan kexue yundong de taolun" (A discussion of how to advance the development of a science education movement). *Zhongguo jiaoyu* (April 1941).

"Zhankai women de yuan Su yundong" (Developing our movement to aid the Soviet Union). *Xinhua ribao* (July 13, 1941).

"Guoji fan fasiqi wenhua de jiaoliu" (The international antifascist cultural trend). *Xinhua ribao* (July 14, 1941).

"Weida de renlei tongqing" (A great compassion for all mankind). *Xinhua ribao* (July 26, 1941).

"Jiu yi ba shi zhounian" (The tenth anniversary of the September Eighteenth movement). *Xinhua ribao* (September 19, 1941).

"Zhu Sulian shiyue geming jie" (On the occasion of the anniversary of the October Revolution in the Soviet Union). *Xinhua ribao* (November 11, 1941).

"Shen Liying furen daoci" (Memorial for Mrs. Shen Liying). *Xinhua ribao* (December 21, 1941).

"Huan yi jiu si er!" (Welcome to the year 1942!). *Xinhua ribao* (January 1, 1942).

"Renshi fasiqi de benxing" (Seeing the true essence of fascism). *Xinhua ribao* (January 3, 1942).

"Xinhua, Xinhua—wo kan zhe ni zhangda," (Xinhua, Xinhua—I have seen you grow up). *Xinhua ribao* (January 11, 1942).

"Kaichang bai" (Opening declaration). *Xinhua ribao* (February 12, 1942).

"Kexue yu jishu" (Science and technology). *Xinhua ribao* (February 16, 1942).

(Suan Shishi) "Sunshu jicai Ke Luya" (The mathematical genius of Ke Luya). *Xinhua ribao* (March 20, 1942).

(Suan Shishi) "Sulian qingnian man suanjia" (A blind young Soviet mathematician). *Xinhua ribao* (March 26, 1942).

"Ji Sulian shenghuaxue lao yuanren" (Congratulations to a venerable Soviet biochemist). *Xinhua ribao* (April 9, 1942).

"Kexue shang de shijian yu lilun" ("Practice and theory in science"). *Xinhua ribao* (April 23, 1942).

"Yi Shouchang" (Remembering Li Dazhao). *Xinhua ribao* (April 29, 1942).

"Wusi dangnian yu jinri" (May Fourth then and now). *Qunzhong* (May 1, 1942).

"Wusi de qingnian xing" (The youthful spirit of May Fourth). *Xinhua ribao* (May 4, 1942).

"Kexue yu minzhu" (Science and democracy). *Xinhua ribao* (May 7, 1942).

"Zhu Luosu qishi" (To Russell, on his seventieth). *Xinhua ribao* (May 21, 1942).

"Suanshu miti" (A mathematical puzzle). *Xinhua ribao* (June 4, 1942).

"Su De xuezhan de yi nian" (A bloody year of war between Germany and the Soviet Union). *Xinhua ribao* (June 26, 1942).

(Lai Muse) "Suanshu de jichu" (The foundation of mathematics). *Xinhua ribao* (July 2, 1942).

"Kexue de fada" (The development of science). *Xinhua ribao* (July 26, 1942).

(Lao Hou) "Daerwen yi wai" (Beyond Darwin). *Xinhua ribao* (July 30, 1942).

"Cong Mojia kan kexue" (Science from the point of view of the Mohists). *Xinhua ribao* (August 15, 1942).

"Weiwu lun de zhongyao" (The importance of materialism). *Xinhua ribao* (August 27, 1942).

(Suan Shishi) "Jialilue yu Naidun jinian" (Commemorating Galileo and Newton). *Xinhua ribao* (September 10, 1942).

"Fasheng yu minzhu" (Speaking out and democracy). *Xinhua ribao* (September 27, 1942).

"Minsheng" (The livelihood of the people). *Minsheng yuekan* (March 10, 1943).

"Minzhu yuanze" (The principle of democracy). *Xinhua ribao* (October 8, 1943).

"Wei guofang kexue xuanquan" (Scientific propaganda for national defense). *Xinhua ribao* (October 10, 1943).

"Sulian shiyue geming ershi liu nian zhounian jinian zhuci" (Congratulations on the occasions of the twenty-sixth anniversary of the October Revolution in the Soviet Union). *Xinhua ribao* (November 7, 1943).

"Xianfa yu funü (Women and the constitution). *Duli yu minzu* (March 1944).

"Di wuci xianzheng zuotan" (The fifth discussion about constitutional government). *Xinhua ribao* (May 1, 1944).

"Yanlun xueshu ziyou de wenti" (Debate on the question of academic freedom). *Xinhua ribao* (June 16, 1944).

"Women wei shenma yao minzhu yu ziyou" (Why we want freedom and democracy). *Xinhua ribao* (September 12, 1944).

"Yi ge huyu" (An appeal). *Xinhua ribao* (January 4, 1945).

"Shiying shijie minzhu chaoliu" (In step with the world democratic trend). *Xinhua ribao* (March 8, 1945).

"Wo ziji de zhexue" (My own philosophy). *Xinhua ribao* (June 23, 1945).

"Qi qi ba zhou" (The eighth anniversary of the July Seventh movement). *Xinhua ribao* (July 7, 1945).

"Dui mengguo youren jiang jiju hua" (A few words addressed to friends in allied nations). *Xinhua ribao* (September 4, 1945).

"Tanpan zhi ji yu wenti de jiejue" (The outcome of negotiations and the resolution of problems). *Xinhua ribao* (September 10, 1945).

"Minzhu tuanjie de jingshen tiaojian" (The spiritual precondition for democratic unity). *Tuanjie zengkan* (September 15, 1945).

"Luoji yu zhengzhi" (Logic and politics). *Minzhu* (October 6, 1945).

Duli yu minzhu (Independence and democracy). Chunqing, 1945.

Si da ziyou (translation of *The Four Freedoms* by F. D. Roosevelt). Chunqing, 1945.

"Qing liji shixian renmin si xiang ziyou" (Please implement promptly the four principles of the people's freedom). *Xinhua ribao* (January 16, 1946).

"Zhongda yanjiang" (Lecture at China University). *Xinhua ribao* (February 9, 1946).

"Zhengxie jueyi yinggai gongtong zhixing" (The decision of the national political conference must be carried out in unison). *Jiefang* (March 9, 1946).

"Shenma shi zhexue?" (What is philosophy?). *Xinwen pinglun* (April 11, 1946).

"Luosu: Xiandai shengcun zui weida de zhexuejia" (Russell: The greatest philosopher alive today). *Xinwen pinglun* (April 12, 1946).

"Lun qingnian tiaoyang" (On the nurturing of youth). *Weimin zhoukan* (May 4, 1946).

"Yu renmin jiehe" (Unite with the people). *Weimin zhoukan* (May 4, 1946).

"Canjia hexie, jianshao jiufen" (Join harmoniously, diminish disputes). *Wenhui bao* (July 11, 1946).

"Dangdai renwu zhi lüe" (A contemporary study in human character). *Renwu zazhi* (November 1, 1946).

"Yi nian zhi zhi" (Reflections on the new year). *Lianhe wanbao* (January 2, 1947).

"Minsheng" (People's livelihood). *Minsheng yuekan* (March 10, 1947).

"You guan renwuzhi" (Concerning a study of human characteristics). *Zhongguo jianshe* (September 1, 1947).

"Kexue fangfa yu kexue zuzhi" (The scientific method and scientific organization). *Zhongguo jianshe* (January 1, 1948).

"Wusi: Huiyi, ganxiang, zhanwang" (May Fourth: Memories, feelings, future hopes). *Beida banyue kan* (May 1, 1948).

"Zhexue yu zhexuejia" (Philosophy and the philosopher). *Zhongguo jianshe* (May 1, 1948).

"Women de zhiqu—Beishe zuzhi yuanqi" (Our aim—the organizational origin of the northern society). *Beishe* (June 1948).

"Qingnian wang he chu qu?" (Where is youth going?). *Shidai qingnian* (June 16, 1948).

"Lun Zhongguo de qulu" (On China's alternatives). *Zhongguo jianshe* (July 1948).

"Shidai qingnian ying bao de taidu?" (What should be the attitude of contemporary youth?). *Shidai qingnian* (July 15, 1948).

"Zhishi fenzi yu xin wenming" (Intellectuals and the new civilization). *Zhongguo jianshe* (August 1, 1948).

"Zhishi fenzi, renmin zai xuyao ni!" (Intellectuals, the people need you!). *Beida banyue kan* (August 5, 1948).

Women de chulu (Our alternative). Beijing, 1948.

"Ren shi sheng ziyou ma?" (Was man born free?). *Ziyou pipan* (October 21, 1948).

"Huyu heping" (An appeal for peace). *Guancha* (October 23, 1948).

"Lixing yu kuangwang" (Reason and madness). *Ziyou pipan* (November 10, 1948).

"Bixu yancheng Hu Feng zhe qun wan'e lietu" (It is necessary to severely chastise the countless evils of Hu Feng and his traitorous clique). *Guangming ribao* (June 7, 1955).

"Zhong xi yi wenti" (The question of Chinese and Western medicine). Unpublished manuscript, dated April 1, 1957.

"Fayang wusi jingsheng: Fang!" (Develop the spirit of May Fourth: Open up!). *Guangming ribao* (April 27, 1957).

"Wo de jiaoyu, zhiye, huodong" (My education, professions, and activities). Unpublished manuscript, dated September 21, 1967.

"Wusi yundong de jinxi" (The May Fourth movement: Its past and present). *Xin wenxue shiliao* (May 1979).

"Jinian Cai Yuanpei xiansheng" (Commemorating Mr. Cai Yuanpei). *Beitu* (March 4, 1980).

"Yi er jiu yundong shizhong" (The December Ninth movement: From beginning to end). Unpublished manuscript, dated April 1980.

"Zhongguo gongchandang jianli qianhou qingkuang de huiyi" (Recollections of the circumstances before and after the founding of the Chinese Communist Party). In *Yida qianhou* (Before and after the First Party Congress). Beijing, 1980.

"Jiandang chuqi de yixie qingkuang" (Certain circumstances surrounding the early period of Party founding). In *Yida qianhou*. (Before and after the First Party Congress). Beijing, 1980.

"Zhang Shenfu tan lu Ou dangtuan zuzhi huodong qingkuang" (Zhang Shenfu speaks about the circumstances surrounding Party organizing in Europe). *Tianjin wenshi ziliao*, no. 15 (May 1981).

"Shi, huo, zhong" (True, lively, moderate). *Zhongguo zhexue shi yanjiu* (July 1982).

"Wo dui Losu de zanpei yu liaojie" (My admiration for and understanding of Russell). Unpublished manuscript, completed March 1983.

"Zhi le ge" (An ode to knowledge). *Zhongguo zhexue shi yanjiu* (January 1984).

"Chouban Huangpu junxia diandi" (Some bits about the founding of Whampoa Military Academy). In *Huangpu junxiao*. Beijing, 1984.

Zhang Shenfu xueshu lunwen ji (A collection of Zhang Shenfu's scholarly essays). Shandong, 1985.

"Liu Fa qianhou wo tong Zhou Enlai tongzhi de yixie jiechu he jiaowang" (Some of my contacts and communications with Zhou Enlai before and after our sojourn in France). In *Jinian Zhou Enlai* (Commemorating Zhou Enlai). Beijing, 1986.

Suosi (Thought as such). Beijing, 1986.

Mingli lun—luoji zhexue lun (translation of *Tractatus Logico-Philosophicus* by Ludwig Wittgenstein). Beijing, 1988.

"Huixiang Beida dangnian" (Recalling those years at Beijing University). *Wenshi ziliao*, no. 121 (September 1990).

"Wo suo renshi de Zhang Shizhao" (Zhang Shizhao as I knew him). *Wenshi ziliao*, no. 121 (September 1990).

INDEX

Alitto, Guy, 36
Amnesia, historical, 1, 6, 76, 78, 94,
   96–97. *See also* Memory
Anti-Japanese war, 2, 16, 21, 37, 81,
   132, 153, 177–83, 187, 198, 204
Antirightist campaign, 192, 200–08

Bai Hua, 9
Bai Yayu, 71, 72
Barbusse, Henri, 113, 133
Before and After the First Party Con-
   gress, 97, 121
Beijing National Library, 48, 97, 201–20
   passim
Beijing University, 10, 14, 25–62 pas-
   sim, 103, 104, 113, 120, 127, 129,
   130, 147, 159–77 passim, 204
Beijing University Library, 8, 47, 58
Bergson, Henri, 137, 138, 140
Black, Dora, 57, 58–59, 61, 92, 127,
   131
Boole, George, 135
Borodin, Mikhail, 7, 169
Buddhism, 14, 31–51 passim, 155
Bukharin, Nikolai Ivanovich, 118

Cai Hesen, 100–01, 105, 107, 120, 121
Cai Xiangming, 208, 209
Cai Yuanpei, 14, 42, 103, 104, 131
Calliens, J., 163
Cao Rulin, 48
Chen Baoyan, 168
Chen Cheng, 178, 180, 183
Chen Duxiu: as dean of Beijing Univer-
   sity, 44, 49; as editor of *New Youth*,
   44, 61; as founder of Chinese Commu-
   nist Party, 44, 53, 94, 97, 98; at fourth
   Party Congress, 121; and friendship
   with Zhang Shenfu, 94, 100, 120,
   210, 220; Liu Qingyang and, 74, 75;
   May Fourth movement and, 49–50,
   220; as Party chief in China, 98, 100,
   104, 115, 117; Zhang Shenfu's letters
   to, 106, 114, 116

Chen Gongpei, 104, 107
Chen Gongpo, 159
Chen Lu, 105
Chen Yannian, 116
Chen Yusheng, 63, 64
Chen Yuzhen, 109, 110
Chenbao, 58, 59, 137, 138
Cheng Hao, 84
China Youth, 83
Chinese civil war, 185, 187, 189,
   193–94, 195, 198, 204
Chinese Communist Party (CCP): alliance
   with the Nationalist Party, 120; Beijing
   cell of, 74, 98–99; Berlin cell of, 8,
   101, 102, 107–16; boycott of National
   Consultative Congress by, 185; Canton
   cell of, 7; distinction between cell and
   Party, 100–01; in Europe, 94–97,
   100–13; founding of, 14, 17, 32, 44,
   48, 53, 75, 94, 97–102, 210, 220;
   historiography of, 6, 9, 13–15,
   97–102, 104–05, 118, 119, 121, 170,
   172, 174, 211; Liu Qingyang in,
   66–69, 74–75, 78, 103, 104, 107,
   111, 156; Montargis group, 105, 106,
   115; Paris cell of, 78, 100–08, 116,
   119, 139, 209; Shanghai cell of, 98,
   99; shortcomings of, 160; and Zhang
   Shenfu's rehabilitation, 96–102,
   119, 208, 211–13, 218–20; Zhang
   Shenfu's withdrawal from, 6, 15, 17,
   33, 83, 115–23, 156, 162, 166, 183,
   190, 220; Zhou Enlai as member of,
   55, 67, 94–122 passim, 209, 210,
   213, 220
Chinese Communist Youth Party,
   101–02, 114, 115–16, 117, 195
Chinese Revolution, 158–60
Civil war. *See* Chinese civil war
Clark, Ronald, 127
Comintern, 75, 114, 117, 120, 169, 195
Communist International. *See* Comintern
Communist Party. *See* Chinese Commu-
   nist Party (CCP)

—works by (*continued*)
lections of the Circumstances Before
and After the Founding of the Chinese
Communist Party," 121; "Revolution
in Science," 111; "Russell: The Greatest Philosopher Alive Today," 132–33;
"Russell's New Views of the Atom,"
142; "Science and Democracy,"
181–82; "Self-Vindication," 166;
"Tell the Truth," 207; *Thought as
Such*, 85–87, 88, 125–26, 146, 148,
150, 217; "True, Lively, and Moderate," 216–17; "Truth Speaking,"
121–22; "Unproblematic Solution to
the Man-Woman Problem," 54–55,
78, 87, 113–14; "What Russell Loves
and What Russell Hates," 141–43;
"Women and Revolution," 85–86;
"Women and the Constitution," 92;
"Wrongdoers Filled with Ten Thou-
sand Evils Such as Hu Feng Must Be
Severely Punished," 202–03
Zhang Shizhao, 104, 105, 164, 165–66,
169
Zhang Songnian. *See* Zhang Shenfu,
given name of
Zhang Tailei, 75, 120, 121
Zhang Xiro, 167
Zhang Yali, 30
Zhang Yanni, 3, 12, 117, 119, 129, 203,
218
Zhang Youyu, 173
Zhao Guangchen, 95, 96

Zhao Lisheng, 160–62, 170–72, 174
Zhao Shiyan, 55, 104, 105–21 passim
Zhao Yuanbi, 104
Zhao Zhang, 10, 25
Zheng Chaolin, 115, 116, 117, 118, 228
Zheng Jiaoxun, 208
Zhongyang ribao (Central Government
Daily), 168–69
Zhou Enlai: during anti-Japanese war,
181; at Communist Party Congress,
120, 121; early years as Communist,
55, 67, 94–122 passim; 209, 210,
213, 220; Enlightenment Society and,
73; father of, 16; Liu Qingyang and,
67, 69, 73, 76; at National Consulta-
tive Conference, 183, 184; photo-
graphs of, 95, 184, 185, 221; *Shaonian*
and, 114; at Whampoa Military Acad-
emy, 118; and Zhang Shenfu, 122,
183, 192, 210, 213; on Zhang Shenfu,
96, 116, 117
Zhou Gucheng, 159
Zhou Zhixin, 98
Zhou Zuoren, 16–17, 19, 163, 164–66,
169
Zhu De, 6, 66, 94, 108, 109, 110
Zhu Denong, 11, 28–32, 34, 38, 39, 41
Zhu Xizhou, 30, 31–32
Zhu Yuhe, 104
Zhu Ziqing, 163, 164
Zhuangzi, 146
Zizan, tradition of, 14–15, 16, 17
Zou Shifang, 220–21